ADVANCES IN ENVIRONMENTAL PSYCHOLOGY

Volume 1
The Urban Environment

Edited by

ANDREW BAUM
Trinity College

JEROME E. SINGER
*Uniformed Services University
of the Health Sciences*

STUART VALINS
*State University of New York
at Stony Brook*

LEA LAWRENCE ERLBAUM ASSOCIATES, PUBLISHERS
1978   Hillsdale, New Jersey

DISTRIBUTED BY THE HALSTED PRESS DIVISION OF
JOHN WILEY & SONS
New York   Toronto   London   Sydney

Lawrence Erlbaum Associates, Inc., Publishers
62 Maria Drive
Hillsdale, New Jersey 07642

Distributed solely by Halsted Press Division

Library of Congress Cataloging in Publication Data

Main entry under title:

The urban environment.

(Advances in environmental psychology; v. 1)
Bibliography: p.
Includes indexes.
1. Cities and towns—Psychological aspects—
Addresses, essays, lectures. 2. Sociology, urban—
Addresses, essays, lectures. I. Baum, Andrew.
II. Singer, Jerome E. III. Valins, Stuart IV. Se-
ries.
HT151.U66   301.36   78-13289
ISBN 0-470-26545-0

Printed in the United States of America

Contents

Preface

Recent years have seen a veritable explosion of concern with factors relating to psychology and environment. The reasons for this interest are many, intimately tied to concern for global environmental deterioration and apparent inadequacies in the theoretical and methodological orientations in a number of disciplines. A great deal of research has been conducted with contextual mediation as a central theme, and interdisciplinary consideration of environmental issues is becoming more common. Unfortunately, investigators and scholars with differing perspectives have employed diverse definitions of the environment and adaptation processes and have used different conceptualizations of basic problems. In part, this diversity is healthy and natural as the convergence of people from different disciplines — sociologists, anthropologists, psychologists, geographers, architects, and the like — brings a number of specialized viewpoints to the field. On the other hand, most of this investigation has been less than cumulative as studies focus on different issues. More importantly, it is often impossible to trace many of the contributions; researchers tend to publish their work within their own familiar journals and disciplines, so that architects do not communicate with sociologists nor psychologists with geographers, even when their contributions share a general framework.

For some of the large disciplines such as psychology, the subfields themselves are almost as far apart as separate disciplines. It is not at all unusual for a social psychologist to be unaware of what has been done in clinical psychology or a clinician to be unaware of what has happened in cognitive psychology. For the concept of control, for instance, there are literally six or seven different literatures and different streams of thought, each with a slightly different but to some extent overlapping foundation of the concept. Until recently, there has been little connection among these conceptions; there still is no unitary concept of control.

Every now and then a contribution that appears in a general publication like *Science,* or in the popular press such as *Time* and *New York,* will capture the public imagination and become well known. By and large, however, most of these studies are relatively unavailable to many of the researchers in the field. Yet, the success and the growth of environmental psychology ultimately depends on the ability of people to cumulate literature and to proceed from one study to another. We are witnessing the emergence of second-generation studies, which move not just from lab to field, for example, but also build on previous research on the same problem. Much as this is to be applauded, the mechanism for accomplishing it is far from institutionalized.

Our intent in this series, *Advances in Environmental Psychology,* is severalfold. First, we hope to be able to present the forefront of research in environmental psychology. Even more, we hope to collate scattered items from different traditions and different fields and put them together in ways that make for a coherent unitary topic. Each of the volumes will have a particular thematic focus: They will not be the equivalent of a journal of environmental psychology in hardback covers. Rather, each volume will bring to bear on a particular topic various articles with differing views of a theme within the field. The current volume, the initial one in the series, deals with life in the cities. The articles range from general exposition of the effects of perceived control on city life, theories about over-stimulation and the city as a locus of excess cognitive demands, criticisms of the casting of social phenomena in the city into psychological terms, studies of urban commuting, etc. These papers do not necessarily report new data, and they are varied in format and style. Some are reinterpretations and reworkings of studies done for one purpose, modified to take advantage of the interaction with and results of other studies; others are primary publications, original studies in journal style; still others are review articles or state-of-the-arts assessments. In many ways they are all enriched versions of what would otherwise appear in isolation if published in a traditional journal with little benefit from related work. All of the articles have the same aim: to provide both the professional specialist and the casual reader with a coherent juxtaposition of the most cogent themes related to a set of particular issues.

The theme, The City, is perhaps the most familiar one with which we could start. It serves as an introduction to the series by illustrating how even so familiar a theme can be embellished by the proper selection of perspectives. Let us consider each of the papers in turn.

Much of the theoretical underpinning of recent environmental psychology has been concerned with the processes of perceived control, choice, and attribution. Sheldon Cohen's paper attempts to redefine these concepts and to integrate them with contemporary theoretical work in cognitive psychology. He accomplishes this by considering the human being as an information processing organism; it must perceive its environment through the allocation of its attention and process what it receives through this allocation. By postulating a sentient organism with a limited attentional capacity, and noting its need to allocate differential attention to separate aspects of the environment, Cohen draws several conclusions about the interaction of processing mechanisms with stressors in the environment, and with factors of predictability and control. By pointing out the circumstances under which attention can be modified by environmental stress, both temporarily and permanently, he highlights some otherwise neglected aspects of environmental stress. Cohen places many of his conjectures in the city, the ultimate laboratory for studies of environmental stress. His discussion of the ways in which the urban environment forces people to reduce the attentional demands and the effects of this reduction are the major topics he addresses.

Of course, cognitive overload is not a concept unique to Cohen. Perhaps chief among those who have been involved in the creation and definition of overload constructs is Stanley Milgram. He and John Sabini implicitly regard the city as a source of social and cognitive overload, and the overload itself as a defining characteristic of the quality of city life. In the present study, the concern is not with the overload itself but rather the tacit norms developed to enable people to shed unwanted stimulation and avoid excessive demands when there are too many things to which they have to attend, respond, and interact. Milgram and Sabini's techniques are also interesting. For them the experimental techniques of social psychology are not to be applied routinely to the problem but rather to be modified, adjusted, and adapted in an amalgam with analogous techniques from other disciplines. They seek to illustrate for us how implicit norms govern and regulate our behavior without our even knowing it; in much the same way, ethnomethodologists show how violation of these norms produces reaction, coping, and return to stability. They explore these issues not as the ethnomethodologist does but with an experimental perspective. It is interesting to note the reactivity on the part of the experimenters who asked people to violate social norms. The reasons for this and what they indicate about our response to urban life are some of the topics that are explored in further detail.

The Milgram and Sabini paper is not the only one to consider what happens to people who ride urban mass transits. The study by Jerome E. Singer, Ulf Lundberg, and Marianne Frankenhaeuser is explicitly directed toward an investigation of the stress provoked by urban commuting — the travel back and forth each day by train from residence to work. This paper provides, within a quasi-experimental design, a merger of several techniques of investigation: psychophysical methods for determining reaction, and physiological measurements for assessing stress. These methods are related to the experimental procedures of selecting groups of people that vary in the distances they commute. The study notes both consistencies in people's self-reporting and physiology and differences between the various systems measured. It is the reconciliation and implication of these consistencies and inconsistencies that provide the basis of the discussion.

The paper by Robert A. Baron discusses two variables that are usually associated with city life. Baron is able to show through a review of studies, mostly his own, that the effect of temperature on aggresssion is not simple but instead is rather complex. An exploration of the relationship between these two factors and the variables mediating them leads him to postulate an inverted U-shaped function such that aggression is minimal at low temperature, peaks at some moderate level of temperature, and decreases as temperature becomes more extreme. The model is even more complex, and Baron shows how aggression does not occur only in response to temperature but interacts with and is affected by the prior dispositional states of people and the affective quality of the environment.

The paper by Charles Korte discusses the city as a group of people interdependently connected to each other. Situations arise in which one person needs another's help: Sometimes that help is forthcoming, sometimes it is not. Korte seeks to look at the conditions under which each of these outcomes prevails. His discussion of bystander helpfulness, and its mirror-image bystander apathy, goes back to one of the earlier themes of the volume — cognitive overload. His discussions center on the ways in which the amount of environmental information to be processed will prime a person to help or not to help another in need. But for Korte, overload is not a sufficient explanation. It, too, has a context, and its context is that of the built environment, the architecture and the physical structure of the city. His proposed nexus between psychological theorizing and recent consideration of environmental quality in architectural discussions provides a bridge between what have been two separate streams of thought.

Daniel Stokols' paper continues with an elaboration of a distinction that is important both theoretically and practically. Density and crowding, he notes, should not be used interchangeably when considering urban stress. Just as psychologists working with sensory processes have insisted upon separation of physical stimuli and their psychological complements, Stokols reiterates his earlier distinctions between physical conditions described by density (i.e., square feet per person or people per square foot) and their psychological complements, including crowding. Furthermore, he considers the role of situational and psychological mediation in the crowding process and discusses the value of viewing crowding as an intervening construct in the density/pathology relationship. He is able to introduce, in one stroke, a simplifying notion that allows us to order previous data and make sense out of what seemed to be contradictory findings. Additionally, the defense, maintenance, and justification of such a concept suggests new views of the urban environment and modification of older models, and it provides implications for future research. The crowding/density distinction is explained not just on its own merits but against the alternatives of competing models that utilize mediational and interventional frameworks.

The recent upsurge in psychologists' concern with the urban environment has produced a rush of ideas — many interesting, some stimulating, some productive of research. The evaluation of this material is a task to which Claude S. Fischer addresses himself. He points out that recent theoretical models must fit into a larger scheme of social relationships and social structure. By assessing some of the urban environmental models for their implications about a model of human nature and a model of environment, his paper begins to critically evaluate the postulates underlying our view of urban phenomena. Fischer considers theoretical orientations in terms of where they fit in a larger historical perspective and within a tradition of a more developed urban sociology. He points out that the very diversity that characterizes the new field of environmental psychology can also result in relatively atomistic models, each of which may be more simplistic than would be the case were they fully integrated.

The volume's concluding paper by Reuben M. Baron and Judith Rodin draws on themes from each of the last two articles. As recommended by Fischer, they seek to integrate studies and models of environmental psychology. Congruent with the suggestions advanced by Stokols, they employ the mediational effects of perceived crowding as an organizing construct. In doing so they make crowding comparable to other environmental factors, such as noise, enabling the development of conceptual linkages between models developed for these other stressors and the somewhat chaotic findings with respect to crowding. The implications of the Baron and Rodin work apply not just for crowding but suggest, rather, that many of the nonphysical variables affecting life in the city are amenable to the same sorts of analyses as have been done more easily for physical variables.

ACKNOWLEDGMENTS

We would like to express our gratitude to our contributors for their cooperation and patience. We feel that what they have written extends the boundaries of recent analysis of the city, and we hope that they stimulate others to further elaborate on the urban environment. We would also like to thank Carlene S. Baum, Glenn E. Davis, and Norman Miller for their helpful comments on some of the manuscripts. We are grateful for suggestions and comments about the development of this series that we have received from colleagues and friends including Irwin Altman, John B. Calhoun, Gary Winkel, and Joachim Wohlwill. And we acknowledge the invaluable assistance of Hilda Streiber and Florence K. Norkin in preparing this volume.

ANDREW BAUM
JEROME E. SINGER
STUART VALINS

ADVANCES
IN
ENVIRONMENTAL
PSYCHOLOGY
Volume 1
The Urban Environment

1
Environmental Load and the Allocation of Attention

Sheldon Cohen
University of Oregon

INTRODUCTION

The modern day urban dweller is bombarded with a wide range of environmental stimulation. Unlike rural or small town counterparts, the city resident continuously encounters complex, intense, surprising, and threatening stimuli. Random bursts of noise, hot and crowded mass transport, and air polluted with ash and carbon monoxide are among the many inputs impinging on daily activities. These conditions have long been recognized by social critics as well as the urbanites themselves and are often alleged to produce behavioral and physical consequences inimical to man. Only recently, however, have specific stressing[1] elements within the urban environment been subject to systematic investigation.

What are the effects of environmental stress on human behavior? A growing body of literature offers some interesting findings that, curiously enough, are often nonintuitive. Of the existing evidence, three substantive and replicable findings stand out as being central to understanding the problem. First, the effects of environmental stress vary according to the task being performed. Thus in some situations it is detrimental, at other times beneficial; but often moderate (i.e., not physiologically damaging) levels of environmental stress have little if any effect on observable behavior (e.g., Broadbent, 1971; Freedman, 1973). Second, environmental stressors that occur unpredictably or are uncontrollable (i.e., cannot be escaped or avoided) have a greater impact on behavior than those that occur predictably and can be controlled (e.g., Averill, 1973; Glass & Singer, 1972;

---

[1]The term "stressor" is used in this paper to refer to stimulation that represents an adaptive threat or potential adaptive threat to the organism.

Pervin, 1963). Finally, prolonged exposure to unpredictable and uncontrollable environmental stress, although often having little if any effect on tasks performed during exposure, does affect poststimulation behavior (e.g., Glass & Singer, 1972; Sherrod, 1974).

Although the above findings have elicited various theoretical interpretations, no one analysis is capable of explaining them all. The present paper attempts to interpret all of these findings within one theoretical framework. The proposed interpretation is based on a capacity model of attention. An individual is regarded as having a limited amount of attention that can be allocated at any one time. Information overload is said to occur when this capacity is exceeded, i.e., when there are too many inputs with which the system must cope or when successive inputs come too fast. Unable to process all the incoming stimuli, the organism develops techniques or strategies to deal with overload. Although maladaptive strategies, such as random omitting of inputs, are sometimes employed (e.g., Miller, 1964), the present analysis focuses on the more adaptive and presumably more usual strategy of using available attention on inputs that are most relevant to the task at hand and thus ignoring inputs that are less relevant or irrelevant to task performance.

This analysis is similar to the one suggested by Milgram (1970) in his paper on the social consequences of the urban environment. Like Milgram, we argue that the city's myriad stimuli often overload processing capacity and that strategies adopted to deal with overload often have considerable impact on interpersonal behavior. However, whereas Milgram's analysis focused on the evolution of urban norms as adaptations to overload, the present analysis is concerned with *individual response* to both short- and long-term attentional overloads. In addition, Milgram's model is primarily concerned with overloads resulting from the urban dweller's contact with vast numbers of people, and it limits its focus to the consequences of overload for social behavior. The intent of the proposed analysis is to extend the use of a capacity model of attention in the study of the effects of urban and environmental stress, demonstrating that physical and social stimulation have similar effects on the attentional processes and that behavioral manifestations of these effects are similarly apparent in perceptual, motor, and social behaviors.

The proposed model is similar in some basic ways and borrows much of its terminology from Kahneman's (1973) analysis of attention. Like Kahneman, we propose that it is limits on available capacity that determine how many activities are carried out. Likewise, we use the terms "capacity," "attention," and "effort" interchangeably. Effort is mobilized in response to the changing demand of the task in which one engages; accordingly, a rise in the demands of ongoing activities causes an increase in the level of effort and attention. Moreover, a standard allocation of effort can be determined for any task, and investment of less than this standard effort causes a deterioration of performance. Unlike previous attentional models, the proposed theory attempts to deal with both the allocation of attention at any one point in time and the effects of prolonged demands on the allocation process. There are four basic assumptions involved:

1. *Humans have limited attentional capacities.* Capacity, however, is not seen as a spatial or temporal concept but is instead viewed as being synonymous with effort. *Thus, a person can invest only a limited amount of effort in the attention process at any one time.*

2. When the demands of the environment exceed capacity, a set of priorities is developed. The usual strategy is to *focus available effort on inputs most relevant to the task at hand at the cost of those that are less relevant or irrelevant to task performance.*

3. *The occurrence, or anticipated occurrence, of an environmental stimulus possibly requiring an adaptive response will activate a monitoring process that evaluates the significance of the stimulus and/or decides on appropriate coping responses.* The amount of effort required to monitor an environmental stimulus is an increasing function of the uncertainty it arouses concerning its adaptive significance.[2] For example, inputs that are predictable, and thus can be incorporated into a plan of a sequence of events to occur, demand less attention than similar inputs that occur unpredictably. Likewise, mild inputs, which are less likely to be viewed as an adaptive threat, often demand less attention than do intense ones. It follows that a person who is exposed to intense, unpredictable environmental stimulation has less attentional capacity available for task performance than he or she would under normal environmental conditions.

4. *Prolonged demands for effort cause a temporary depletion in capacity.* The rate of capacity depletion increases with both the momentary effort required by an ongoing activity (including that required by extraneous inputs) and the duration of the activity. Thus, an individual can attend to fewer inputs after enduring prolonged demands than he or she can in a rested state. It follows that attentional overload can occur in low-demand situations following prolonged periods of substantial demands on capacity. Recovery of capacity occurs with rest.

The proposed model suggests conditions under which overload occurs but makes no direct predictions about its effects on behavior. There is, however, a

---

[2]The present paper is concerned primarily with environmental stimuli that are monitored because they are potentially threatening. However the term "adaptive" is used here in its broadest sense, encompassing those stimuli that may provide an opportunity for positive pursuits as well as those posing a potential threat. A discussion of "salient" stimuli that, because of biases that have been built in the organsim, demand attention is provided by Kaplan (1977).

direct link between the model's assumption and certain modes of behavior occurring under conditions of attentional overload. As stated in the second assumption, it is presumed that the adaptive strategy most often employed under conditions of overload is the focusing of available attention on those cues that are perceived by the individual as being most relevant to the task at hand and neglecting less relevant cues. Thus, a person *does not perceive* (i.e., is not aware of) many environmental inputs, both physical and social, that are perceived under less demanding conditions. The effects of this "focusing" of attention vary depending on the ongoing activity; task performance can be hurt if a portion of the neglected inputs are task-relevant and improved if the processing of neglected inputs would have distracted from task performance. Similarly, interpersonal behavior can be adversely affected when another's subtle (and sometimes gross) social cues are not processed but positively affected if these neglected cues are disturbing or disrupting.

Before discussing the specific implications of the model, it is appropriate to consider the evidence on which it is based. Factors involved in the allocation of attention are considered first and the fatigue effect, second. Although it is tempting to suggest that the proposed model can predict the effects of any environmental stressor, for the present the discussion is limited primarily to noise and crowding, two pervasive urban stressors. The great majority of research cited in this paper has been conducted in a performance setting. Moreover, studies of noise far outnumber those of crowding.

OVERLOAD AND THE ALLOCATION OF ATTENTION

Information overload is said to occur when there are too many inputs with which the system must cope or when successive inputs come too fast (Milgram, 1970). Further, when overload does occur (i.e., when the demands on attention exceed available capacity), the organism sets priorities, allocating attention to relevant cues at the cost of subsidiary ones. A number of studies on the effects of stimulus overload on task performance indicate that such a reallocation of attention does occur. For example, it has long been known that a subject's attention capacity can be overloaded by requiring the performance of two tasks at the same time.[3] Studies on the performance of simultaneous tasks suggest that rather than equally dividing available attention between the two tasks, subjects tend to maintain performance on one task and to allow the other to suffer (literature reviewed by

_____

[3]It is important to note tha dual tasks create overloads even when one task is auditory and the other visual (e.g., Mowbray, 1952, 1953, 1954). Thus, one's limitation on performing dual tasks does not seem to be sensory but rather the results of overloading of some central mechanism.

Welford, 1968). In cases where the subject is instructed as to which task is more important, attention is focused on that task.

This tendency to maintain priority-task performance allows the dual-task procedure to serve as a means of assessing the load imposed by the primary task under differing conditions, because increases in primary-task demand appear as degradations in secondary-task performance (cf. review by Kerr, 1973). The dual-task procedure has been used, for example, to assess the effects of differing primary loads on subsidiary short-term memory tasks. In a study reported by Brown and Poulton (1961), subjects driving a car through either a residential or shopping area listened to eight-digit numbers presented aurally every 4 seconds. One digit changed between each group and the next, and the subject indicated which had changed. Errors on the secondary task were greater in shopping areas, where there were presumably more competing inputs, than in residential areas. Similarly, Murdock (1965) studied the effects of maintaining performance on card-sorting tasks of varying difficulty on the immediate recall of 20-word lists. Recall of the lists was worse when the sorting was based on two or more dimensions than when it was based on one. Poulton (1958) likewise reports greater deterioration of short-term memory when the priority task involves monitoring six dials as opposed to two.

Whereas the above studies induced overload by increasing the number of inputs, similar effects on the reallocation of attention are obtained when subjects are forced to increase their processing speed, either because they are given less time to complete a task or because of a higher rate of stimulus input. For example, Kalsbeek (1965) required subjects to press right and left pedals in response to 2000 cps. and 250 cps. tones respectively. The signals were presented at fixed rates of from 10 to 120 per 2-minute interval. Performance on a subsidiary spontaneous-writing task deteriorated with increased speed of the primary task. Increased demands on capacity associated with increasing signal rates are also reported by Brown (1962, 1965) and Gould and Schaffer (1967).

Also of interest is the work assessing the effects of signal predictability on primary-task load. Several studies report that the capacity demanded by tasks requiring response to unpredictable signals is greater than that needed for equivalent performance with predictable signals. For example, Dimond (1966) required subjects to press a key in response to a light appearing at intervals of from 4 to 10 seconds. A subsidiary six-choice key-pressing task was performed simultaneously. After practice (required to learn predictable nature of the signals), secondary-task performance was better when the signals in the primary task were predictable than when they were unpredictable. Likewise, in a study reported by Bahrick, Noble, and Fitts (1954), subjects performed a five-choice reaction-time task with either repetitive or random patterns of signals and, at the same time, gave answers to simple arithmetic problems read aloud by the experimenter. Again, after practice, the arithmetic task was performed better when primary-task signals were predictable than when they were random. Similar effects of predictability are reported by Bahrick and Shelley (1958).

A closer examination of the allocation of attention under overload suggests that focusing occurs not only at the *macrolevel* of performing one task at the cost of the subsidiary one but also in the selection of cues on a single task (the subsidiary task in the dual-task paradigm), where there is some but not enough available attention. The typical strategy is to focus on centrally located signals at the cost of peripheral ones. Thus, in a study reported by Webster and Haslerud (1964), both an auditory (counting clicks) and visual (counting flashes) primary task had equally detrimental effects on both the number of responses and reaction time to peripheral lights in a subsidiary visual-detection task. Similar results are reported by Leibowitz and Appelle (1969), who found that luminance thresholds to peripheral lights increased with the difficulty of a primary foveal-fixation task.

Rate of processing has a similar effect on secondary-task focusing. Youngling (1967), using a central tracking task with a multiposition peripheral-light detection task, found that as the tracking target rate increased, there was a funneling or systematic loss of response to peripheral signals that was greater the more peripheral the light position. Furthermore, he found no difference between time-on-target scores at the different tracking rates. Thus, the extra attention that was needed to maintain primary-task performance was preempted from the secondary task. Moreover, the attention deficit on the detection task resulted in a reallocation of available attention to central cues at the cost of peripheral detections.

Although we are arguing that there is a focusing of attention on *relevant cues* when there is insufficient capacity to maintain normal task performance, the evidence cited up to this point demonstrates focusing based on spatial (i.e., central versus peripheral) cues and not on a relevance or importance criterion. Focusing on central cues can, of course, be interpreted as the best strategy in a detection or tracking task in which central and peripheral signals are equiprobable. They can also be considered the most important cues if their probability of occurrence is greater than the probability of peripheral occurrences. In fact, Hockey (1970b) suggests that central cues in tasks of this sort often have a higher subjective probability than peripheral ones. These interpretations, of course, are only speculative. However, a study varying both task load and cue value (Kanarick & Petersen, 1969) provides concrete evidence that attentional focusing is based on "relevance" rather than "spatial" criteria. Rather than using a dual-task procedure, Kanarick and Petersen required subjects to track several visual inputs simultaneously under differing signal rates. They report that high-input-rate subjects pay proportionately more attention to high-value information sources at the expense of monitoring low-value sources, where high value refers to those signals earning more points. Because spatial position of high-payoff channels was counterbalanced, the results suggest focusing based on cue relevance rather than position.

Several conclusions are supported by the studies reviewed thus far:

1. A task's demand on capacity increases with (a) rate of signal input (whether varying time or number of inputs), and (b) unpredictability of the signal sequence.

2. When performing simultaneous tasks whose combined demands exceed total available capacity, attention is focused on the task deemed more important at the expense of the subsidiary task.

3. When there is not enough capacity to maintain normal performance on a task, whether a subsidiary task or a single task with high-capacity demands, available attention is focused on relevant task cues at the cost of less relevant cues.

EVALUATING THE SIGNIFICANCE OF ENVIRONMENTAL STIMULI

The research cited in the previous section suggests that demands on attentional capacity increase with the sequential rate of task-relevant signals. It is clear that subjects performing these tasks according to instructions, and thus attempting to attend to many inputs simultaneously, experience attentional overload. The urban experience, however, differs in an important way from these experimental situations. Many of the additional stimuli in the urban environment are *not* task-relevant. They are "background" stimulation. Is capacity also expended on competing stimuli not relevant to the task at hand?

The effects of task-irrelevant stimuli are more easily understood if examined in the context of mechanisms involved in the allocation of attention. It is possible to view the allocation of attention as being determined by two sets of factors: the momentary task intentions of voluntary attention, and the more enduring dispositions that control involuntary attention (Kahneman, 1973). These enduring dispositions cause us to pay more attention to some stimuli than to others. Thus, stimuli that are novel, intense, surprising, complex, conflicting, or having some special learned significance elicit an apparently automatic response (Berlyne, 1960). The characteristic response made to these classes of stimuli has been called the "orienting response" (Sokolov, 1963). The orienting response (OR) occurs because the organism is uncertain about the adaptive significance of a stimulus and thus responds with attention and alertness (Glass & Singer, 1972). The response is characterized by an increase in sensitivity to the stimulus source on both the physiological and cognitive levels. The individual focuses attention on novel stimuli and readies him- or herself to act.

Individuals are, however, capable of attenuating even complex, intense, and novel stimuli. Evidence concerning the OR suggests that such a filtering mechanism is operative. After repeated presentation of a particular stimulus, the OR habituates. The stimulus is no longer novel and thus no longer elicits response. For example, when a subject is instructed to "listen to tones," the first and perhaps the second tones elicit very substantial ORs, but after several presentations, the response is no longer elicited (Uno & Grings, 1965). The habituation of the OR does not, however, imply that the stimulus is no longer analyzed (Kahneman, 1973); rather, it implies that the stimulus is expected to occur predictably. When the expectation is violated, an OR is elicited. A demonstration of this effect is provided by Sokolov (1969). When a single flash of light is omitted from a regular series, an OR occurs soon after the omitted light was due. Similar results are reported by Badia and Defran (1970).

An input evaluation process similar to that suggested by research on the OR is proposed by Lazarus (1966) in regard to evaluating the potential harmfulness of stimuli. Lazarus introduces the concept of threat appraisal as the process intervening between stimulus presentation and stress reaction. In order for a situation to be deemed threatening, the stimulus must be evaluated as harmful. This process is presumed to depend on two classes of antecedent conditions: the psychological structure of the individual, and the cognitive features of the stimulus situation (e.g., predictability). When a stimulus is evaluated as threatening, an appropriate coping response is chosen by means of a second process. Thus, potentially dangerous inputs are monitored in order to evaluate their adaptive significance and to decide on appropriate coping responses when necessary.

These approaches suggest that attention level and responsivity to a stimulus depend on the degree of uncertainty elicited by its occurrence or nonoccurrence. It follows that competing (i.e., task-irrelevant) stimuli that are intense and unpredictable, and thus arouse uncertainty concerning their adaptive significance, often demand a greater allocation of attention than do milder and more predictable inputs. Stressors such as noise and crowding can thus be most profitably viewed in terms of the uncertainty they arouse, i.e., their information value. Those that occur in a predictable sequence, eliciting little uncertainty, can be monitored at an attenuated level (e.g., Sokolov, 1969) with a small but not substantial demand on capacity. However, those that occur unpredictably, (i.e., eliciting high levels of uncertainty) demand a continual monitoring and evaluation process even after repeated presentation. Thus, even when voluntary attention is task directed, some capacity is required in the low-level processing of environmental stressors.

STRESS, OVERLOAD, AND
THE ALLOCATION OF ATTENTION

If effort is expended in the monitoring of irrelevant inputs, we would expect that a person exposed to intense and/or unpredictable environmental stimulation could process fewer task-relevant inputs than he or she could in a less distracting environment. Research using the dual-task procedure to assess attentional demand imposed by exposure to environmental stress suggest that this, in fact, is the case. As described earlier, this procedure allows us to assess increases in priority task load by monitoring performance on the subsidiary task. Thus, any effect of a stressor sufficient to require the use of excess capacity to maintain primary task performance is evidenced as a secondary task decrement.

In a study reported by Evans (1975), subjects performed simultaneous tasks while in a crowded or uncrowded room. (Density was manipulated by varying spatial parameters with both large and small rooms containing 10 people.) The primary task was a figure-matching task requiring subjects to choose matching pairs of figures from stimulus sheets containing 80 figure pairs. Simultaneously, subjects listened to a story read aloud on which they were to be tested later. Whereas the primary task was unaffected by crowding, the subsidiary task — recognition memory for the story — was poorer in the crowded group than in the uncrowded group. Thus, it appears that the additional attention required to maintain primary-task performance under crowded conditions was preempted from the subsidiary task.

Similar effects of subsidiary-task performance occur under noise. In an experiment by Boggs and Simon (1968), subjects performed two tasks simultaneously under quiet conditions and also while exposed to unpredictable, 92-decibel noise. The primary task was a visual reaction-time (RT) task, the secondary one an auditory monitoring task. Although exposure to noise did not affect performance on the RT task, there was task degradation on the auditory-monitoring task in noise, as compared with quiet, and this degradation was greater when the primary task was complex rather than simple. (Because secondary task stimuli were presented during intervals between noise bursts, degradation in auditory monitoring cannot be attributed to masking.) Thus, it appears that the additional effort required to perform under noise consumed enough attentional capacity to impair task performance on the secondary task.

Research on the maintenance of items in immediate memory similarly suggests that effort is expended in the monitoring of noise. If extraneous environmental stimulation is capacity consuming, we would expect that the addition of noise during item presentation or during performance of a task intervening between presentation and reproduction would, by preempting capacity allocated to item rehearsal, cause memory decay (cf. Posner & Rossman, 1965). Evidence reported by Rabbitt (1968) suggests that this is the case. Results of a first study indicate that lists of digits are less likely to be correctly recalled when they are presented through noise than when presented in quiet. (The noise had no effect on performance when lists of digits were to be recognized or transcribed, and thus the effect cannot be attributed to masking.) Therefore, it can be argued that the process of recognizing digits through noise preempted the processing capacity necessary for their efficient retention. In a second experiment, subjects presented with two consecutive groups of digits recalled the first group of digits better if the second group was presented in quiet than if it was presented in noise. There was no evidence that presentation of the first group through noise affected recognition of the second group. This is consistent with the assumption that the rehearsal of the first group of digits is inhibited, because the needed capacity was preempted by the task of recognizing a second group through noise. Similar results were obtained in a replication of these two experiments using lists of nouns instead of digits and measuring recognition instead of recall (Rabbitt, 1966).

Studies on recall of peripheral stimuli also find performance degradation under environmental stress. It is difficult to determine whether this effect can be attributed to a lack of attention paid to task-irrelevant stimuli or to the subject's inability to retain these items in memory. In either case, however, the performance deficit can be attributed to a focusing of attention on task-relevant cues under noise. O'Malley and Poplawsky (1971) presented subjects with a series of slides each containing a four-letter word printed in the center in heavy black capitals and a three-letter word in small, light print located in the periphery. Subjects were given standard serial anticipation instructions with no mention of the periphery words. The slides were presented in 75-, 85-, and 100-decibel noise, or quiet. A free-recall test indicated that subjects in the 85- and 100-decibel noise conditions learned fewer of the peripheral words than did subjects in the 75-decibel noise and quiet conditions.

An exploratory study (Saegert, 1973) found a similar lack of memory for peripheral cues under conditions of high density. Subjects were brought to the shoe department of a New York department store at a time chosen to assure either high or low density. Their task was to write short descriptions of 12 shoes in the area. After the task was completed, the subject was taken to a secluded part of the store where she was asked to describe the same shoes she had previously described, in the same order, and to draw a map of the shoe section in as much detail as she could remember. High-density subjects drew maps that had a less detailed and less correct picture of the area in which they were working. (Scoring was based on memory for large objects that would be visible under high-density conditions.) Thus, subjects in the high-density condition either did not originally attend to, or could not remember, peripheral cues irrelevant to their ongoing task.

The capacity-consuming nature of irrelevant stressing stimuli has also been reported in the clinical literature. Research and clinical observation on the applied use of noise stress (Licklider, 1961) suggests that noise is an effective supressor of pain. Thus, dental patients who previously required a conventional anaesthetic or analgesic agent to undergo dental operations undergo audio analgesia without serious pain or unpleasantness. The patient wears earphones and controls the acoustic stimulation through a control box held in his or her lap. There are two control knobs, one for music and a second for white noise. When the patient feels any discomfort, the volume on the music control is increased; at the first sign of any pain, he or she turns up the noise knob. The noise level can be set as high as 116 decibels. Audio analgesia seems to be effective in 65% of the cases.

Predictability, Controllability, and
Demands on Capacity

Of special interest is the effect of increasing the randomness or unpredictability of unwanted stimuli on attentional capacity and allocation. It was suggested earlier that unwanted inputs that are unpredictable require greater expenditures of capacity than similar inputs that occur predictably. In line with this is a study reported by Finkelman and Glass (1970). Subjects working on simultaneous tracking-and digit-recall tasks showed performance degradation on the secondary task under unpredictable noise but not under predictable noise. Performance on the primary task was unaffected by either type of stimulation. Thus, although primary task performance under unpredictable noise demanded enough additional capacity to cause a reallocation of available attention, equivalent performance under predictable noise had no significant effect on the distribution of attention. Several additional studies similarly suggest that performance under unpredictable noise requires greater processing capacity than equivalent performance under predictable stimulation. The effects of unpredictable noise include increasing the variability of performance across subjects in paper and pencil tasks (Sanders, 1961), degrading tracking-task performance (Plutchik, 1959), and producing a reduction in complex psychomotor performance (Eschenbrenner, 1971). Similarly, research on audio analgesia (Licklider, 1961) suggests that random noise is more effective in supressing pain than predictable sounds.

The stressing effects of unpredictably occurring events have received considerable attention and suggest a conceptual framework in which to view the allocation of attention under stress. For example, Mandler and Watson (1966) suggest that inputs that can be incorporated into a plan of the sequence of events to occur are less anxiety provoking than those that cannot be incorporated into a plan. Thus a predictable input, because it can be planned for, elicits less anxiety than an unpredictable input. Likewise, an input whose onset or offset can be controlled, and thus incorporated into a plan, is less aversive than an uncontrollable input. This analysis leads us to expect that the ability to control the onset and/or offset of an aversive stimulus may have similar effects on attentional capacity and allocation as the ability to predict its occurrence. Although there are no noise or crowding studies relevant to this suggestion, a study by Wachtel (1968) using threat of electric shock as a stressor does suggest support. A tracking task and a subsidiary peripheral-light detection task were performed simultaneously. Subjects threatened with uncontrollable electric shock performed no differently than an unthreatened group on the primary task but had significantly longer RTs to lights in the subsidiary detection task. Subjects who were told that they could avoid the shock with good performance on the tracking task showed no such increase in RT. Thus, the anticipation of uncontrollable shock preempted attention from the subsidiary task, whereas the anticipation of controllable shock required little, if any, attention.

Predictability and Crowding

In the context of noise research, unpredictability refers to stimulation occurring when it is not expected. For example, noise is considered predictable when bursts occur at fixed intervals and unpredictable when bursts occur at random intervals. It is less obvious, however, how the concept of predictability fits into the crowding literature. Some clarification of this point is provided in a recent theoretical paper by Rapoport (1975). Rapoport suggests that a condition of high density is unpredictable when there are no social—cultural norms, physical barriers or markers to structure behavior. Thus, when expectancies of how others will behave are vague, nonexistent, or nonoperative, the situation is unpredictable. On the other hand, under similar conditions of spatial limitation, when social—cultural norms and physical markers and barriers effectively structure behavior (i.e., expectancies are accurate), the situation is considered predictable. Rapoport further suggests that unpredictable density demands a substantial allocation of attention and that this allocation decreases with increased predictability. As a consequence, "crowding" effects are more likely to occur under unpredictable than predictable density. The foregoing analysis is consistent with the model developed earlier. That is, the stimuli that occur in dense conditions are demanding (i.e., capacity consuming) only to the extent that uncertainty is aroused concerning their adaptive significance.

Conclusions.   It is clear that noise and crowding have similar effects on attentional capacity and allocation, as do overloads induced by increasing number and rate of inputs. In line with the conclusions made earlier, research on the effects of noise and crowding on attentional capacity and allocation indicate the following:

1. Environmental stress creates demands on attentional capacity, and these demands increase when the stressor is (a) intense, (b) unpredictable, and (c) uncontrollable.

2. When simultaneous tasks are performed under conditions of environmental stress, attentional load increases, resulting in a decrement in subsidiary-task performance.

3. When simultaneous tasks are performed under environmental stress, there is a focusing of attention on relevant cues to the neglect of less relevant ones on the subsidiary task.

These results provide strong support for points (1), (2), and (3) of the attentional model presented earlier. Most important, overloads induced by the occurrence of moderate physical stressors (e.g., noise) have the same effects as those induced by more conventional means.

COGNITIVE FATIGUE EFFECT

The term "fatigue" is usually employed to describe the "detrimental effects of work upon work, whatever the nature of those effects" (Broadbent, 1953a, p. 173). However, deeper probing reveals that there are many aspects of the problem, many different mechanisms that may result in lower work output. The term "cognitive (or mental) fatigue" is used in this context to delineate one such mechanism, a decrease in total available attentional capacity. This depletion of capacity is reflected both in the amount of information that can be handled at any one instant and in the amount that can be handled in a given period, and hence in slowness of perception, choice, and so on (Welford, 1968, p. 247). Although it is similar to neuromuscular fatigue in that it disappears with rest, cognitive fatigue is viewed as a change in the state of a central process, whereas neuromuscular fatigue is usually seen as a peripheral process.

The proposed model assumes that the rate of cognitive fatigue — of depletion of attentional capacity — increases with both the amount of attention required by a task and the duration of the task. Thus, subjects performing complex tasks, more than one task at a time, or performing under environmental stress, show signs of capacity depletion earlier than those performing on less demanding tasks. These decrements in attentional capacity are manifest in an inability to provide the attention demanded by many situations and thus in a reduction in performance and in the focusing of attention associated with attentional overloads.

There is considerable evidence in the performance literature indicating that task performance becomes worse over prolonged working periods. A difficulty arises, however, in distinguishing the effects of monotony (or boredom) from those of cognitive fatigue, because tasks that are fatiguing are often repetitious as well. One factor that aids in delineating the effects of monotony and fatigue is a tendency for a subject, when given the opportunity, to distribute efforts over a working period so as to minimize fatigue (Forrest, 1958; Katz, 1949; Saufley & Bilodeau, 1963). Thus, a subject will adjust pace to the expected length of the working period right from the beginning (Welford, 1968). This means that fatigue effects are more likely if subjects work on paced tasks or under pressure for speed for an unknown period than if they work at their own pace for a time known in advance. It is difficult to attribute these differences between paced and unpaced tasks to associated fluctuations in boredom. It is likely that self-paced subjects who are bored would rush through a task as quickly as possible rather than slow down. Second, we expect that fatigue, and consequently the rate of performance degradation, will accelerate when tasks are complex as opposed to simple and when they are performed under intense environmental stimulation as opposed to normal environmental conditions. Monotony, however, would likely be lessened under these conditions and thus performance improved. Finally, tasks impaired by cognitive fatigue should show significant improvement after short periods of rest; boring tasks would be less likely to show such reversals. The evidence that follows can be attributed, by at least one of the foregoing criteria, to cognitive fatigue. Although interpretation of some of these results is somewhat ambiguous, the overall picture lends strong support to the fatigue hypothesis.

It has generally been found that performance on serial reaction-time tasks becomes progressively worse over time. Thus, Broadbent (1953b) reports that subjects performing a self-paced, serial reaction-time task show a decrease in the rate of work and an increase in the variability of the rate. However, this degradation in performance did not appear until the last 10 minutes of the 1-hour task. When the task was paced, on the other hand, subjects showed an increase in errors after only 10 minutes. Similar indications of task performance declining uniformly as a function of time are reported for vigilance tasks wherein subjects must remain alert for relatively long periods during which they must note small changes on one of a complex of dials, lights, or clocks (Poulton, 1970).[4] Performance on these tasks can be restored, however, by a short rest period (Mackworth, 1970). Thus, Mackworth (1950) reports that performance on the Jump Clock test declines over the first half-hour and declines further over the second half-hour. A half-hour rest, however, restored performance to the original level.

A direct relationship between time on task and decline in performance on a variety of tasks is suggested in a paper by Mackworth (1964). In her review of performance decrement in vigilance, threshold detection, and high-speed perceptual motor tasks, Mackworth concludes that decrements in performance found on these tasks appear to be a linear function of the square root of time on task. She argues that "continuous attention to a simple decision-making task leads to a decrement in performance over a wide range of stimuli and responses [p. 221]." Moreover, this decrement is due to a *decreased ability to perceive the stimulus*. The results from a number of the studies reviewed by Mackworth are shown in Fig. 1.1. The figure shows the results of five different studies. Thus, in a study on auditory thresholds, Solandt and Partridge (1946) report an increased range of pitch discrimination as the test proceeded. Likewise, Bakan (1955) reports

---

[4]Decreases in vigilance performance over time are especially difficult to interpret. Some vigilance tasks seem to require little attention and thus are unlikely candidates for cognitive fatigue. Moreover, decrements on those that are attention demanding (e.g., Jump Clock Test) are attributable to shifts in decision criterion (Swets, 1973). Thus, a progressively more conservative decision criterion (less hits but also proportionally fewer false alarms) comes about over time. It is, however, possible to interpret conservative criterion shifts in terms of the reallocation of attention under overload. As time elapses, capacity decreases, and available attention is allocated to only the most relevant (i.e., "sure hit" signals).

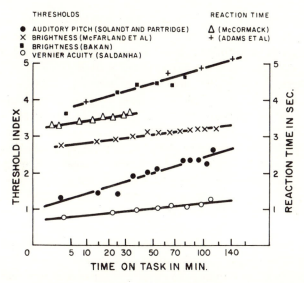

FIG. 1.1. Changes in thresholds and reaction time as a function of the square root of time on watch. (From Mackworth, 1964, fig. 2, p. 214.)

that thresholds for a flash of light increased with time on task. Similar effects on visual threshold are reported by McFarland, Holway, and Hurvich (1942) and Saldanha (1957). Reaction-time studies by Adams, Stenson, and Humes (1961) and McCormack (1960) also show performance decrement as a function of time on task.

Mackworth (1964) also points out that declines in performance on these tasks can be prevented by rest pauses. For example, Bergum and Lehr (1962) report that rest pauses of 10 minutes every half-hour were sufficient to maintain performance in a vigilance task. McFarland et al. (1942) found marked recovery on a visual threshold task following 10 minutes of exercise, and McCormack (1958) showed that a rest pause of 5 minutes after 30 minutes of testing improved RTs but did not restore performance to its original level, whereas a pause of 10 minutes was sufficient to do so.

Declines in performance over time occur because a point is reached at which available attentional reserves are inadequate. As discussed earlier, such a state of overload requires a reallocation or focusing of attention. Thus, prolonged task duration should be reflected in a focusing of attention on relevant task cues as well as the more gross measure of overload — performance decrements. In fact, attentional focusing after prolonged performance is reported in a series of experiments by Drew (reported in Davis, 1948). Drew tested subjects for 2-hour spells in a simulated aircraft cockpit under blind flying conditions. He reports that most subjects tended to pay less and less attention to the more peripheral parts of the task as time on task increased, giving their main attention increasingly to the controls in constant use. For example, the fuel indicator had to be reset every 10 minutes but came to be more often neglected.

It was suggested earlier that environmental stress, by increasing demands on capacity, should increase the rate of cognitive fatigue. Evidence consistent with this assumption is reported under a variety of conditions. Several studies (e.g., Broadbent, 1954; Jerison, 1959) find that performance degradation on a serial RT is accelerated in time under noise as opposed to quiet. Thus Broadbent (1953b) reports that 100-decibel "white" noise as opposed to quiet reduces the accuracy of repetitive serial responding, but only during the last 30 minutes of the test. Similar results are reported by Corcoran (1962) and Wilkinson (1963). Sanders (1961) found an increase in variability of performance on a serial responding task performed under 75-decibel noise, appearing in the last half of a 30-minute session. Likewise, Hartley (1973) found that the number of errors produced by noise on a serial reaction-time task depends on the duration of noise exposure. Subjects who worked on tasks for 40 minutes, but were exposed to noise for only the last 20 minutes, showed less impairment of performance than those exposed for the entire session.

The relationship between length of the working period and whether or not a stressor impairs performance is discussed by Wilkinson (1969) in a review of the effects of environmental stress on performance. After reviewing the research on the effects of noise, heat, cold, sleep deprivation, hypoxia, vibration, and acceleration, Wilkinson (1969) concludes that "duration of work is an important factor to be considered in any attempt to predict or simulate their impact on performance. In almost all cases, furthermore, this influence is in the direction of increasing the adverse effect of the stress as time wears on [p. 262]." He suggests that this tendency is so common that it is tempting to conclude that it reflects some factor common to most stresses that increases with exposure to the associated task. Thus, it appears that prolonged task performance under environmental stress results in increasing task degradation — an effect attributable to a depletion of available attention.

Task duration under experimental conditions is usually limited to between 20 minutes and 1 hour. Although this may be sufficient to cause a significant decay in available capacity, it may not affect performance on the primary task, which by that point is well practiced and requires little effort. However, subsequent tasks demanding considerable attention on the part of the subject, would be sensitive to fluctuations in available processing capacity. Thus, we would expect depletions in attentional capacity resulting from prolonged task and environmental demands to be manifest in deficits on tasks administered immediately after termination of the principal task.

Aftereffects of demanding cognitive tasks have, in fact, been reported. Rey and Rey (1963) report that after 45 minutes of work at a cancellation task, RT became larger, CFF lower, and rate of tapping more irregular. Takakuwa (cited by Welford, 1968) found that the accuracy of aiming at a target over a period of 1 minute deteriorated after a number of tasks regarded as mentally fatiguing. A direct test of the relationship between principle-task load and duration on the performance of aftereffects tasks has recently been completed in our own laboratory (Cohen & Spacapan, 1978). The principle task required subjects to respond to 12 colored lights (four each of red, green, and yellow) by pressing one of three corresponding colored response keys as quickly and accurately as possible. The lights occurred at either a high [200 millisecond interstimulus interval (ISI)] or low (800 millisecond ISI) rate, and the task lasted either 15 or 30 minutes. After completing the principle task, subjects were immediately ushered into a second room where a second experimenter administered the Feather tolerance-for-frustration task (cf. Glass & Singer, 1972). The subjects were led to believe that the task was part of a different experiment than the RT task. Results indicate that high-load subjects performed more poorly on the tolerance-for-frustration task than did low-load subjects. Moreover, subjects required to perform the principle task for 30 minutes performed more poorly than those required to work on the task for 15 minutes, although this latter effect was only marginally significant. These results do suggest that cognitive fatigue, and therefore performance on aftereffects tasks, is related to both the amount of attention required by and the duration of the principle task.

Similar evidence suggesting a decreased ability to perform attention-demanding tasks after prolonged demands on capacity is provided by the research on the aftereffects of environmental stress. Thus, in an experiment by Glass, Singer, and Friedman (1969), subjects worked for 25 minutes on a simple arithmetic task. During this period, they were exposed to predictable or unpredictable 110 or 56-decibel noise. A control group worked in quiet. Subjects working under unpredictable noise, in contrast to predictable noise and no noise, showed degradations in performance on attention-demanding tasks administered after stimulation was terminated. These effects were more pronounced when the unpredictable noise was delivered at 110 decibels as compared to 56 decibels. A second experiment reported in the same paper showed that the adverse poststress effects following loud, unpredictable noise were substantially reduced if the subjects believed they had control over the termination of the noise. Glass and Singer report similar results for the effects of electric shock (Glass & Singer, 1972; Glass, Singer, Leonard, Krantz, Cohen, & Cummings, 1973).

These results are consistent with the assumption that more capacity is expended in performance under unpredictable and uncontrollable stressors than under predictable and controllable ones. Because there is a greater expenditure of effort in these conditions, capacity depletion is accelerated and fatigue effects are more likely to occur after a relatively short period of time. Subjects exposed to unpredictable, uncontrollable noise show a degradation in task performance on a second task that is indicative of a depletion of total available capacity. Degradation in performance on a second task as a function of duration of noise/work exposure on a first task is reported by Hartley (1973). Errors on a serial reaction-time task were made more often by subjects working under noise in a pretest period and quiet during the testing period than by those who spent the pretest period in quiet and the test period in noise. Thus, it appears that prior exposure to noise (task during pretesting period was either the same RT or reading) results in a depletion in total available capacity and a consequent inability to adequately perform a subsequent task.

In a study on the aftereffects of density by Sherrod (1974), a noncrowded group of subjects, a crowded group, and a crowded group who were told that they could leave the room if they felt too uncomfortable (perceived control over termination of stress) worked for 1 hour on either a simple or complex task. Immediately afterward, all subjects worked in a noncrowded situation on two additional tasks, one involving frustration tolerance and the other involving quality of proofreading performance (cf. Glass & Singer, 1972). Crowding had no effect on simple or complex task performance. In the postcrowding situation, however, crowding resulted in negative behavioral aftereffects on the frustration tolerance measure, although perceived control ameliorated these aftereffects. There were no significant aftereffects on the proofreading measure.

The work on audio analgesia in the suppression of pain also suggests the existence of aftereffects. Licklider (1961) reports that "stimulation of intense noise appears to have a more or less persistent aftereffect on pain. In some instances, after long or intense exposure, it has been possible for patients to undergo ordinarily painful operations without further presentation of noise [p. 52]."

Evidence reported in this section lends support to Assumption (4) of the proposed model. Available attention appears to be depleted by prolonged spells on demanding tasks. Moreover, performance under conditions of environmental stress accelerates this depletion.

SUMMARY OF THE MODEL

A short summary of the important points of the model is appropriate at this point. As suggested by earlier theorists, information overload occurs at any time that the demand for attention exceeds total available capacity. The present model diverges from previous theory in suggesting that total available capacity is not fixed and in fact "shrinks" when there are prolonged demands on attention. Thus, an individual can attend to fewer inputs after prolonged demands than he or she can in a rested state. The model further suggests that the presence of an environmental stressor, because it requires an allocation of capacity, is likely to create informational overload. Finally, the most usual strategy employed to deal with overload is the focusing of available attention on the aspects of the environment most relevant to task performance at the cost of less relevant inputs.

IMPLICATIONS FOR PERFORMANCE

Because the proposed model is presented in the language of the performance literature, many of the implications of the theory for performance are evident. It is, however, necessary to clarify an important point. Under what conditions is task performance adversely affected, and under what conditions is performance positively affected by attention overload?

As discussed earlier, the less available attention, the fewer the inputs that can be processed. The first inputs to be reduced (dropped out) are those that are irrelevant or only partially relevant to task performance. As available capacity decreases, task-relevant cues are also neglected. In some tasks, proficiency demands the use of a wide range of cues (e.g., dual-task performance or single tasks requiring the integration of information from many sources). Any reduction in available capacity is likely to adversely affect performance on such tasks, because remaining attention would likely be less than that required to process task-relevant cues. In other tasks, proficiency demands the use of only a restricted range of cues. Such tasks improve with moderate decreases in available attention (improvement in performance occurs only to the extent that reducing competing cues facilitates a particular task) but are detrimentally affected when available capacity falls below that required to process task-relevant cues. Thus, continued reduction in capacity will improve and then impair proficiency.

Recent analyses of the effects of noise on task performance (e.g., Hockey, 1970a) suggest support for this interpretation. Because noise is assumed to require capacity, there is less attention available for tasks performed in noise than in quiet. Thus, in reviewing the effects of acoustic noise on visual monitoring efficiency, Hockey finds that multisource tasks, requiring the integration of information from many sources, are generally impaired by noise, whereas single-source tasks, on which performance is improved by a focusing of attention, are generally performed better under noise than quiet. In fact, all the reviewed experiments using more than one source (e.g., Broadbent, 1951, 1954; Broadbent & Gregory, 1963) are impaired by noise. In contrast, those studies using single-source tasks (e.g., Davies & Hockey, 1966; Kirk & Hecht, 1963) characteristically result in increments in task performance or in no effect.

The negative effects of noise on performance in the dual-task studies cited earlier are consistent with the proposed effects of overload and with the findings of Hockey's review. To complete the picture, it is appropriate to examine a task in which performance is improved when competing stimuli are ignored. One such task is the Stroop Color-Word (CW) test (Jensen & Rohwer, 1966; Stroop, 1935). The task stimuli are the names of four colors (green, red, orange, and blue), each of which is printed in one of the other three colors. That is, the word "green" may be printed in either red, orange, or blue. The four color words are presented randomly over a series of trials, and the subject is asked to say aloud the color in which the word is printed. In order to be successful at the task, the subject must ignore the word itself and attend only to the color in which it is printed. Thus, focusing attention on relevant cues (color) to the detriment of irrelevant cues (words) should improve task performance. In fact, the facilitative effect of noise on Stroop performance is reported by several investigators (Hartley & Adams, 1974; Houston, 1969; Houston & Jones, 1967; O'Malley & Poplawsky, 1971). In contrast, a similar task not requiring the subjects to ignore competitive stimuli (reading sets of colored asterisks) is not affected by noise (Hartley & Adams, 1974;[5] Houston, 1969).

Evidence for the improvement and subsequent impairment of proficiency as available attention decreases is also provided by the research on the Stroop. Stroop performance is better when the test is administered under noise than when administered in quiet. Thus, attention that, under quiet, is allocated to competing cues is being consumed in the monitoring of noise. However, there is a decrement in Stroop performance when the test is given after prolonged exposure to noise (Glass & Singer, 1972; Hartley & Adams, 1974). Thus, there is not enough available attention after prolonged performance under noise (cognitive fatigue effect) to process relevant task cues.

IMPLICATIONS FOR SOCIAL BEHAVIOR

In order to understand the implications of the proposed model, some translation from performance jargon to the language of social behavior is necessary. The term "task-relevant" is interpreted as meaning relevant to fulfilling one's own personal needs and wants. Thus, attentional overload results in a focusing of attention on environmental inputs relevant to one's own goals, neglecting other cues, social and nonsocial alike.

Important social cues that are often neglected when attention is restricted include those that carry information concerning the moods and subtly expressed needs of others. The neglect of such cues results in a lowered probability of help-

---

[5]This "focusing-of-attention" effect is often attributed to fluctuations in arousal. Thus Easterbrook (1959) suggests that increases in arousal are associated with increased neglect of environmental cues. At first, irrelevant cues are dropped out, and as arousal increases, task-relevant cues are neglected. Hockey (1970a) suggests a similar analysis viewing the effect of arousal as a change in the information-selection strategy of the organism. Although the evidence seems to bear out that a focusing of attention does occur under conditions that are expected to cause arousal, autonomic indices often find no perceptible physiological changes (e.g., Houston, 1969). It is also possible to interpret conditions that are usually associated with arousal as increasing attentional load. Moreover, many situations that are not expected to induce physiological arousal but are designed to overload attentional capacity (e.g., Kanarick & Petersen, 1969) also result in attentional focusing.

ing another, expressing sympathy for another, or reacting appropriately to another's needs. The experience of attentional overload can affect the probability of such helping responses in three ways:

1. The cue that suggests that a helping response may be required is *not even perceived*. Thus, if a husband doesn't see the distressed look on his wife's face, he cannot know that she is in need of sympathy. Likewise, if a potential helper does not see a man lying on the sidewalk, he cannot give him aid.

2. The cue is perceived, but a lack of available attention makes the person *incapable of evaluating its significance*. Because distress cues are often ambiguous, an evaluation is usually required in order to determine whether a cue actually represents distress and whether intervention on the part of the potential helper is appropriate (cf. Latané & Darley, 1970). This evaluation requires a substantial allocation of attention. Thus, a husband may perceive an emotional expression on his wife's face but not interpret its meaning. Likewise, a man lying on the sidewalk may be seen but his plight not recognized.

3. The distress cue is perceived and evaluated, but aiding the person in need *requires effort that is not available* or that is being reserved for an ongoing activity judged more important. This analysis is not meant as an explanation for neglecting someone who is clearly in desperate need but rather suggests that many situations that may, under less demanding conditions, elicit token aid are ignored under conditions of attentional overload. Thus, a husband recognizes that his wife is distressed but finds it more important to use his available effort to go over the accounts. Likewise, even though it is clear that the man lying on the sidewalk has fainted, the bystander decides to use his remaining efforts to complete his work at the office.

An attentional interpretation of decreases in sensitivity to others under overload assumes that social cues are ignored in the same way as nonsocial cues. There is, however, at least one fundamental difference between social and nonsocial cues that suggests that they may be processed differently. It is likely that people are more interesting and/or more response-demanding than nonsocial objects. For example, social situations may induce sympathy, empathy, or pity — responses unlikely to be elicited by nonsocial stimuli.

In order to determine the effects of environmental stress on sensitivity to task-irrelevant (peripheral) social cues, we (Cohen & Lezak, 1977) have recently conducted a study of memory for incidental social cues presented under noise. Subjects were presented with six stimuli, each consisting of two slides presented side by side. One of the slides contained a nonsense syllable, and the other (the social cue slide) pictured a person or persons engaged in an interaction or task. Subjects were told that their task was to remember the nonsense syllables in the order that they were presented and that any other visual or auditory stimulation occuring during the experiment was part of our effort to determine the effects of distraction on memory. After stimulus presentation, half of the subjects were given the expected recall test for nonsense syllables. The remaining subjects were told that although we and asked them to learn the nonsense syllables, we would like them to try and remember everything they could about the "distraction" pictures. They were then administered a memory recognition questionnaire that required them to choose out of several choices the "correct" descriptions of the social slides. Individual subjects viewed the stimuli either under 95-decibel random intermittent noise or in quiet. For all subjects, half of the social cue slides portrayed a person(s) in *distress*, and the other half pictured a *calm* person(s). Results indicated that although noise did not affect memory for the nonsense syllables — task-relevant cues, social cue slides — task-irrelevant cues, regardless of whether they depicted calm or distressed persons, were remembered less well under noise than under quiet. Thus, it appears that peripheral cues that are social in nature are ignored (or not deeply processed) under conditions of environmental stress and that the probability of these peripheral cues being processed is not affected by their meaning (distress/calm).

Does this apparent attenuation of peripheral social cues translate into decreased helping? Much of the research on the influence of information overloads on helping behavior is inferential, comparing behavior in urban settings, where many other factors besides information overload are acting, to behavior in less urban settings (cf. Milgram, 1970). However, direct evidence for decreased helping under conditions of attentional overload is provided by several recent experimental studies.

In a study conducted in Holland, Korte, Ypma, & Toppen (1975) used sound level, traffic count, pedestrian count, and a number of visible "public" buildings to specify areas that they characterize as either high or low on environmental inputs. They report that regardless of whether the area is in a city or town, people in low-input areas are more likely to assist a lost person and to grant a street interview than people in high-input areas. A similar lack of helping subjects in high-load environments is reported by Krupat and Epstein (1975) in a laboratory setting. They find that subjects assigned to very heavy work loads are less likely to grant a favor that required interruption on their assigned tasks (subject was to provide some information by writing a letter) than those assigned to light work loads.

Evidence that acoustic noise causes decreases in helping is reported by Matthews and Canon (1975). Subjects were less likely to aid a person who had dropped a pile of books when a loud lawnmower was running than when it was quiet. Moreover, a subtle cue suggesting the legitimacy and degree of need for assistance — a cast on the victim's arm — increased helping under ambient conditions but did not affect the level of helping under noise. This result can be interpreted as supporting an attentional focusing hypothesis. Under noise, subjects did not act on a subtle cue (the arm cast), whereas under quiet, that cue was perceived, evaluated, and acted on.

Two field studies on the effect of density on helping report a similar lack of sensitivity to the needs of others (both studies are reported in Bickman, Teger, Gabriele, McLaughlin, Berger, & Sunaday, 1973). In the first study, students living in low-, medium-, and high-density dormitories were confronted with "lost" letters, apparently dropped by their senders and needing mailing. Results indicated that the greatest percentage of letters were returned by those living in low-density dorms, followed by medium-density dorms, with the least helping occurring in high-density dormitories. In the second study, the lost-letter finding was replicated, and an additional helping measure, whether dorm residents would save milk cartons for an art project that other students were conducting, similarly indicated that the least helping occurred in high-density housing and that medium- and low-density dorms (although not significantly different from each other) helped more. Both studies suggest that those living in high-density — high-load — environments are less responsive to others' needs than those living in lower density — lower load — environments.

An experiment by Sherrod and Downs (1974) investigated the social aftereffects of overload. Subjects were required to proofread a prose passage, underline the errors as they read, and at the same time monitor an audio taped series of random numbers. In the nonoverload conditions, the random numbers were superimposed over a recording of a soothing simulated seashore. In the stimulus-overload condition, the random numbers were superimposed over a recording of Dixieland jazz plus a second male voice reading nonrelevant prose. In a final condition, subjects experienced the same treatment as the stimulus overload condition but were told that they could terminate the distracting stimulation if they found it necessary (perceived control). After the completion of the 20-minute experiment, subjects left the laboratory and were confronted by a second experimenter who asked for voluntary help in pretesting some experimental materials. Subjects in the nonoverload condition were most helpful, followed by subjects in the overload condition with perceived control treatment, and finally by the overload condition. These results are consistent with two earlier suggestions: first, that the experience of overload without perceived control demands a greater allocation of effort than overload with control; and second, that the amount of capacity available following an ongoing activity is inversely proportional to the total demands of the ongoing activity. It follows that the experience of overload without control results in less available effort for perceiving, interpreting, and acting on a distress cue.

Similar results were found in a study of the aftereffects of density and task load that we have recently conducted in a large shopping center (Cohen & Spacapan, 1978). Subjects were required to perform high- or low-information rate shopping tasks during periods in which the shopping center was crowded or un-crowded. After completing their task, subjects (on their way to meet the experi-menter) entered a deserted corridor where they encountered a woman who feigned dropping a contact lens. Those subjects who performed high-load tasks and/or were crowded helped less often and for less time than their low-task-load, uncrowded counterparts. The least help (0%) was offered by those who per-formed high-load tasks under crowded conditions, and the most help (80%) was offered by those who performed low-load tasks under uncrowded conditions. These results are consistent with those of Sherrod and Downs and suggest that cognitive fatigue (and the consequent focusing of attention) can result in insensi-tivity to the needs of others.

The research reviewed up to now supports the argument that a person is less likely to offer simple assistance under environmental stress than under ambient conditions. It is important to note, however, that none of these studies defini-tively establishes that decreased sensitivity to the needs of others is due to an at-tentional deficit. One strong alternative, for example, would attribute these decreases in helping to a negative affective state induced by overload. That is, "I feel bad, therefore I will not help" (cf. Moore, Underwood, & Rosenhan, 1973). Further research is necessary in order to clarify the roles of attentional and affec-tive mechanisms in response to overload.

Another possible (not as yet researched) effect of attentional focusing is to oversimplify and distort perceptions of complex social relationships. Thus, it in-volves less effort to view the relationship between two groups as either clearly positive or clearly negative than it does to view the more subtle similarities and differences between groups. A similar distortion of information can likewise occur in the perception of individuals. Gross cues like group membership are likely to be overemphasized, because effort is not available to process and inter-pret a wider range of information. Evidence of stress-induced distortion in the perception of individuals is provided in a recent paper by Siegel and Steele (1976). In judging individuals on the basis of profiles, subjects making their judgments in noise were more likely to generalize from inadequate information and were more sure of their judgments than those working in a quiet environment.

A similar analysis can be applied to communication under conditions of over-load. The focusing of attention on the major theme and consequent neglect of the more subtle nuances can result in a gross distortion of a communication, es-pecially when it is complex or includes qualifications. Although the distortion of communications under overload poses a major problem in formal communica-tions networks, interesting social implications include the effect of overload on the transmission of rumors and other informal intra- and intergroup messages.

It is clear from the foregoing analyses that the focusing of attention under conditions of overload has a wide variety of implications for both social and non-social behavior. It should be emphasized that the aforementioned effects are likely to occur as aftereffects of stress (or of any high demand conditions) as well as during periods of attentional demand and that the source of inputs demanding attention include stress and nonstress conditions alike.

ACKNOWLEDGMENTS

The author would like to thank Robyn Dawes, Gary Evans, Dave Glass, Harold Hawkins, Stephen Kaplan, Beth Kerr, Ray Klein, Mike Posner, Myron Rothbart, Susan Saegert, Jock Schwank, and Jeff Summers for their comments on the manuscript. A special thanks is due Steve Keele for his patience and guidance during earlier discussions. Research reported in this paper was done in collaboration with Shirlynn Nichol (cognitive fatigue studies) and Anne Lezak (social cue study) and was supported by a grant from the National Science Foundation (SOC 75-09224).

REFERENCES

Adams, J. A., Stenson, H. H., & Humes, J. M. Monitoring of complex visual displays, II. Effects of visual load and response complexity on human vigilance. *Human Factors,* 1961, *3,* 213–221.

Averill, J. R. Personal control over aversive stimuli and its relationship to stress. *Psychological Bulletin,* 1973, *80,* 286–303.

Badia, P., & Defran, R. H. Orienting responses and GSR conditioning: A dilemma. *Psychological Review,* 1970, *77,* 171–181.

Bahrick, H. P., Noble, M., & Fitts, P. M. Extra-task performance as a measure of learning a primary task. *Journal of Experimental Psychology,* 1954, *48,* 298–302.

Bahrick, H. P., & Shelly, C. Time sharing as an index of automatization. *Journal of Experimental Psychology,* 1958, *56,* 288–293.

Bakan, P. Discrimination decrement as a function of time in a prolonged vigil. *Journal of Experimental Psychology,* 1955, *50,* 387–390.

Bergum, B. O., & Lehr, D. J. Vigilance performance as a function of interpolated rest. *Journal of Applied Psychology,* 1962, *46,* 425–427.

Berlyne, D. E. *Conflict, arousal and curiosity.* New York: McGraw-Hill, 1960.

Bickman, L., Teger, A., Gabriele, T., McLaughlin, C., Berger, M., & Sunaday, E. Dormitory density and helping behavior. *Environment and Behavior,* 1973, *5,* 465–490.

Boggs, D. H., & Simon, J. R. Differential effect of noise on tasks of varying complexity. *Journal of Applied Psychology,* 1968, *52,* 148–153.

Broadbent, D. E. *The twenty dials test and the twenty lights test under noise.* (Research Rep., 160–171). Cambridge, England: Medical Research Council/Applied Psychology Research Unit, 1951.

Broadbent, D. E. Neglect of the surroundings in relation to fatigue decrements in output. In W. F. Floyd & A. T. Welford (Eds.), *Symposium on fatigue.* London: H. K. Lewis & Co., for the Ergonomics Research Society, 1953. (a)

Broadbent, D. E. Noise, pace performance and vigilance tasks. *British Journal of Psychology,* 1953, *44,* 295–303. (b)

Broadbent, D. E. Some effects of noise on visual performance. *Quarterly Journal of Experimental Psychology,* 1954, *6,* 1–5.

Broadbent, D. E. *Decision and stress.* New York: Academic Press, 1971.

Broadbent, D. E., & Gregory, M. Vigilance considered as a statistical decision. *British Journal of Psychology,* 1963, *54,* 309–323.

Brown, I. D. Measuring the "spare mental capacity" of car drivers by a subsidiary auditory task. *Ergonomics,* 1962, *5,* 247–250.

Brown, I. D. A comparison of two subsidiary tasks used to measure fatigue in car drivers. *Ergonomics,* 1965, *8,* 467–472.

Brown, I. D., & Poulton, E. C. Measuring the spare "mental capacity" of car drivers by a subsidiary task. *Ergonomics,* 1961, *4,* 35–40.

Cohen, S., & Lezak, A. Noise and inattentiveness to social cues. *Environment and Behavior,* 1977, *9,* 559–572.

Cohen, S., & Spacapan, S. The aftereffects of stress: An attentional interpretation. *Environmental Psychology and Nonverbal Behavior,* 1978, in press.

Corcoran, D. W. J. Noise and loss of sleep. *Quarterly Journal of Experimental Psychology,* 1962, *14,* 178–182.

Davies, D. R., & Hockey, G. R. J. The effects of noise and doubling the signal frequency on individual differences in visual vigilance performance. *British Journal of Psychology,* 1966, *57,* 381–389.

Davis, D. R. *Pilot error* (Air Ministry Publication A.P. 3139A). London: Her Majesty's Stationery Office, 1948.

Dimond, S. J. Facilitation of performance through the use of the timing system. *Journal of Experimental Psychology,* 1966, *71,* 181–183.

Easterbrook, J. A. The effect of emotion on cue-utilization and the organization of behavior. *Psychological Review,* 1959, *66,* 183–201.

Eschenbrenner, A. J. Effects of intermittent noise on the performance of a complex psychomotor task. *Human Factors,* 1971, *13,* 59–63.

Evans, G. W. *Behavioral and physiological consequences of crowding in humans.* Unpublished doctoral dissertation, University of Massachusetts, Amherst, 1975.

Finkelman, J. M., & Glass, D. C. Reappraisal of the relationship between noise and human performance by means of a subsidiary task measure. *Journal of Applied Psychology,* 1970, *54,* 211–213.

Forrest, D. W. Influence of length of task on rate of work and level of muscular tension. *Occupational Psychology,* 1958, *32,* 253–257.

Freedman, J. L. The effects of population density on humans. In J. T. Fawcett (Ed.), *Psychological perspectives on population.* New York: Basic Books, 1973.

Glass, D. C., & Singer, J. E. *Urban stress: Experiments on noise and social stressors.* New York: Academic Press, 1972.

Glass, D. C., Singer, J. E., & Friedman, L. N. Psychic cost of adaptation to an environmental stressor. *Journal of Personality and Social Psychology,* 1969, *12,* 200–210.

Glass, D. C., Singer, J. E., Leonard, H. S., Krantz, D., Cohen, S., & Cummings, H. X. Perceived control of aversive stimulation and the reduction of stress responses. *Journal of Personality,* 1973, *41,* 577–595.

Gould, J. D., & Schaffer, A. The effects of divided attention on visual monitoring of multichannel displays. *Human Factors,* 1967, *9,* 191–201.

Hartley, L. R. Effect of prior noise or prior performance on serial reaction. *Journal of Experimental Psychology,* 1973, *101,* 255–261.

Hartley, L. R., & Adams, R. G. Effects of noise on the Stroop test. *Journal of Experimental Psychology,* 1974, *102,* 62–66.

Hockey, G. R. J. Effect of loud noise on attentional selectivity. *Quarterly Journal of Experimental Psychology,* 1970, *22,* 28–36. (a)

Hockey, G. R. J. Signal probability and spatial location as possible bases for increased selectivity in noise. *Quarterly Journal of Experimental Psychology,* 1970, *22,* 37–42. (b)

Houston, B. K. Noise, task-difficulty, and Stroop color–word performance. *Journal of Experimental Psychology*, 1969, *82*, 403–404.

Houston, B. K., & Jones, T. M. Distraction and Stroop color–word performance. *Journal of Experimental Psychology*, 1967, *74*, 54–56.

Jensen, A. R., & Rohwer, W. D., Jr. The Stroop color–word test: A review. *Acta Psychologica*, 1966, *25*, 36–39.

Jerison, H. J. Effects of noise on human performance. *Journal of Applied Psychology*, 1959, *43*, 96–101.

Kahneman, D. *Attention and effort.* Englewood Cliffs, N.J.: Prentice-Hall, Inc., 1973.

Kalsbeek, J. W. H. Measure objective de la surcharge mentale: Nouvelles applications de la méthode des doubles tâches. *Travail Humain*, 1965, *1–2*, 122–132.

Kaplan, S. Tranquility and challenge in the natural environment. In *Children, nature and the urban environment. Symposium Proceedings Northeastern Forest Experiment Station.* Upper Darby, Pa.: U.S.D.A. Forest Service, 1977.

Kanarick, A. F., & Petersen, R. C. Effects of value on the monitoring of multichannel displays. *Human Factors*, 1969, *11*, 313–320.

Katz, D. Gestalt laws of mental work. *British Journal of Psychology*, 1949, *39*, 175–183.

Kerr, B. Processing demands during mental operations. *Memory and Cognition*, 1973, *1*, 401–412.

Kirk, R. E., & Hecht, E. Maintenance of vigilance by programmed noise. *Perceptual and Motor Skills*, 1963, *16*, 553–560.

Korte, C., Ypma, A., & Toppen, C. Helpfulness in Dutch society as a function of urbanization and environmental input level. *Journal of Personality and Social Psychology*, 1975, *32*, 996–1003.

Krupat, E., & Epstein, Y. *I'm too busy: The effects of overload and diffusion of responsibility on working and helping.* Unpublished manuscript, Rutgers University, 1975.

Latané, B., & Darley, J. M. *The unresponsive bystander: Why doesn't he help?* New York: Appleton-Century-Crofts, 1970.

Lazarus, R. S. *Psychological stress and the coping process.* New York: McGraw-Hill, 1966.

Leibowitz, H. W., & Appelle, S. The effect of a central task on luminance thresholds for peripherally presented stimuli. *Human Factors*, 1969, *11*, 387–392.

Licklider, J. C. R. On psychophysiological models. In W. A. Rosenblith (Ed.), *Sensory communications.* Cambridge, Mass.: MIT Press, 1961.

Mackworth, J. F. Performance decrement in vigilance, threshold, and high speed perceptual motor tasks. *Canadian Journal of Psychology*, 1964, *18*, 209–223.

Mackworth, J. F. *Vigilance and attention.* Baltimore: Penguin Books, Inc., 1970.

Mackworth, N. H. *Researches on the measurement of human performance* (Spec. Rep. No. 268). London: Medical Research Council, 1950.

Mandler, G., & Watson, D. L. Anxiety and the interruption of behavior. In C. D. Spielberger (Ed.), *Anxiety and behavior.* New York: Academic Press, 1966.

Mathews, K. E., Jr., & Canon, L. K. Environmental noise level as a determinant of helping behavior. *Journal of Personality and Social Psychology*, 1975, *32*, 571–577.

McCormack, P. D. Performance in a vigilance task as a function of length of inter-stimulus interval and interpolated rest. *Canadian Journal of Psychology*, 1958, *12*, 242–260.

McCormack, P. D. Performance in a vigilance task as a function of length of inter-stimulus interval. *Canadian Journal of Psychology*, 1960, *14*, 265–268.

McFarland, R. A., Holway, A. N., & Hurvich, L. M. *Studies of visual fatigue* (Rep.) Cambridge, Mass.: Harvard Graduate School of Business Administration, 1942, 160 *et seq.*

Milgram, S. The experience of living in cities: A psychological analysis. *Science*, 1970, *167*, 1461–1468.

Miller, J. G. Psychological aspects of communication overloads. In R. W. Waggoner & D. J. Carels (Eds.), *International psychiatry clinics: Communication in clinical practice.* Boston: Little, Brown, 1964.

Moore, B., Underwood, B., & Rosenhan, D. L. Affect and altruism. *Developmental Psychology,* 1973, *8,* 99–104.

Mowbray, G. H. Simultaneous vision and audition: The detection of elements missing from over-learned sequences. *Journal of Experimental Psychology,* 1952, *44,* 292–300.

Mowbray, G. H. Simultaneous vision and audition: The comprehension of prose passages with varying levels of difficulty. *Journal of Experimental Psychology,* 1953, *46,* 365–372.

Mowbray, G. H. The perception of short phrases presented simultaneously for visual and auditory reception. *Quarterly Journal of Experimental Psychology,* 1954, *6,* 86–92.

Murdock, B. B. Effects of a subsidiary task on short-term memory. *British Journal of Psychology,* 1965, *56,* 413–419.

O'Malley, J. J., & Poplawsky, A. Noise induced arousal and breadth of attention. *Perceptual and Motor Skills,* 1971, *33,* 887–890.

Pervin, L. A. The need to predict and control under conditions of threat. *Journal of Personality,* 1963, *31,* 570–587.

Plutchik, R. The effects of high intensity intermittent sound on performance, feeling, and physiology. *Psychological Bulletin,* 1959, *56,* 133–151.

Posner, M. I., & Rossman, E. Effect of size and location of informational transforms upon short-term retention. *Journal of Experimental Psychology,* 1965, *70,* 496–505.

Poulton, E. C. *Environment and human efficiency.* Springfield, Ill.: Charles C Thomas, 1970.

Poulton, E. C. Measuring the order of difficulty of visual-motor tasks. *Ergonomics,* 1958, *1,* 234–239.

Rabbitt, P. M. A. Recognition: Memory for words correctly heard in noise. *Psychonomic Science,* 1966, *6,* 383–384.

Rabbitt, P. M. A. Channel-capacity, intelligibility and immediate memory. *The Quarterly Journal of Experimental Psychology,* 1968, *20,* 241–248.

Rapoport, A. Toward a redefinition of density. *Environment and Behavior,* 1975, *2,* 133–158.

Rey, P., & Rey, J. P. Les effets comparés de deux éclairages fluorescents sur une tâche visuelle et des tests de "fatigue." *Ergonomics,* 1963, *6,* 393–401.

Saegert, S. Crowding: Cognitive overload and behavioral constraint. In W. F. E. Preiser (Ed.), *Environmental design research: Proceedings of EDRA IV Conference.* Stroudsberg, Pa.: Dowden, Hutchinson & Ross, Inc., 1973.

Saldanha, E. L. *Alternating an exacting visual task with either rest or similar work* (A.P.U. 289). Cambridge, England: Applied Psychology Unit, 1957.

Sanders, A. F. The influence of noise on two discrimination tasks. *Ergonomics,* 1961, *4,* 253–258.

Saufley, W. H., & Bilodeau, I. Protective self-pacing during learning. *Journal of Experimental Psychology,* 1963, *66,* 596–600.

Sherrod, D. R. Crowding, perceived control, and behavioral aftereffects. *Journal of Applied Social Psychology,* 1974, *4,* 171–186.

Sherrod, D. R., & Downs, R. Environmental determinants of altruism: The effects of stimulus overload and perceived control on helping. *Journal of Experimental Social Psychology,* 1974, *10,* 468–479.

Siegel, J. M., & Steele, C. M. *The effects of environmental distraction and anticipation of future interaction on interpersonal judgments.* Unpublished manuscript, University of Washington, 1976.

Sokolov, E. N. [*Perception and the conditioned reflex*] (S. W. Waydenfold, trans.). Oxford: Pergamon Press, 1963. (Originally published, 1958.)

Sokolov, E. N. The modeling properties of the nervous system. In M. Cole & I. Maltzman (Eds.), *A handbook of contemporary Soviet psychology*. New York: Basic Books, 1969.

Solandt, D. Y., & Partridge, D. M. Research on auditory problems presented by naval operations. *Journal of Canadian Medical Service*, 1946, *3*, 323–329.

Stroop, J. R. Studies of interference in serial verbal reaction. *Journal of Experimental Psychology*, 1935, *18*, 643–662.

Swets, J. A. The relative operating characteristics in psychology. *Science*, 1973, *187*, 990–1000.

Uno, T., & Grings, W. W. Autonomic components of orienting behavior. *Psychophysiology*, 1965, *1*, 311–321.

Wachtel, P. L. Anxiety, attention, and coping with threat. *Journal of Abnormal Psychology*, 1968, *73*, 137–143.

Webster, R. G., & Haslerud, G. M. Influence on extreme peripheral vision of attention to a visual or auditory task. *Journal of Experimental Psychology*, 1964, *68*, 269–272.

Welford, A. T. *Fundamentals of skill*. London: Methuen & Co., 1968.

Wilkinson, R. T. Interaction of noise, with knowledge of results and sleep deprivation. *Journal of Experimental Psychology*, 1963, *66*, 332–337.

Wilkinson, R. T. Some factors influencing the effect of environmental stressors upon performance. *Psychological Bulletin*, 1969, *72*, 260–272.

Youngling, E. W. The effects of thermal environments and sleep deprivation upon concurrent central and peripheral tasks. *Dissertation Abstracts International*, 1967, *1*, 348–B.

2 On Maintaining Urban Norms: A Field Experiment in the Subway

Stanley Milgram
John Sabini
Graduate Center,
The City University of New York

ABSTRACT

This study attempted to probe residual norms of everyday life by means of experimental techniques. An experiment was conducted in which a norm of the New York subway was violated by experimenters who asked passengers, "Excuse me. May I have your seat?" Contrary to expectations, a majority of requests (68.3%) resulted in the offer of a seat. In other conditions, where experimenters offered a trivial reason for wanting the seat, or forewarned the subject of the request, there was significantly less success at obtaining a seat (41.9% and 37.5%, respectively). Most experimenters reported an acute and intense inhibition before making the request, and that they felt compelled to act sick if a seat was offered. Three additional experimental conditions assessed the role of justification, surprise, and mode of communication for the compliant response. The results are interpreted in terms of Berger and Luckmann's (1967) argument that the sheer objectivity of the social world is the primary and essential means of social control. The study represents a fusion of ethnomethodological questions with techniques of experimental analysis.

INTRODUCTION

The general question that motivated this research was: How are social norms maintained? Our focus was on the type of norm described by Garfinkel (1964) as "routine grounds of everyday activity," norms which regulate everyday activity and which are neither made explicit nor codified. Scheff (1960) refers to this class of norms as "residual rules," residual in the sense that they are the restraints on behavior that persist after the formal social norms have been sorted out of the analysis. Scheff isolates these rules on the basis of two criteria: (1) people must be in substantial agreement about them; and (2) they are not noticed until a violation occurs. These rules have been likened to the rules of grammar in that one can follow them without an explicit knowledge of their content and yet notice a violation immediately.

The fact that these residual rules are usually unexpressed creates a serious obstacle to their study: We are virtually inarticulate about them. When compared with formal laws, for example, which have been explicitly codified, residual rules have been left unarticulated by the culture.

An important distinction between these residual rules and laws can be drawn in terms of enforcement. The mechanism for the maintenance of laws is obvious. The entire law enforcement establishment is charged with the responsibility of keeping behavior within the law. The society is quite explicit about the consequences of breaking the law and about who should administer punishment. But who is charged with maintaining residual rules? What consequences should the residual rule breaker expect? Scheff posits a negative feedback system through which the rule breaker is returned to the straight and narrow, but he does not elaborate on the feedback process itself. Scott (1971), in an analysis of social norms from the point of view of the operant conditioning paradigm, defines social norms as "patterns of sanctions" and sanctions as the "reinforcing effect of interaction [p. 85]." In this formulation, norms are maintained by the negative consequences of the violation. If this is the case, it should be possible to identify the negative consequences that are supposed to befall the violator. This, then, determined our strategy: we would violate a residual rule and observe the consequences to the violator.

The idea for studying this class of norms by their violation was introduced by Garfinkel (1964); his accounts contain qualitative evidence about the consequences of norm violation. The present research goes further in measuring the effects of violating a residual norm; it centers on a discrete and measureable response to the rule-breakers's action. We are thus able to quantify how people react to violated norms and by systematically changing features of the encounter, to treat the matter experimentally.

The residual rule selected for study was a rule of social behavior on the New York City subway system. The requirements of appropriate social behavior on the subway are, on the face of it, simple. People get on the subway for a very clear and specific reason: to get from one place to another in a brief period of time. The amount of interaction among the riders required for this purpose is minimal and the rules governing this interaction are widely adhered to. One rule of subway behavior is that seats are filled on a first-come, first-served basis. Another implicit rule is one that discourages passengers from talking to one another. Even though riders are often squeezed into very close proximity, they are rarely observed to converse. The experimenters in this study violated these rules by asking people for their seats. This procedure allowed for discrete, measurable responses: People could either give up their seats or refuse to do so.

Several notions about the outcome of such a request may be formulated:

1. Scott's analysis predicts that such a violation would result in "negative consequences."

2. Scheff suggests that a possible outcome of a residual rule violation is a process of "normalization." Normalization is the attribution of a meaning to the violation that would make it seem not to be a violation at all. The attribution — "the experimenter is asking because he is sick" — would be such a "normalization."

3. Most of the experimenters expected not only refusal but some form of active rebuke.

4. Common sense suggests that it is impossible to obtain a seat on the subway simply by asking for it.

Harold Takooshian obtained data on this last point. He asked 16 people to predict what percentage of requests would result in the offer of a seat. Answers ranged from 1% to 55%; the median prediction was that 14% of those who were asked would give up their seats.

Before we describe the experimental procedure, it is worth pointing out some things that the procedure was *not*. The procedure was not an attempt to obtain seats by demanding that riders give them up. Experimenters were instructed to be sure to phrase their requests as requests, not as demands. The procedure was not designed to question the subjects' right to their seats. The subjects' right to their seats was affirmed in the request; you do not request things from people which they do not rightfully possess. The procedure does *not* involve some momentous or unreasonable request. Nothing of any great or lasting value was requested from the subjects. It is, in fact, the observation that this request is so reasonable and yet so rare that suggests the operation of some strong inhibitory social force.

PROCEDURE

The experimenters were six male and four female graduate students. One woman was black; the other experimenters were white. Experimenters worked in pairs; as one performed the manipulation, the other recorded the data and observations.

The passengers on several mid-town routes of the New York City subway system formed the subject pool for the experiment. Experimenters were free to select their own subjects under the following constraints: Each experimenter asked one passenger from each of the following categories: man under 40 (by experimenter's approximation), woman under 40, man over 40, woman over 40. One member of each category was approached by each experimenter in each of the three conditions described in the following. Experimenters approached members of their own race only.

1. In the first condition (no justification), the experimenter approached a seated subject and said, "Excuse me. May I have your seat?" The observer recorded the age and sex of the subject, whether or not the subject gave up the seat, and other reactions of the subjects and other passengers. Information about the time of day, subway line, and nearest station was also recorded.

As Table 2.1 shows, 56% of the subjects got up and offered their seats to the experimenters. An additional 12.3% of the subjects slid over to make room for the experimenter. (Experimenters had been instructed to ask for seats only if

TABLE 2.1
Subway Experiments: Responses in Each
Experimental Condition[a]

No Justification Condition n = 41	
Subjects who gave up their seats	56.0%
Subjects who slid over to make room for E	12.3%
Subjects who did not give up their seats	31.7%
Trivial Justification Condition n = 43	
Subjects who gave their seats	37.2%
Subjects who slid over to make room for E	4.7%[b]
Subjects who did not give up their seats	58.1%
Overheard Condition n = 41	
Subjects who gave up their seats	26.8%
Subjects who slid over to make room for E	9.8%[c]
Subjects who did not give up their seats	63.4%
Written Condition n = 20	
Subjects who gave their seats	50.0%
Subjects who slid over to make room for E	0.0%[d]
Subjects did not give up their seats	50.0%

[a]Overall chi squared for four conditions collapsing subjects who gave up their seats with those who slid over = 9.44, $df = 3$, $p < 0.05$.

[b]Z test between No Justification and Trivial Justification conditions (collapsing as above): $Z = 2.3$, $p < 0.05$.

[c]Z test between No Justicication and Overheard Condition (collapsing as above): $Z = 2.7$, $p < 0.05$.

[d]Z test between No Justification Condition and Written condition (collapsing as above): not significant.

all of the seats in a car were taken, but it sometimes occurred that, although there did not appear to be any seats, room could be generated if the passengers squeezed together.) If these two responses are combined, we see that 68.3% of the subjects obtained seats by asking for them.

2. A second condition tested the hypothesis that subjects gave up their seats because they assumed the experimenters had some important reason for requesting it. In order to rule out this assumption, experimenters were instructed to say "Excuse me. May I have your seat? I can't read my book standing up." The experimenter stood holding a paperback mystery. It was expected that by supplying this trivial reason, experimenters would receive fewer seats. The expectation was confirmed; experimenters received significantly fewer seats (41.9% of the requests, $z = 2.3$ p <0.05). In Scheff's terms, the trivial justification prevented the process of "normalization;" subjects could not as easily create some adequate justification for the request.

3. A third condition was included because we believed that subjects might have been so startled by the request that they didn't have time to formulate an adequate reply.[1] It seemed that they might have surrendered their seats because it was easier to do so than to figure out how to refuse in the brief time allowed. This condition was, therefore, designed to allow more time to formulate a reply.

To do this, it was necessary to alert the passenger that a seat might be requested. An experimenter and confederate entered the subway car from different doors and converged in front of the subject. They then engaged in the following conversation, while giving the impression that they were strangers: E to confederate, "Excuse me. Do you think it would be alright if I asked someone for a seat?" The confederate replied, "What?" E repeated, "Do you think it would be alright if I asked someone for a seat?" The confederate replied, noncommitally, "I don't know."

This conversation was enacted in a sufficiently loud voice so that the passengers seated in front of the pair would definitely overhear it. The seated passengers would be alerted to the possibility that one of them might be approached with a request to surrender his or her seat. It gave the seated passengers time to formulate a response to the request, eliminating the startle component of the earlier conditions.

Thus, after acting out the foregoing exchange, the experimenter paused for approximately 10 seconds, then turned to the nearest seated passenger, and re-

---

[1]Although it might seem to be a simple matter to say "No" to the request, as Goffman (1971) points out, requests demand either compliance or an "accounted denial." That is, one does not merely say "no" to a polite request, one gives a justification for saying "no." It takes time to realize that a justification is not required in this case or to construct one. Many subjects may have given up their seats simply because they didn't know how *not* to.

quested his or her seat. In this condition, experimenters received seats only 36.5% of the time, compared to 68.3% in Condition 1. The additional time between the overhearing of the conversation and the direct request was used to advantage. Subjects were better prepared to turn down the request.

4. Finally, we wished to separate the content of the request from the oral manner in which it was delivered. An orally delivered question directed to a person seems to demand an immediate oral response. We wondered whether a written message would reduce the demand for an immediate and obliging response. Accordingly, in this condition, the experimenter stood in front of the subject and wrote the following message on a sheet of notebook paper: "Excuse me. May I have your seat? I'd like very much to sit down. Thank you." The experimenter then passed the message to the subject, saying, "Excuse me." We expected fewer seats than in the basic variant, as the request on paper seemed less direct and somewhat more distant, especially since the subject was not forced to engage the experimenter in eye contact as he formulated a reply. Our expectation was wrong. Experimenters received seats 50.0% of the time, a nonsignificant decrease from the initial condition. (Each experimenter carried out this procedure twice rather than four times; the overall n equaled 20.) The reason for this result is not clear. This method seemed to add a touch of the bizarre to the procedure, perhaps adding to the subject's eagerness to end the whole interaction by simply giving up his seat.

Observers also recorded other aspects of the subjects' reactions. Subjects often had a vacant and bewildered facial expression. Of the subjects who gave up their seats in the initial condition, 70% did so without asking, "Why?"[2] Other subjects responded by simply saying, "No." Some subjects didn't seem to be distressed at all. Subjects who attributed sickness to the experimenter were often very concerned and comforting.

Information was also gathered about the reactions of other passengers who witnessed the incident. On a few occassions, other passengers openly chided a subject who had given up a seat. A more common reaction was for one rider to turn to another and say something such as, "Did you see that? He asked for a seat!" Such a comment points to the abnormal nature of the event and invites criticism of it. Witnesses to the exchange often turned and stared at the experimenter as he or she left the car.

The effects of the sex and age of experimenters and subjects are noted in Tables 2.2 and 2.3. Although these variables yield substantial differences in results, they are somewhat tangential to our main thesis and are not discussed in detail here.

---

[2]If subjects asked, "Why," experimenters were instructed to respond, "I'm very tired." If the subject proposed a reason, "Are you sick?" the experimenter was to agree.

TABLE 2.2
Effect of Sex of Experimenter and Subject
on Acceding to Request (For All Conditions)

Sex of Experi- menter	Sex of Subject	No. of Subjects (n)	Responses		
			Got Up (% of n)	Didn't Get Up (% of n)	Slid Over (% of n)
M	M	45	40.0	53.3	6.7
	F	40	30.0	65.0	5.0
Total	(M + F)	85	35.3	58.8	5.9
F	M	30	66.7	26.7	6.7
	F	29	34.5	51.7	13.8
Total	(M + F)	59	50.8	39.0	10.2

TABLE 2.3
Effect of Experimenter Sex and Subject
Age on Acceding to Request (For All Conditions)

Age of Subject	Sex of Experi- menter	No. of Subjects (n)	Responses		
			Got Up (% of n)	Didn't Get Up (% of n)	Slid Over (% of n)
Under 40	M	42	54.7	42.8	2.5
	F	30	63.3	30.0	6.7
Total	(M + F)	72	58.3	37.5	4.2
Over 40	M	43	27.9	62.9	9.2
	F	29	37.9	48.2	13.9
Total	(M + F)	72	31.9	57.0	11.1

An important aspect of the maintenance of social norms is revealed in the emotional reaction of the experimenters. Most students reported extreme difficulty in carrying out the assignment. Students reported that when standing in front of a subject, they felt anxious, tense, and embarrassed. Frequently, they were unable to vocalize the request for a seat and had to withdraw. They sometimes feared that they were the center of attention of the car and were often unable to look directly at the subject. Once having made the request and received a seat, they sometimes felt a need to enact behavior that would make the request appear justified (e.g., mimicking illness; some even felt faint).

We introduced our study partly in terms of the operant conditioning paradigm by Scott as a framework for the understanding of social norms. What implications do our results have for his position? The answer depends on how one interprets "patterns of sanctions" which Scott holds maintain social norms. If this phrase is interpreted in its most simple and direct sense, and in a way consistent with the operant paradigm, it means the objectively specifiable response of the social environment to the violation. If we use this interpretation, the operant analysis does not work. The response on the part of others to a request for a seat is usually to grant the request. The 68.3% rate with which experimenters received seats corresponds to a variable ratio schedule of positive reinforcement (VR2). Skinner (1953) has found that behavior reinforced under this schedule is enhanced rather than discouraged. If we take "patterns of sanctions" to include the internal, emotional effects of the request which are not produced by the environment but which are direct accompaniments of the experimenters' behavior, the analysis has some merit, but it leads directly to the question: Why does the act of making this simple request cause such an acute emotional response?[3]

One might approach this question by focusing on the content of the request; after all, the experimenters did ask for a seat from someone when they had no clear right to do so. But this focus on the seat seems misguided. The intensity of the emotion the experimenters experienced is incommensurate with the small cost involved in the subjects' giving up their seats. The significance of the request lies not in the seat (that is not the heart of the matter), but in the redefinition of the immediate relationship between experimenters and subjects that the request involves. Since it is this disruption of relationships that constitutes the essence of the violation, it can better be understood as a breach of a structure of social interaction than as merely a violation of rules of equity in interaction.

One analysis of the structure of social interaction that may help us to understand the sources of this affect has been provided by Goffman (1959). His description of the breakdown of interaction that results when an actor discredits his role fits well the description our experimenters gave of their experiences:

> At such moments the individual whose presentation has been discredited may feel ashamed while the others present may feel hostile, and all the participants may come to feel ill at ease, nonplussed, out of countenance, embarrassed, experiencing the kind of anomy that is generated when the minute social system of face-to-face interaction breaks down [p. 12].

---

[3]Even if we allow this more liberal interpretation of "patterns of sanctions" (more liberal, probably, than Scott intended), an operant analysis of the problem is not without its problems. Such an analysis would be required to argue either that all of our experimenters had been severely traumatized by asking for a seat in the subway in the past (an improbable assumption, especially for those experimenters new to the city), or that the emotion results from "stimulus generation" from similar experiences. This notion of generalization is both vague and, as Chomsky (1959) has pointed out, mentalistic.

One might argue with some cogency that the experimenters were playing a social role, that of a subway rider, and that they discredited it by asking for the seat. But this use of 'role' and 'discrediting' seems strained and forced. Our results indicate, rather, that this 'anomy' is a more general phenomenon resulting directly from doing something that 'just isn't done' in a particular setting, whether it is related to the performance of any important social role or not.

This interpretation is consistent with Berger and Luckmann's argument (1967, cf. pp. 53—67) that the primary and essential means of social control is the sheer objectivity of the social world. They argue that it is the immediate and unreflective perception by actors of 'the way things are done' which stabilizes individual conduct and *ipso facto* the social order. Under this perspective, both the sanctions that Scott considers and the discrediting of identity that Goffman has explored are secondary; that is, they are derivative of this basic means of control.

To be sure the concept of "those things that just aren't done" is itself a complex one, containing both a statistical proposition (such actions *do not* occur) and a normative proposition (such actions *ought not* to occur). Moreover, there remains the problem of specifying the precise content of those things that "just aren't done," a discussion we shall not develop here.

The results of our experience in doing something that 'just isn't done' suggest that knowledge of the objective social order controls behavior not only cognitively (people may simply never have thought of asking for a seat), but emotionally: action outside of understood routine paths appropriate to the social setting, at least in this case, give rise to an intense, immediate, inhibitory emotion. This emotion[4] restricts individual action to the routine patterns that constitute the stable background of everyday life.[5]

---

[4]The exact nature of this inhibitory emotion is open to further inquiry. It might be argued that the affect produced was *guilt* over either taking the seat or bothering the passenger. But the seat is not a very important matter, nor were the riders lastingly disturbed. Further, the emotion was confined to the subway car itself. As soon as experimenters left the car tey felt thoroughly at ease. This emotion, rooted in the situation, seems closer to embarrassment than guilt.

Harold Takooshian (1972) has proposed an empirical test. He has suggested that the procedure be changed such that an experimenter stands before a confederate (preferably an older woman) and bluntly ask her for her seat, which she reluctantly surrenders. She is then to stand in front of the experimenter as he makes himself comfortable in her seat. The question is whether the experimenter would feel great tension even though there is absolutely no reason for him to feel guilt. The experimenter may find himself feeling embarrassed nonetheless sitting there in the sight of the other passengers.

[5]A question remains as to whether this inhibition against substantial interaction among riders is functional. On the one hand, this inhibition simplifies the situation considerably for users of the subway. Since it is common knowledge that everyone minds his own business on the subway, a rider is free to assume a passive posture with regard to other riders. He need not be prepared to respond to demands from all those who surround him either for his attention or for more substantial involvement. On the other hand, daily contact with the by now clichéd "faceless masses" of fellow riders may contribute to the alienation and anonymity often associated with urban life.

ACKNOWLEDGMENTS

The study reported in this paper was carried out in the context of two research seminars conducted by first author at The City University of New York. Among those who participated in the study were: Harry From, Ira Goodman, David Greene, Robert Johnson, Elinor Manucci, Bruce Parker, and Maury Silver. Also, Jerry Cahn, David Carraher, Maria Garriga, Kathryn Krogh, Robert Massey, John Sabini, Harold Takooshian, Edward Weir, Jacqueline Williams, and Barbara Wolf. Thanks also to Drs. Stuart Albert and Irwin Katz, who participated in the seminars. The second author is now affiliated with the Department of Psychology, University of Pennsylvania.

REFERENCES

Berger, P., & Luckmann, T. *The social construction of reality.* New York: Doubleday Anchor, 1967.

Chomsky, N. Review of *Verbal behavior. Language,* Jan.–Mar. 1959, *35,* pp. 26–58.

Garfinkel, H. Studies of the routine grounds of everyday activity. *Social Problems,*Winter 1964, *11*(3), pp. 225–250.

Goffman, E. *The presentation of self in everyday life.* New York: Anchor Doubleday, 1959.

Goffman, E. *Relations in public.* New York: Harper, 1971.

Scheff, T. *Being mentally ill: A sociological theory.* Chicago: Aldine, 1960.

Scott, J. F. *Internalization of norms.* Englewood Cliffs, N. J.: Prentice-Hall, 1971.

Skinner, B. F. *Science and human behavior.* New York: Macmillan, 1953.

Takooshian, H. *Report on a class field experiment.* Unpublished manuscript, 1972.

3
Stress on the Train:
A Study of Urban Commuting

Jerome E. Singer
Uniformed Services University of the Health Sciences

Ulf Lundberg
Marianne Frankenhaeuser
University of Stockholm

ABSTRACT

Regular male passengers commuting on the Nynäshamn–Stockholm line participated in a 4-day investigation aimed at studying the stress that arises from day-
to-day commuting from a suburban home to a central-city job. All subjects rode
a morning train; one group boarded the train at its first stop, and the other
midway on its trip. The times of travelling were 79 and 43 min., respectively. On
each day the subjects made quantitative reports concerning the travelling conditions on the train, and on the third day urine specimens from each passenger
were also collected and analyzed for adrenaline and noradrenaline. The mean
number of passengers/car increased progressively as the train approached
Stockholm and a corresponding increase occurred in the magnitude of the estimates expressing various forms of discomfort. The subjects with the longer trip
(Nynäshamn) were found to have a lower rate of adrenaline excretion on the
train than the subjects with the shorter one (Västerhaninge). The results indicate
that the stress involved in travelling varies more with the social and ecological
circumstances of the trip than with its length or duration.

INTRODUCTION

There has been a recent growing interest in the application of theoretical
psychology to problems of modern life and the environment. A century-old
tradition of experimental laboratory psychology has generated a wide variety of
models and supporting data for theories concerning human function, performance,

and adjustment. Because of a desire to test these theories in circumstances less restrictive than the laboratory, and also because of a desire to make a meaningful contribution to current pressing social problems, more and more field studies deriving from laboratory procedures are being conducted.

A prime candidate for such field explorations is the study of various forms of stress. Already there is a sizeable body of literature exploring stress in nonlaboratory situations. The work by Janis (1958) on patients facing surgery, and by Cohen, Glass, and Singer (1973) on the effects of environmental noise on children's reading abilities can all serve as illustrations. Although these studies are interesting and, in a sense, pioneer efforts, they are caught in an unfortunate methodological dilemma. Their strength is precisely the fact that they study a real problem, in vivo, so that whatever contribution they make is directly understandable and applicable. Their weakness lies in the fact that experimental randomization, the procedure which can so effectively rule out other possible or even implausible alternatives, is absent from situations studied in the real world. Consequently, field studies on environmental psychology represent a compromise: a balance of the greatest possible experimental rigor in a situation which resistantly defies attempts at experimental intervention. It is our belief that this compromise, which possesses a sort of hybrid vigor, is their greatest asset.

One area of special concern to psychologists, planners, and lay people alike, is that of the stresses involved in a person's daily life and routine. To the extent that governmental, social, and cultural factors shape the way people live and work, they commit people to a certain style or way of life. This style of life carries with it certain positive and negative consequences that is, (an accompanying quality of life). It is concern over the current state and future prospects of this life quality (Frankenhaeuser, 1974) that has been the impetus for a new thrust in psychological discussion and research. Even a preliminary study of life quality, however, quickly confronts a dilemma. Although many people, including the researchers, can give anecdotal evidence of an unpleasant quality of life, it is difficult to find documentation for these effects (cf. Glass & Singer, 1972): For example, a quick summary of what is known about the effects of a simple stressor, noise, may indicate the nature of the problem.

1. People adapt so quickly and rapidly to routine stressors that it is difficult to detect behavioral effects. Behavioral deficits, reports of unpleasantness, or even some physiological mechanisms may cease to occur after continued presentation of what was once stressful.

2. People's self-reports of the bothersomeness of a situation may be related to folklore and cultural truisms about the stressor rather than to physiological or behavioral performance data. If everyone in a society "agrees" that driving an automobile on a motorway is stressful, people may so answer when asked even though some of them may enjoy driving.

3. Even in cases where people adapt to stressors, various sorts of deficits — behavioral, interpersonal, and attitudinal — show up as aftereffects. People who

are able to adapt to stressful environments may pay a price for the actual or attempted adaptation, so that a worker in a noisy factory may do well at work but be irritated at home with the family in the evening.

4. The context in which the stressor is administered is a prepotent factor in its consequences. In particular, subjective feelings of control over the environment can greatly ameliorate otherwise stressful events. To a lesser extent, the predictability of a stressor also diffuses its power as do, to a lesser extent, social factors such as relative deprivation and the like. For example, whether one is irritated or amused by the play and noise of active children will depend more on the setting, at the beach or at an opera, than on level of disruption produced by the children.

All of these considerations provided the framework for our present study, which is an attempt to study the stress and the circumstances modifying it that arise from day-to-day commutation by public transport from a suburban home to a central-city job. It is an attempt to explore self-reports of the stresses involved in commutation and to examine their correlations with well-established physiological measures of stress, as well as a quasi-experimental examination of some of the factors involved in point 4 above.

The need for a study of the effects of daily commutation is self—evident. This pattern of travel to and from work is a common life style in most industrialized Western and some non-Western cities, and is a valuable object of study in its own light. Recent political events, as well as accompanying shortages and high prices for energy and fuel, have made the study of commutation particularly salient and cogent.

We attempted to relate our study design to the four points listed above as follows:

1. The failure to find nonadapted effects of stress is logically equivalent to trying to prove the null hypothesis. It might well be that different measures or procedures, as yet unapplied to this aspect of stress, could detect the effects of a stressor while the ones traditionally used reflected adaptation.

2. Although self-reports may not correlate with behavioral or physiological measures, there may be a systematic pattern to both types of measure. And it certainly would be worthwhile to establish the relationship of each individually to the application of an ongoing stress.

3. The presence of aftereffects is a clear indication that some process must be occurring during the seemingly adapted stressful situation. Once again, a better choice of dependent measures may provide evidence for ongoing stressful processes.

4. Any study that examines the effects of a stressor will be of much greater utility if it can vary some aspects of the social context providing similar subjects with similar stresses under different circumstances, and may be the most effective way of highlighting the remedial aspects of the situation.

The present study explored the effect of riding to work by public transportation by morning commuters in Stockholm. Urban commuters give self-reports of the crowdedness, comfort and unpleasantness of their trips using psychophysical scaling methods. These measurements represented a continuation of a usual procedure for obtaining self-reports from subjects concerning urban experiences; they differ in being more precise and methodologically sophisticated than most surveys, (Oborne & Clarke, 1973) as well as being conducted during the stress rather than being collected retrospectively. A psychophysiological measure of stress was also utilized: In particular, the rate of adrenaline secretion as reflected in urinary excretion, which has been shown to be an accurate and powerful general indicator of the effects of stress, as well as having more construct validity for the particular study of stress than most similar indicators (see, e.g., Frankenhaeuser, 1971, 1975).

Social context was varied by studying two groups of commuters on the same train. One group boarded the train at its first stop, the other midway on its trip. The groups differ in two respects. Obviously, the length of their train trips was different. Not so obvious, but we believe of at least equal importance, was the fact that they boarded the train with a different social context. Those coming in at the first stop entered an empty train. They had their choice of seats; they could sit with whomever they chose; they could arrange their parcels and coats, and otherwise have a relatively flexible control over their immediate environment. The group boarding the train in midtrip were constrained as to where they sat, with whom they could associate, and in how they could comfort themselves. Their environment was much less responsive to their own wishes and arrangements.

A study of this sort does not have hypotheses in the usual rigorous, deductive sense. We did, however, have certain expectations and beliefs about the results. First, we felt that people's scaling reports and the characteristics of their train trip would be consistent, uniform, and reliable, and would reflect the increasing stress (or, at least, norms in belief that stress increases) as the train became more and more crowded on its way to the central station. We believed that the use of urinary catecholamine assays would enable us to detect the level of ongoing stress during the train trip, and that we could examine how this psychophysiological indicator of stress related to the scaled reports. Further, we could compare both kinds of reports for the two groups of passengers. We had no way of telling in advance which of two counterposed factors would produce more stress: the longer trip for those who boarded at the first stop or the loss of environmental control for those who boarded in the middle of the trip.

To recapitulate, we conducted a study of some subjective and psychophysiological correlates of urban commuting in the Stockholm metropolitan area. The major aims of the study were directed toward establishing procedures and methodologies for field studies and experiments, as well as the specific aims of establishing measures of stress in two different contexts.

METHOD

Overview of the Study

Regular male passengers commuting between two suburban locations and Stockholm participated in a 4-day study of perceived and actual commutation stress. All passengers rode a morning train on the Stockholm—Nynäshamn line for four successive days, Monday through Thursday. On each day, they made psychophysical judgments concerning travelling conditions on the train; and, on the third day, urine specimens from each passenger were collected and analyzed for adrenaline and noradrenaline.

Subjects

The subjects for the study were recruited in a two-stage process. Approximately two months prior to the scheduled experimental days, research assistants rode several commuter trains on the evening runs from Stockholm out to the suburbs, distributing envelopes to all male passengers. Printed on the outside of the envelopes was a brief description of the purposes of the study (i.e., that we were a group of researchers investigating social and medical aspects of the stress involved in commuting on trains). Passengers were asked to help in the study by volunteering to fill out forms while riding (at some unspecified future time) and were told of the inclusion of urine analyses as part of the study. In the envelope were a brief questionnaire and a postage-paid reply envelope. The passengers were informed that, if selected, they would receive a 1-month commutation ticket ("50 card") in exchange for their cooperation.

When the volunteer applications came in, they were screened, and two groups were selected according to the following criteria:

1. They had to commute from one of the target stations all the way to the central station to arrive at their daily employment in Stockholm.
2. They must have been regular commuters making the same run at approximately the same time on a daily basis.
3. They must have been commuting on this line for at least 6 months.
4. They must have been between 20—50 years of age. (One subject of 67 was also included in order to make the number of subjects in each group equal.)
5. They must have been either nonsmokers or moderate smokers.

These criteria were utilized for two major purposes: (1) the matching of the subject samples and to avoid the inclusion of acute stress for infrequent travelers; and (2) to avoid selecting subjects whose personal habits, etc., might interfere with the catecholamine analysis. When the samples were drawn, potential subjects were contacted to assure their cooperation.

Two groups of 19 subjects were chosen; absences on one or another day of the study, other miscellaneous reasons for dropping out, and inability to urinate reduced the sample sizes for different analyses. The final sample consisted of 15 men in each of the two groups, although the number for a given comparison or a given day may have been somewhat less.

The Train Trip

Within the greater Stockholm area, all bus, subway, and commuter-train service is essentially under the control of a single company. Although, as for most transport, fares are related to distance, regular travelers may purchase a "50 card." This card, so named for its monthly 50-kronor cost, entitles its recipient to utilize any of its company's transport services for a month with no additional charge. For commuters, then, distance traveled is independent of cost. The particular line chosen, the Stockholm–Nynäshamn, was the longest commuter run included within the use range of the "50 card." Between Nynäshamn and the Stockholm Central Station, the train made seventeen stops and took 79 minutes. The intermediate station selected, Västerhaninge, was the eighth station in the line, 36 minutes from Nynäshamn and 43 minutes from the Stockholm Central Station.

On the morning run utilized, the train became progressively more crowded as it moved toward Central Station; however, at no time was the train more than 85–90% crowded so that all passengers had seats.

Scaling of Subjective Experiences

The subjects were tested June 4, 5, 6, and 7, Monday through Thursday, 1973. The study materials were mailed to each subject prior to this time together with instructions for their use. The subjects from Nynäshamn (longer trip) made ratings at seven stations each day. The ratings were made on preprinted response booklets concerning the degree of crowdedness, comfort, boredom, and unpleasantness experienced by the subjects at the various parts of the trip. These booklets were mailed to the subject, one for each day of the study, less than a week prior to the start of the experiment. The subjects also counted and reported the number of passengers in their cars after having finished each set of subjective ratings. In similar fashion, the subjects from Västerhaninge (shorter trip) reported their subjective experiences and the number of passengers at the last four corresponding stations.

Each subject compared a leg of the journey — the trip between two stops — to a previous leg used as a standard. The first rating for each leg was made on a continuous graphical scale ranging from 0 to 100, where the endpoints were described (in Swedish) as, for example, "not crowded at all" and "more crowded than ever before," respectively. The ratings that followed were made on a continuous graphical percentage scale, where 100% denoted, for example, "exactly

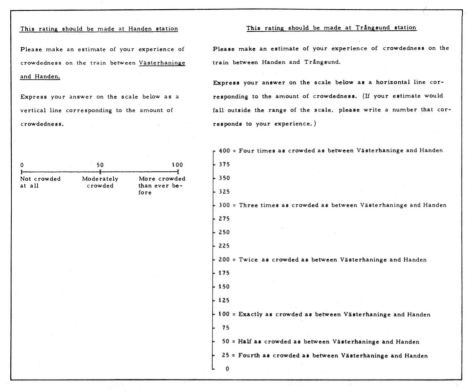

FIG. 3.1. Sample graphical rating forms for judgments of the trip characteristics. The one on the left was used for the first ratings on the train and the one on the right for the following ratings. The original Swedish forms, corresponding to the reduced (in size) English versions presented above, were used by the subjects from Västerhaninge for the scaling of crowdedness on the first two parts of the trip.

as crowded as between the previous two stations," 50% "half as crowded as between the previous two stations," 200% "twice as crowded as between the previous two stations," etc. The scaling technique may be described as a modified version of the method of magnitude estimation (see, e.g., Ekman & Sjöberg, 1965; Stevens, 1972). Figure 3.1 contains specimen forms of the rating scale. At the conclusion of their trip, the subjects mailed the forms to the experimenter in a previously distributed postage-paid, reply envelope. On June 6, however, the forms were given directly to the experimenters at Stockholm's Central Station, where the urine samples were also collected.

Psychophysiological Measures

Rate of adrenaline excretion was studied by the analysis of two successive urine samples from each subject. On June 6, the third morning of the investigation, each subject was asked to urinate into a previously provided specimen bottle immediately prior to his leaving home for the station and to note the exact time for voiding. The bottles were collected by an experimenter waiting at the station where, for each sample, urine volume was measured, the pH was adjusted to 3.0 with 2 N HCl, and the urine was stored at $-18°C$ until analyzed by the fluorimetric method of Euler and Lishajko (1961).

The second urine sample was obtained from each subject at the Stockholm Central Station. After the train's arrival on the morning of June 6, the subject went directly to a specially equipped lavatory situated near the platform (the subjects had been shown the location the previous evening). Each subject then gave a urine specimen to an experimenter who treated it as noted previously.

RESULTS

The data of the 4 consecutive days were analyzed separately, and it was found that the results were almost identical (i.e., no marked changes occurred with regard to the subjects' experiences or to their travel conditions over the 4 days of the investigation). Therefore, only the results from June 6, when psysiological measures also were obtained, are reported in this paper. From each group, 15 subjects participated in the study that day.

Number of Passengers on the Train

The subjects traveled in several early morning trains and the results are summed across trains. The number of passengers/car on the trains is shown in Fig. 3.2 for the two groups of subjects. The mean number of passengers/car increased progressively as the trains approached Stockholm. At the station before the last one, however, almost no one entered the trains, although a few people got off; as a result, the mean number of passengers decreased a little between the last two stations. The subjects from Västerhaninge tended to travel with the more crowded trains and have therefore reported more passengers/car than the other subjects at the corresponding stations.

Subjective Experiences

The geometric means of the rating data were calculated for each group of subjects. Geometric means were considered more appropriate for the present type of data (ratio estimations) than arithmetic means (cf. Stevens, 1972). Four subjects from Nynäshamn were excluded from the calculations because there was no positive correlation (rank) between their estimates of crowdedness and the number of passengers in their car. It is very likely that these subjects had not followed the instructions regarding the scaling technique. As the subjects were instructed by mail, there was no way of ascertaining that they had understood

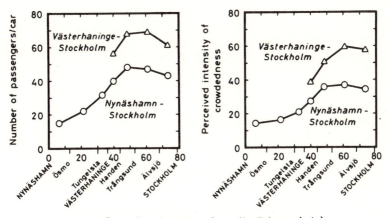

Time after departure from Nynäshamn (min)

FIG. 3.2. Number of passengers/car at seven stations for subjects from Nynäshamn and at four stations for subjects from Västerhaninge.

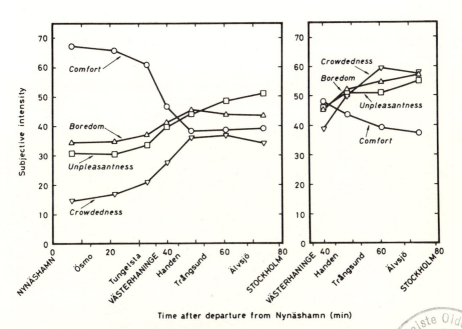

Time after departure from Nynäshamn (min)

FIG. 3.3. Perceived intensity of crowdedness, comfort, boredom, and unpleasantness at seven stations for subject from Nynäshamn and at four stations for subjects from Västerhaninge.

the directions until after the data were collected. Under these circumstances, attrition was actually quite low.

The rating data of the subjects from Nynäshamn and Västerhaninge are shown in Fig. 3.3. The three variables tapping discomfort — crowdedness, boredom, and unpleasantness — showed a similar, progressively increasing trend as the train approached Stockholm. The feeling of comfort decreased as the train approached Stockholm and the number of passengers increased. The results for the subjects from Nynäshamn and Västerhaninge show a similar trend at the corresponding part of the trip. The difference between the two groups with regard to the magnitude of perceived crowdedness corresponds quite well with the difference in number of passengers/car. As there is no way to discount systematic scale usage differences or endpoint references on the part of different groups, our attention is focussed on the similarity of the two functions obtained rather than on the absolute values.

Catecholamine-Excretion Rate

Table 3.1 shows means and standard errors for adrenaline and noradrenaline excretion for the two groups of subjects. The night—rest samples were given to the experimenter at the boarding station, and the "on—the—train" samples were collected upon arrival at Stockholm Central Station. Since adrenal—medullary activity is generally low during night rest, the fluorimetric method was not sensitive enough to yield reliable measures of adrenaline excretion for all subjects. For this reason night—adrenaline data are reported for 16 subjects only. "On—the—train" adrenaline values are missing for two Västerhaninge subjects who were unable to void at arrival in Stockholm.

The most striking picture of the data is the pronounced increase in both catecholamines during the train trip as compared with the preceding night. The

TABLE 3.1
Means and Standard Errors for Adrenaline and
Noradrenaline Excretion for Subjects Traveling by Train
from Västerhaninge and Nynäshamn to Stockholm[a]

		Night Rest		On the Train	
Variable		Västerhaninge	Nynäshamn	Västerhaninge	Nynäshamn
Adrenaline (ng/min)	M	0.88	1.29	4.72	3.21
	SE	0.22	0.47	0.70	0.86
	n	9.00	7.00	13.00	14.00
Nonadrenaline (ng/min)	M	16.86	18.29	29.55	28.07
	SE	1.20	1.99	2.14	2.42
	n	16.00	15.00	13.00	14.00

[a]Urine excretion varied between 0.67 and 0.79 ml/min in the different conditions.

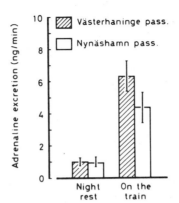

FIG. 3.4.   Mean and standard error of adrenaline excretion on the train and resting at night for six subjects from Nynäshamn and six from Västerhaninge.

rise in adrenaline excretion was significant at the 0.01 level for both groups (t = 5.41, df = 6, for Västerhaninge subjects). Similarly, the increases in noradrenaline excretion were significant at the 0.01 level for Nynäshamn subjects (t = 3.25) and at the 0.001 level for the Västerhaninge subjects (t = 5.29). These results are consistent with earlier data showing that urinary catecholamine measures are sensitive indicators of behavioral activity level (Frankenhaeuser, 1971). The most interesting comparison, however, concerns the magnitude of the increase in catecholamine excretion induced in each of the two samples of riders. Knowledge from previous studies (Frankenhaeuser, 1971, 1975) has made it clear that adrenaline levels tend to reflect changes in the psychosocial environment, including crowding and controllability, whereas noradrenaline output is not sensitive to such influences. The present data fit into this picture: noradrenaline excretion did not differ between the Nynäshamn and Västerhaninge groups (Table 3.1), but the increase of adrenaline excretion did. Figure 3.4 shows mean adrenaline excretion during night rest and during train trips for the six Nynäshamn subjects and the six Västerhaninge subjects, respectively, for whom complete sets of catecholamine data were available. It is seen that the increase in adrenaline was relatively larger in the Västerhaninge group, although in this small sample of subjects the difference between the groups did not reach a statistically significant level (t = 1.40, df = 10). When all subjects (i.e., also those for whom night values were not available) were included in the comparison, the difference between the groups approached statistical significance, the Nynäshamn subjects raising their adrenaline level more than Västerhaninge subjects (t = 1.74, $0.10 > p > 0.05$).

DISCUSSION

The basic results of the study can be easily summarized. Regular passengers on a commuter train can report consistently upon the conditions of their travel. This consistency is threefold: It is consistent between passengers so that there is a uniform perception of the characteristics of the trip; it is consistent across days so that the same characteristics are reported for several sequential trips; and, when adjusted for the location of the standard, it is consistent irrespective of the entry point of the passengers. Subject reports concerning travel time and number of passengers in the car tend to be veridical. The analysis of urinary adrenaline indicates that stress is greater for the Västerhaninge passengers, those who board at midtrip, than for those who board at Nynäshamn, at the train's origin.

These results have a number of interesting implications, but first let us turn to a discussion of some of the limitations of the study and the procedure used. This field study produced a number of difficulties. Foremost among these is the fact that subjects could not be randomly allocated to the two groups. Extensive efforts were made to match these groups on relevant characteristics, but the success of such a match is always a moot point. Our particular samples did not differ materially with respect to age, type of job, or length of time they had been commuting. The restriction to male subjects and the fact that travel costs were identical also served to eliminate some potential differences between the samples. The two groups did differ, however, in their residential distances away from the city. Although there is a shortage of housing in the Stockholm area, and choice of residential location may be partially constrained by availability, we cannot ignore the fact that some self-selection may have occurred between those who chose to live further away from the central city while continuing to work there, and that psychological mechanisms following this choice may influence stress reactions to the train journey. Although such a sampling problem cannot be discounted for this study, we discuss ways in which it could be controlled in future research.

There is another form of subject selection. Subjects dropped out from day to day because of illness, a start of a vacation, because they missed their train, or other such factors. In addition, not all subjects were able to give the two necessary urine samples. Although there is no evidence that the missing data are selective in any fashion, their omission complicates several of the analyses and makes it difficult for certain correlations to be computed.

Although simple in theory, it should not be overlooked that a field study such as this poses enormous logistic problems. The use of psychophysical scaling is a standard procedure; it is usually administered to college-student subjects in a laboratory situation, in which instructions can be given, checked, and readministered as needed. We were confronted with the problem of instructing subjects (who, by and large, were not of college level in sophistication with verbal materials) in psychophysical procedure, by mail, with no chance to check on their comprehension of the details. In addition, the collection of urine samples necessitated the presence of research assistants at several train stations simultaneously. Besides these technical difficulties, the usual problems of communication with potential subjects, the coordination of a large research team, the securing of permission and cooperation from various authorities, as well as the collaboration of large organizations such as the transportation company and postal service, were all necessary. Although none of these difficulties is insurmountable, they do provide the background for the rather simple nature of the experimental design. The feasibility of many of the procedures had yet to be established; so we made a decision to simplify the study in an effort to make it workable. Although we were certainly able to construct a more comprehensive experimental plan, devise several alternate control groups, and formulate additional questions and procedures, these were ultimately discarded in our planning as operational necessities forced us to adapt to a "bare-bones design."

Even so, the study reveals some unexpected and interesting results. The Nynäshamn subjects with the longer trip showed a lower rate of catecholamine excretion. To this extent, the inference is clear. Those people with a longer trip were, on the average, less stressed on the train than those with the short one. Considering that all subjects had seats, these differences cannot be attributed to differential activity, movement, or the like. Clearly, some factor related to the environment at Nynäshamn must have ameliorated the stress of the train ride (or alternatively some factor at Västerhaninge may have exacerbated it). The subjects from Västerhaninge traveled under more crowded conditions than the subjects from Nynäshamn (Figs. 3.2 and 3.3). It is our contention that the greater options for selection of seats, the ability to arrange costs and parcels, and the freedom to choose with whom to sit at the first station, Nynäshamn, as subjects boarded the train were the potent factors in reducing the stress of their trip. It should be mentioned that the interpretation of these results has received support in a subsequent study with the same subjects (Lundberg, 1976). Conceptually, this can be thought of as feelings of control, or predictability (Frankenhaeuser & Rissler, 1970; Glass, Singer, Leonard, Krantz, Cohen, & Cummings, 1973), or the chance to optimize territoriality (Sommer, 1969) for the Nynäshamn subjects; it may also be conceived of as interruption of behavior (Mandler & Watson, 1966), learned helplessness (Seligman, Maier, & Solomon, 1971) for the Västerhaninge passengers, or both. The important inference is not which of these mechanisms are involved, as it may be that they are all related, but rather that length of time exposed to the stress of traveling is not as important as the context or the conditions under which the trip occurred. It is also instructive to note that the psychophysical and psychophysiological methods used, usually restricted to laboratory studies, were adaptable to the most complex and difficult field situation. Indeed, these methodological refinements enabled us to find indications of ongoing stress under circumstances in which only adaptation had been previously noted. In all probability, nonregular commuters who were passengers on the train might have shown even greater stress but that is not the point at issue.

We realize, of course, that the stress phenomena we are exploring only utilizes a small range of many possible physical parameters. Clearly, a commutation of but one station had a ride lasting only 3 minutes might not prove stressful at all. Or a commutation of 4 hours might well signal an entirely different life style and adjustment than our longest one of 79 minutes. We obviously do not mean to suggest that our finding of greater stress for shorter rides is generalized to the limits of the function; even relatively minor changes might well wash out this relationship. Nevertheless, large numbers of people commute to central cities from suburbs; and they spend anywhere from 5 minutes to 2 hours making a one-way trip. Within broad bands of that time spectrum, we are implying that the routine stress involved varies more with the social and ecological circumstances of the trip than with its length or duration. We regard the explanation and investigation of this phenomenon as more intriguing than the systematic variation of the magnitudes of our variables in an effort to get precise borders for our finding.

The alternative explanation that the subjects were different to begin with cannot be completely discounted. Both our matching procedures and the particular circumstances determining residential location in the Stockholm area make us feel comfortable in minimizing them. And, now that the procedures have been operationalized and such studies are feasible, it is clear that a future study avoiding the selection bias can be run. We studied commuters going from the first station to central in the morning. If our explanation for our results is correct, there is an inverse relationship between residential distance from the city and loss of control: The closer one lives to the city, the more the inner environment of the train is fixed when one boards it. Such a relationship would not exist for the return journey. Commuters board the train in the central city. The first ones on the train have more control than the last ones, but there is no reason to expect that time of entering the homebound train is related to distance traveled. A study, then, that explores stress during train riding for subjects on both legs of their daily trip, should reveal a distance relationship for the trip to the city and a time of boarding one, independent of distance, for the trip home.

There is another important contribution that we feel our study has made. As psychologists turn to considerations of their environment, it is all-important that studies be done of the environment itself. Theoretical or laboratory work can provide theories, hunches, and a host of detailed studies concerning the effects of selected and isolated variables, but they cannot substitute for a study of its aspects of the work outside the laboratory to which they are addressed. It thus requires acts of faith and extrapolation to move from a laboratory phenomena to recommendations of real application. Our present work was conducted on the commuter train. Its findings, its lessons, and its implications can be applied to the stresses of that train ride. We regard this direct applicability as our reward for undertaking this type of study. The organizational complications and interpretive difficulties are, we feel, more than offset by our ability to find out something about environmental stress and not just simulations or analogs of it. For us, at least, the present study provides a partial model for meaningful psychological studies of environmental factors.

Intriguing as the present results are, they represent the first phase of an attack on our ignorance concerning the details of the psychology of the environment. Replication, corroboration, and extension of these findings should prove valuable not merely in our greater understanding, but also as an aid to planners and designers in modifying environments, internal arrangements, and schedules to minimize the adverse effects of necessary environmental stresses.

ACKNOWLEDGMENTS

The study was conducted while the first author was a guest researcher at the Psychological Laboratories of the University of Stockholm. Support for the study was provided by grants from the Swedish Medical Research Council (Project No. 997X), the Social Science Research Council, and the U.S. National Science Foundation (GS-34329). We are indebted to the Swedish Railways Company (SJ), which helped us in organizing and performing the investigation. We also wish to thank Eva Bella-Hottovy, Hans Bjurström, Bernard Devine, Anita Elgerot, Björn Lindström, Ulf-Johan Olson, and Margareta Norrman, research assistants at the University of Stockholm, who assisted in the recruiting of subjects and the collection of data. The catecholamine analyses were performed by Lars Holmberg.

REFERENCES

Cohen, S., Glass, D. C., & Singer, J. E. Apartment noise, auditory discrimination, and reading ability in children. *Journal of Experimental Social Psychology*, 1973, *9*, 407–422.

Ekman, G., & Sjöberg, L. Scaling. *Annual Review of Psychology*, 1965, *16*, 451–474.

Euler, U. S. v., & Lishajko, F. Improved technique for the fluorimetric estimation of catecholamines. *Acta Physiologica Scandinavica*, 1961, *51*, 348–355.

Frankenhaeuser, M. Behavior and circulating catecholamines. Review article. *Brain Research*, 1971, *31*, 241–262.

Frankenhaeuser, M. Aspects of research on man in future society. Reports from the Psychological Laboratories, The University of Stockholm, Suppl. 24, 1974 [Also in L. Levi (Ed.), *Society, stress and disease* (Vol. IV). *Working life.* London: Oxford University Press, 1974.]

Frankenhaeuser, M. Experimental approaches to the study of catecholamines and emotion. In L. Levi (Ed.), *Emotions. Their parameters and measurement.* New York: Raven Press, 1975.

Frankenhaeuser, M., & Rissler, A. Effects of punishment on catecholamine release and efficiency of performance. *Psychopharmacologia*, 1970, *17*, 378–390.

Glass, D. C., & Singer, J. E. *Urban stress.* New York: Academic Press, 1972.

Glass, D. C., Singer, J. E., Leonard, H. S., Krantz, D., Cohen, S., & Cummings, H. X. Perceived control of aversive stimulation and the reduction of stress responses. *Journal of Personality*, 1973, *41*, 577–595.

Janis, I. L. *Psychological stress: Psychoanalytic and behavioral studies of surgical patients.* New York: Wiley, 1958.

Lundberg, U. Urban commuting: Crowdedness and catecholamine excretion. *Journal of Human Stress*, 1976, *2*, 26–34.

Mandler, G., & Watson, D. L. Anxiety and the interruption of behavior. In C. D. Spielberger (Ed.), *Anxiety and behavior.* New York: Academic Press, 1966.

Oborne, D. J., & Clarke, M. J. The development of questionnaire surveys for the investigation of passenger comfort. *Ergonomics,* 1973, *16,* 855–869.

Seligman, M. E. P., Maier, S. F., & Solomon, R. L. Unpredictable and uncontrollable aversive events. In F. R. Brush (Ed.), *Aversive conditioning and learning.* New York: Academic Press, 1971.

Sommer, R. *Personal space.* Englewood Cliffs, N.J.: Prentice-Hall, 1969.

Stevens, S. S. *Psychophysics and social scaling.* Morristown, N.J.: General Learning Press, 1972.

4 Aggression and Heat: The "Long Hot Summer" Revisited

Robert A. Baron
Purdue University

INTRODUCTION

It has frequently been contended that ambient temperature exerts an important, facilitating effect upon human aggression. More specifically, the view that exposure to uncomfortable heat contributes to the outbreak of both individual and collective acts of violence has won widespread, seemingly general acceptance (e.g., U.S. Riot Commission, 1968). While the roots of this suggestion appear to rest largely in "folk wisdom," common sense, and informal observation, two indirect types of empirical evidence have often been marshaled in its support.

First, the results of several laboratory studies conducted by William Griffitt and his colleagues (Griffitt, 1970; Griffitt & Veitch, 1971) point to the conclusion that as suggested by informal observation, we are indeed often more irritable, prone to outbursts of temper, and more negative in our reactions to others under uncomfortably hot than comfortably cool environmental conditions. Second, systematic observation reveals that it is in fact the case that a large proportion of the serious instances of collective violence which erupted in American cities during the late 1960s and early 1970s took place during the hot summer months, when heat wave or near heat wave conditions prevailed (Goranson & King, 1970; U.S. Riot Commission, 1968).

Together, these observations and findings seem to provide fairly convincing support for the existence of an important and relatively straightforward link between high ambient temperatures and the occurrence of overt aggression. But is this actually the case? Does exposure to uncomfortable heat always — or even usually — facilitate the later development of assaults against others? After more than five years of research concerned with such issues, our answer must be a

57

qualified "no." While there does indeed seem to be a link between ambient temperature and aggression, it has turned out to be far more complex and intricate in nature than that suggested by such phrases as "hot under the collar," "the heat of anger," or "the long hot summer." In fact, the findings of our research suggest that under appropriate conditions, uncomfortable heat can actually inhibit — as well as facilitate — overt acts of aggression. And additional aspects of our work seem to point to the conclusion that the link between aggression and heat, while it exists, may simply represent one aspect of a larger and more general relationship between the presence of *any* unpleasant, negative-affect inducing conditions and the occurrence of such behavior. In short, while uncomfortably hot environmental conditions may indeed affect the occurrence of physical aggression, their impact in this respect is quite different from that suggested by "common sense."

As might well be expected, our investigations concerning the impact of ambient temperature upon aggression have involved many false starts, blind alleys, and discarded hypotheses. Moreover, they have encompassed repeated changes in methodology, as we sought to refine the techniques and dependent measures of our research. Taken as a whole, then, they do not represent the completely smooth and orderly process we might wish. Yet, in retrospect, our work in this area seems to fall fairly readily into three distinct phases. For want of more appropriate titles, these might be labeled: (1) naive empiricism; (2) preliminary theory construction; and (3) later theory construction and validation. The remainder of this chapter, then, will consist largely of a description of our work during each of these phases, and a final, concluding section concerning possible implications of this research.

NAIVE EMPIRICISM:
IS THE "LONG HOT SUMMER" REALLY HOT?

Our first investigation of the impact of high ambient temperatures upon aggression (Baron, 1972) was, in an important sense, purely empirical in nature. For several years, mass media accounts of the frightening riots occurring in many major cities had attributed such events to the irritating influence of the "long hot summer." That is, such descriptions suggested that it was prolonged exposure to temperatures in the high 80's or 90's F, which had shortened tempers, increased irritability, and so set the stage for the outbreak of collective violence.

On the face of it, such suggestions seemed quite reasonable. Moreover, they fit very well with findings reported by Griffitt (1970), which suggested that individuals exposed to extremely hot and uncomfortable ambient temperatures did indeed report feeling more tense and irritable, and indicated less positive feelings toward strangers than persons exposed to comfortably cool conditions. Yet, as far as we could tell, the view that high temperatures facilitated aggression had never been subjected to direct, empirical test. Given this fact, we decided to examine this hypothesis in the simplest and most direct manner possible. Thus, our first investigation involved a simple 2 x 2 design in which male subjects were either angered or not angered prior to an opportunity to aggress, and participated in the experiment under comfortably cool or uncomfortably hot environmental conditions. The basic idea behind this early research was that of conclusively demonstrating the aggression-facilitating impact of high temperatures. Once such effects had been established, we believed, it would be possible to go on to examine the possible interaction of such environmental conditions with other determinants of aggression, such as exposure to aggressive models (Bandura, 1973), or the presence of aggressive cues (Berkowitz, 1974). Because the procedures used in this investigation have also been employed (with certain modifications) in all of our subsequent studies, they are now described in some detail.

Initial Investigation: Basic Procedures

When subjects arrived for their appointments, they found a male confederate already seated in the waiting room. Shortly thereafter, the experimenter arrived and conducted both individuals to the first experimental room. Once there, she explained that the first part of the study was concerned with attitudes and opinions, and requested that both persons complete a 23-item questionnaire dealing with a wide variety of issues (e.g., student protests, belief in God, the draft). In reality, this task was employed solely as a *time filler,* in order to insure that subjects spent sufficient time in the experimental rooms for any influence of ambient temperature on their behavior to become apparent.

After allowing both the subject and confederate (who worked in an adjacent room, out of subjects' sight) to complete the questionnaire, the experimenter announced that the second part of the study would be concerned with the effects of stress on problem-solving ability. She then indicated that in order to study this problem, one of the two individuals present would serve as a problem solver and the other as an evaluator. The subject was then chosen to play the first role and the confederate to play the second. The experimenter then explained that the problem solver's (i.e., the subject's) task would consist of writing a solution to a complex social problem (the control of rising crime rates), knowing that his work would be evaluated in two ways by the evaluator. This individual (the confederate) would write his overall reaction to the subject's solution on a form which the subject would later see, and would also deliver from 0 to 10 shocks to him according to the rule that the poorer his work, the greater the number of shocks he would receive. In reality, this portion of the study was employed to vary subjects' degree of anger toward the future victim (the confederate). Thus, in the *nonangry* condition, the confederate delivered only 1 shock to the subject and wrote a very positive statement about his solution. In the *angry* condition, however, he delivered 9 shocks to this individual and wrote a very negative statement about his work. These procedures were adapted from those employed in earlier research conducted by Leonard Berkowitz and his colleagues (e.g., Berkowitz & Geen, 1966), and had been found in such research to exert strong effects both upon subjects' level of aggression toward the confederate, and their reported feelings of anger toward this person. The shocks received by subjects in both the angry and nonangry groups consisted of 67 volt, 0.5 second pulses, and were delivered by means of stainless steel finger electrodes. Every precaution was taken in the design of the shock-delivery equipment to insure that no harm could possibly befall participants in the study.

After completing the above procedures, the experimenter conducted both the confederate and subject to yet another room, where she explained that the final part of the study would be concerned with the effects of punishment on learning. She then stated that in order to examine this topic, one of the individuals would act as a *teacher* and the other as a *learner*. The teacher would attempt to teach the learner a list of nonsense syllable pairs, rewarding him for correct responses and punishing him with electric shock for errors. The experimenter then noted that since the confederate had acted as the evaluator in the previous part of the study, he should now consent to serve as learner. He agreed to this request, and the experimenter then conducted him to a third room where she provided instructions for his task in the study and appeared to attach shock electrodes to his arms.

After completing these activities, she returned and provided the subject with detailed instructions for his task as teacher. These instructions indicated that each time the learner made a correct response on the memory task, the teacher should reward him by pushing a "correct" button on the apparatus. However, whenever the learner made an error, the teacher should choose and depress one of the 10 shock buttons in order to punish this individual (see Fig. 4.1). It was carefully explained that the higher the number of the buttons chosen by the teacher, the stronger the shocks to the learner, and that the longer any shock button was depressed, the longer these shocks would last. In order to convince the subject that the shock apparatus was in fact operational, she then administered sample shocks from Buttons 4 and 5 to this individual. The shocks produced by these buttons were 36 and 50 volts, respectively, and were generally perceived as moderately unpleasant by subjects.

Following these activities, the experimenter returned to the room where the learner was waiting and signaled the subject to begin teaching his list of nonsense syllables to this individual. The learner appeared to make a total of 20 prearranged errors during the experiment, but gradually seemed to master the list as the session progressed. Following the final shock trial, subjects completed a postexperimental questionnaire on which they rated (on 7-point scales) their anger toward the victim, and their current feelings along the dimension of comfortable—uncomfortable and pleasant—unpleasant. After completing the questionnaire, subjects received a thorough de-briefing, during which the major purposes of the study were carefully and fully explained.

FIG. 4.1. The apparatus used
to measure aggression in the author's research.

Ambient temperature was manipulated by means of air conditioners and
electric heaters. In the *cool* condition, air conditioning was used to lower the
temperature in the experimental rooms to comfortable levels (the low 70's F),
whereas in the *hot* condition, this equipment was turned off, and the heaters were
employed to raise the temperature in these rooms to uncomfortably high levels
(the low to mid-90's F). Readings of ambient temperature were taken both before
and after each session in both experimental rooms. In the cool condition, the
average before and after readings were 74.2°F and 84.3°F in the first room, and
74.6°F and 75.0°F in the second room. In the hot condition, the corresponding
readings were 93.9°F and 91.1°F in the first room, and 95.2°F and 91.8°F in
the second.

Initial Investigation: Some Surprising Results

As may be recalled, the major hypothesis under investigation in this preliminary
study was quite straightforward: In the face of prior provocation, exposure to
uncomfortable heat would facilitate subsequent aggression. Much to our surprise,
however, results failed to confirm these predictions. Although previously angered
subjects did in fact demonstrate higher levels of aggression than those who had
not been so provoked, exposure to uncomfortable heat seemed to reduce rather
than enhance such behavior. Further, this was the case for both dependent measures employed, the duration ($F = 4.54$, $df = 1/36$, $p < 0.05$) and intensity
($F = 3.00$, $df = 1/36$, $p < 0.10$) of shocks directed by subjects against the confederate (see Figs. 4.2 and 4.3).

Our first thought was that perhaps the attempted manipulation of ambient
temperature had failed, and that subjects had not been exposed to such condi-

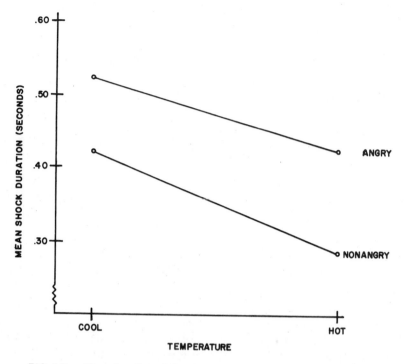

FIG. 4.2.   Mean duration of the shocks directed against the confederate
by subjects in four experimental groups. (From Baron, 1972, fig. 1, p. 186.)

tions for a long enough period to allow the expected effects of uncomfortable
warmth to appear. Additional findings, however, argued against the acceptance
of this suggestion. In particular, subjects in the hot condition rated themselves
as feeling significantly less pleasant and comfortable than those in the cool
condition. Thus, we were left facing the apparent fact that contrary to common
sense, the findings of previous research (Griffitt, 1970; Griffitt & Veitch, 1971),
and our own expectations, high ambient temperatures actually seemed to inhibit
rather than facilitate overt assaults against others.

Once we succeeded in overcoming our initial puzzlement over these unexpected findings, several possible explanations for their occurrence came quickly
to mind. First, it seemed possible that subjects in the hot condition reduced the
strength of their attacks against the victim because they perceived this individual
as having shared with them the unpleasant experience of participating in the
study under uncomfortable environmental conditions. Previous research (Latané,
Eckman, & Joy, 1966) indicated that the perception of shared suffering with another often leads to increased liking for this person, and such positive reactions
might well have caused subjects in the hot condition to lower the strength of
their attacks. Second, it seemed possible that subjects in the hot condition directed weaker assaults against the victim than those in the cool condition because

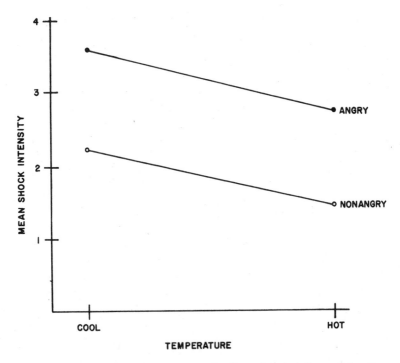

FIG. 4.3.   Mean intensity of the shocks directed against the confederate by subjects in four experimental groups. (From Baron, 1972, fig. 2, p. 187.)

they assumed that like themselves, he was perspiring profusely and so found the shocks he received especially painful.

Although both of these possibilities seemed plausible, a third explanation, suggested by comments from subjects themselves, appeared to be somewhat more compelling. In many cases, participants in the hot condition volunteered the information that they had found the experimental rooms to be so unpleasant that they sought to complete the study as quickly as possible. More specifically, several noted that they had employed shocks of short duration and relatively low intensity in order to avoid doing anything "controversial" which might prolong the session. In short, it appeared that for some subjects, at least, escape from the stifling laboratory was a stronger behavioral tendency than aggressing against the confederate. In retrospect, this was far from surprising; after all, even subjects in the angry condition had experienced only a relatively mild instigation to aggression. However, it raised an interesting and theoretically important question: What would happen if aggression were a somewhat stronger and more dominant response in subjects' behavior hierarchies? Would high ambient temperatures tend to facilitate subsequent aggression under such conditions? These questions, in turn, suggested a possible link between our puzzling findings and a theoretical framework for understanding aggression proposed by Albert Bandura (1971). At this point, then, we turned our major attention to the task of adapting Bandura's suggestions to the task of explaining the effects of high ambient temperatures upon aggressive behavior.

EARLY THEORY CONSTRUCTION: HEAT AS A SOURCE OF AROUSAL

Not very surprisingly, Bandura's (1971, 1973) social learning theory of aggression is both sophisticated and complex. The portion of this framework most relevant to our research, however, seemed quite straightforward. Basically, it held that virtually any type of aversive treatment serves to induce heightened emotional arousal among the individuals subjected to such conditions. This heightened arousal, in turn, would then enhance the frequency or strength of later aggressive behavior under conditions in which these persons were "prone to behave aggressively" (Bandura, 1973, p. 56). In short, Bandura's theory proposed that almost any type of aversive, unpleasant treatment or experience — anything from severe frustration through actual physical pain — might facilitate later aggression when such behavior represents a strong or dominant response among subjects. When other response, especially those incompatible with aggression, are dominant, however, aversive treatment might actually inhibit rather than enhance such behavior.

Given the fact that most individuals find exposure to high ambient temperatures quite unpleasant (Baron, 1972; Griffitt, 1970), and the finding that such conditions do indeed induce increments in arousal (Provins & Bell, 1970), it seemed possible that this portion of Bandura's theory could readily explain our previous findings. That is, if responses other than aggression could be assumed to have been dominant in subject's behavior hierarchies, the finding that high ambient temperatures reduced overt aggression would be predicted. As noted previously, comments by many participants suggested that this was actually the case, and that attempts to escape from the study or minimize discomfort were stronger or more dominant than tendencies to aggress against the confederate. Thus, the social learning theory of aggression seemed to provide a reasonable explanation for our previously puzzling results.

Even more important, the theory seemed capable of specifying those conditions under which uncomfortably high temperatures might facilitate or actually inhibit subsequent aggression. Specifically, it suggested that uncomfortable heat would facilitate later aggression when such behavior represented a dominant behavior tendency among subjects, but would inhibit aggression when it represented only a weak, subordinate response. In order to test these interesting predictions, we then designed and conducted two separate studies.

In the first (Baron & Lawton, 1972), we reasoned that two factors which might strongly influence the dominance of subjects' tendencies to aggress were: (1) the degree of provocation they experienced; and (2) exposure to the actions of an aggressive model. Previous research concerning the effects of these variables (Berkowitz, 1970) suggested that if subjects were strongly provoked and then witnessed the behavior of an aggressive model before being permitted to attack their tormentor, aggression would represent a dominant or prepotent response in their behavior hierarchies. Thus, it was predicted that under such conditions, exposure to high ambient temperatures would tend to facilitate such behavior. However, since aggression was clearly *not* made dominant by anger arousal alone in our previous study (Baron, 1972), it was also expected that high ambient temperatures would fail to enhance such actions, or possibly even reduce them, under conditions in which subjects were provoked but not exposed to the behavior of the model.

In order to examine these predictions, male subjects were first angered in the manner previously described. Next, they were either exposed to the actions of an aggressive model (another confederate of the experimenter who pushed only Buttons 8, 9, and 10 on the apparatus) or were not exposed to such a model. Finally, they were provided with an opportunity to aggress against the individual who had previously annoyed them by means of electric shock. For half of the participants, all of these procedures were conducted under comfortably cool conditions (temperatures averaging 75.0°F); for the remainder, all were performed under uncomfortably hot conditions (temperatures averaging 97.5°F). The results of the investigation are summarized in Table 4.1, where it can be seen that the expected pattern of findings seemed to emerge. That is, as anticipated, high ambient temperatures facilitated aggression when subjects had been both angered and exposed to the actions of the model but actually seemed to inhibit such behavior when participants had been only angered. Unfortunately, however, neither of these effects attained acceptable levels of statistical significance. Thus these findings, though promising, were quite inconclusive.

TABLE 4.1
Median Intensity of Shocks Delivered to the Confederate
By Subjects in Four Experimental Groups

Model Condition	Ambient Temperature	
	Cool	Hot
No model	4.28	3.78
Model	5.50	6.93

Some Methodological Changes and
a Second Attempt

The encouraging pattern of results obtained in the preceding study seemed to point to the necessity for various methodological refinements. That is, it seemed quite possible that by strengthening the manipulations of the two variables employed (i.e., anger arousal and exposure to the actions of an aggressive model) stronger and perhaps more clear-cut findings might be obtained. In order to examine this possibility, we undertook several changes in procedure.

First, with respect to the manipulation of anger arousal, we decided to adopt approaches that had been employed with great success in several previous investigations (e.g., Baron, 1973; Doob & Wood, 1972). Briefly, these proceeded as follows. Under the guise of studying the manner in which individuals form first impressions of others, both the subject and confederate (i.e., the future victim) were asked to write brief sketches of their own personalities. These sketches were then ostensibly exchanged, and on the basis of the information they contained, both persons were asked to rate their partners on a number of different dimensions (e.g., intelligence, likability, sincerity, maturity, etc.). Finally, these ratings, too, were exchanged, presumably so that each person could see the kind of impression he or she had made on his or her partner. In reality, of course, both the personality sketch and ratings subjects received from the confederate followed a prearranged pattern. In the *nonangry condition,* the personality sketch supposedly written by the confederate suggested that he was a pleasant, modest, and friendly individual. Moreover, the ratings he assigned to the subject were quite favorable and flattering (e.g., he described the subject as being highly intelligent, likable, sincere, masculine, etc.). In contrast, in the *angry condition,* the self-description ostensibly prepared by the confederate indicated that he was a nasty, conceited, hostile person. Further, his ratings of the subject were highly unfavorable and quite derogatory. As might well be expected, these general procedures had been found to produce sharply different levels of self-reported anger among subjects. Thus, it was anticipated that they would provide a more adequate manipulation of this factor than that obtained in our previous investigations (Baron, 1972; Baron & Lawton, 1972). Moreover, they offered the advantage of eliminating actual shocks to subjects during this portion of the study — a procedure that raised important ethical issues.

Second, an attempt was made to strengthen the manipulation of the modeling factor by: (1) having the model push Buttons 9 and 10 more frequently and Button 8 less frequently than in the previous study; and (2) pretraining the model to depress these buttons for longer periods of time (2.0–3.0 seconds) than was true in the earlier experiment.

In addition to these alterations, one other, and fairly major, change was instituted. Specifically, the standard "teacher-learner" paradigm devices by Buss (1961) was replaced by another, seemingly more effective technique. The results of several studies (e.g., Baron & Eggleston, 1972) suggested that the measure of aggression yielded by the Buss approach was somewhat contaminated by various altruistic motives. For example, subjects often reported pushing higher-numbered buttons on the shock apparatus in order to help the victim learn, and so avoid any further shocks. In short, a positive correlation had been found to exist between their stated desires to help the victim, and the intensity of the shocks they employed ($r = +0.45$; Baron & Eggleston, 1972). As a means of lessening such difficulties, a different, and hopefully more neutral set of procedures was developed. Within the context of these procedures, subjects were informed that the purpose of the investigation was that of examining the effects of unpleasant stimuli such as electric shock upon physiological reactions. In order to study this topic, one of the individuals present (the confederate who had previously angered the subject) would serve as a *responder,* and receive a series of electric shocks of varying intensity from the remaining individuals (the subject and other confederate), who would act as *stimulators.* It was further explained that the responder's physiological reactions would then supposedly be monitored with great care in order to determine the precise impact of the shocks upon his reactions. Previous findings (Baron & Eggleston, 1972) suggested that under these conditions, the strength of the shocks directed by subjects against the victim was negatively related to their stated desires to help him ($r = -0.55$). Thus, it was reasoned that these procedures yielded a somewhat more useful measure of aggression than the standard "teacher-learner" paradigm. Another advantage of these general procedures was that they provided an apparently reasonable "cover story" for the very high temperatures encountered by subjects in our hot condition. Essentially, we explained that the study was concerned with the effects of temperature and humidity upon physiological reactions to electric shock. This "cover" turned out to be quite effective, and was accepted without question by the vast majority of our subjects.[1] On the basis of these advantages, the procedures outlined above were adopted for use in all of the remaining studies described in this chapter.

All of these procedural alterations were incorporated into our second attempt to apply Bandura's theoretical suggestions to the effects of uncomfortable heat upon aggression (Baron & Bell, 1975). The study we conducted, then, consisted of a 2 x 2 x 2 factorial design in which subjects were angered or not angered, exposed to the actions of an aggressive model or not so exposed, and participated

---

[1]No attempt was made to conceal the experimenter's interest in the impact of ambient temperature because: (1) the equipment employed to vary this factor could not safely or readily be disguised; and (2) pilot data suggested that all subjects exposed to high temperatures would guess that this was one of the factors under investigation, regardless of any attempts by the investgators to disguise this fact. As a result, it was deemed more effective to admit concern with ambient temperature, but then to divert subjects' attention away from the major purposes of the investigation by means of appropriate cover stories.

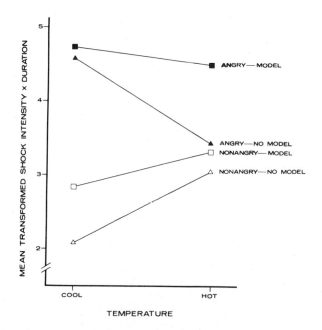

FIG. 4.4.   Mean level of aggression (transformed shock intensity ×
duration) delivered to the confederate by subjects in each of eight experimental groups. (From Baron & Bell, 1975, fig. 1, p. 829.)

in the investigation under comfortably cool or uncomfortably hot temperatures.
As was the case in our earlier study, the investigation was conducted in three distinct but related phases. In the first, which served as a *time filler* portion, subjects
were asked to work on selected jigsaw puzzles, ostensibly to examine the impact
of environmental factors upon their performance. In the second, they were exposed to the manipulation of anger arousal, and in the third, they were exposed
to the model or not, and provided with an opportunity to aggress against the victim by means of electric shock. On the basis of Bandura's theory and our
previous findings, it was predicted that high ambient temperatures would tend to
facilitate aggression under conditions in which subjects had been both strongly
provoked and exposed to the factions of the model but would fail to exert such
effects when only one (or neither) of these conditions prevailed.

The results of the study are represented in Fig. 4.4, where it can be seen that
our predictions were definitely *not* confirmed.[2] Instead, it appeared that regard-

---

[2]Because our original two dependent measures, shock intensity and shock duration,
generally yielded identical patterns of results, they were combined into a single index of
aggression through multiplication (Shock Intensity × Duration) in this and subsequent
studies. In order to eliminate heterogeneity of variance, the scores so obtained were then
subjected to a simple square root transformation ($X = \sqrt{x} + \sqrt{x + 1}$).

less of exposure or lack of exposure to the model, high ambient temperatures increased later aggression by nonangered subjects while actually inhibiting such behavior by those who had previously been provoked. Statistical analyses performed on these data indicated that, as suggested by Fig. 4.4, the interaction between anger arousal and ambient temperature was significant ($F = 9.94$, $df = 1/56$, $p < 0.005$).[3] Moreover, subsequent comparisons between the appropriate means revealed that high ambient temperature significantly facilitated aggression by nonangry subjects ($p < 0.005$), while actually inhibiting such behavior by those who had previously been annoyed ($p < 0.05$).

Needless to say, these findings were quite unexpected. Both the aggression data themselves, and subjects' replies to items on our postexperimental questionnaire suggested that the manipulations of anger arousal and modeling had been successful. Thus, according to our reasoning, and the results of past research, aggression should have been a strong or dominant response in the case of individuals who had been provoked and then exposed to the model's actions. Yet, contrary to our predictions, high ambient temperatures actually led to less rather than more aggression under such circumstances.

Given the surprising nature of these results, it seemed only reasonable to attempt to replicate them. We undertook this task at once, in a follow-up investigation identical to the preceding study in all major respects except for the addition of a warm condition (temperatures in the mid-80's F) and omission of the modeling factor (Baron & Bell, 1976, Experiment I). Once again the same pattern of findings emerged: High ambient temperatures facilitated aggression by subjects who had been treated in a friendly manner by the confederate, but actually inhibited such actions by those who had previously been provoked (the interaction between type of evaluation and ambient temperature was significant; $F = 4.33$, $df = 2/29$, $p < 0.025$). Moreover, it appeared that similar effects were produced by warm as well as hot environmental conditions.

Together, the findings of these two investigations seemed to cast considerable doubt upon the usefulness of applying Bandura's (1973) theory to the impact of uncomfortable heat upon aggression. But how, then, were the effects of such environmental conditions to be explained? If arousal was not the crucial mediating variable in this complex relationship, what was? Fortunately, a tentative answer to this question was provided by our subjects, both in their replies to items on our postexperimental questionnaires, and in their comments during lengthy debriefing sessions. It was largely on the basis of such input, then, that we formulated a revised theoretical framework.

------

[3]Despite the apparent pattern of findings in Fig. 4.4, the three-way interaction between anger arousal, modeling, and ambient temperature failed to attain significance ($F = 2.93$, $df = 1/56$, $p \cong .10$). Thus, the interaction between anger arousal and ambient temperature took essentially the same form in both the model and no model conditions.

LATER THEORY CONSTRUCTION AND VALIDATION:
HEAT AND NEGATIVE AFFECT

In all of the studies described up to this point, subjects were asked to rate their feelings along several different affective dimensions (e.g., comfortable—uncomfortable; pleasant—unpleasant, etc.). Separate analyses performed upon these data indicated that without exception, participants experienced considerably more negative reactions under hot environmental conditions than under comfortably cool ones. Moreover, in several cases (Baron & Bell, 1975; Baron & Lawton, 1972), the most negative feelings were reported by individuals who had been exposed to prior provocation and taken part in the study in the presence of uncomfortable heat. Such findings, of course, are neither surprising nor very informative in and of themselves. When combined with other data, however, they take on a much more suggestive meaning.

In two of the studies conducted (Baron & Bell, 1975; Baron & Bell, 1976, Experiment I), subjects were also asked to indicate the strength of their desire for the experiment to end. In both instances, those exposed to the combination of high ambient temperatures and prior provocation (the hot-angry groups) reported by far the strongest desires to gain release from the study. As we noted previously, these findings from the postexperimental questionnaire were supported by informal comments volunteered by many individuals during debriefing sessions. At that time, many noted that they had been primarily concerned with completing the study as quickly as possible, in order to escape from what they found to be an extremely unpleasant situation. The following are indicative of subjects' comments in this respect: "My main concern was finishing up so I could get a breath of fresh air;" "The only thing I thought about was getting the hell out of here."

Together, these data regarding subjects' current affective states and their expressed desires to escape from the experimental session pointed to an interesting possibility: perhaps the crucial psychological process underlying the impact of ambient temperature upon aggression was not general arousal in response to aversive conditions, as we had believed, but rather the degree of induced negative affect. More specifically, it seemed possible that in the context of a negative evaluation from another person, high ambient temperatures served as the proverbial "last straw," causing subjects in the hot-angry group to feel so uncomfortable that minimization of discomfort rather than aggression became the dominant response in their behavior hierarchies. In the context of a positive evaluation from the confederate, however, the negative affect induced by high temperatures may have served only to annoy or irritate subjects to the point where aggression became more dominant than would otherwise have been the case; thus, such behavior was enhanced.

In short, the possibility of a curvilinear relationship between the level of negative affect experienced by subjects and the strength or dominance of aggression

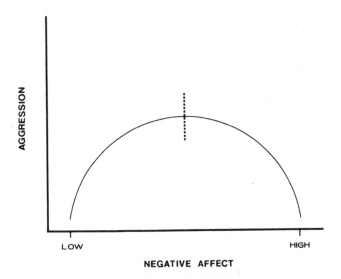

FIG. 4.5.   Hypothesized curvilinear relationship between negative affect and aggression. (From Baron & Bell, 1976, fig. 2, p. 254.)

in their behavior hierarchies was suggested. This hypothetical relationship is illustrated in Fig. 4.5: verbally, it may be described as follows. Up to some determinable point, aggression becomes increasingly dominant as negative affect — induced by high temperatures, negative evaluations from others, or any other factor — rises. Beyond this point, however, the tendency to engage in such behavior may decrease as other responses incompatible with aggression (e.g., escaping from the extremely aversive situation) became increasingly prepotent.

Although these suggestions fit our previously collected data quite well, they could not, of course, be accepted with any degree of confidence until subjected to independent empirical test. Thus, we went on to conduct three additional investigations designed primarily to provide information on the possibility that the impact of ambient temperature upon aggression was mediated by subjects' level of negative affect.

Reducing Negative Affect: The Effects Of A Cooling Drink

In the first of these experiments (Baron & Bell, 1976, Experiment II), we reasoned that if the effects of high ambient temperatures upon aggression are in fact mediated by negative affect, then factors serving to reduce such reactions should also tend to counteract the influence of this type of unpleasant environmental conditions. While a number of different treatments might be expected to be effective in this respect, one which seemed almost certain to counteract the unpleasant feelings induced among subjects by high ambient temperatures was the provision of a cooling drink. Thus, in one investigation, we attempted to determine whether the presence of such liquid refreshment would tend to lessen the previously observed effects of high ambient temperatures upon aggression.

The general procedures of this investigation were quite similar to those of our previous research in all respects save one: immediately prior to their opportunity to aggress against the victim, half of the participants were provided with an 8 ounce cup of cold lemonade and asked to drink all of this liquid. The remaining subjects were not provided with any lemonade, and of course, no mention of its presence was ever made. The explanation provided to individuals who received the lemonade was quite straightforward: The experimenter noted that one of the purposes of the study was that of determining whether liquid intake would influence their physiological reactions to variations in temperature and humidity.[4] Basically, then, the study employed a 2 x 2 x 2 factorial design in which subjects received either positive or negative evaluations from the confederate, a drink of lemonade or no liquid refreshment, and participated in the experiment under comfortably cool (71–73°F) or uncomfortably hot (92–94°F) conditions. On the basis of the theoretical framework described above, it was predicted that in the absence of liquid refreshment, results highly similar to those obtained in previous studies (Baron & Bell, 1975) would be observed, while in the presence of a cooling drink, the effects of high ambient temperatures upon aggression would be reduced. More specifically, we predicted that under the latter conditions, high ambient temperatures would produce smaller increments in aggression on the part of individuals exposed to a positive evaluation, and smaller reductions in aggression on the part of subjects exposed to a negative evaluation.

The results of the experiment are presented in Table 4.2, where it can be seen that all of these predictions were confirmed. Under conditions where subjects failed to receive a drink of lemonade, findings identical to those reported in our earlier research were obtained: high temperatures facilitated aggression by subjects who had received a positive evaluation, but inhibited such behavior by those who had received negative, derogatory feedback. In contrast, when subjects had been provided with a cooling drink, such effects were either reduced in size, or entirely eliminated. Consistent with this apparent pattern of findings, an analysis of variance performed upon the appropriate data yielded significant interactions between type of evaluation and ambient temperature ($F = 5.23$, $df =1/56$, $p < 0.025$) and between type of evaluation and presence of a drink ($F = 3.76$, $df = 1/56$, $p = 0.05$). Follow-up comparisons performed to more closely examine the nature of these interactions indicated that in the no drink condition, high ambient temperatures significantly facilitated aggression by subjects receiving

---

[4]In order to lend credibility to this rationale, readings of subjects' blood pressures were actually taken by means of a standard manometer at several points during the study. Unfortunately, background noise from the temperature control equipment rendered these data too unreliable for statistical treatment.

TABLE 4.2
Mean Level of Aggression[a] Delivered to the Confederate
by Subjects in Eight Experimental Groups

	No Drink		Drink	
Evaluation	Cool	Hot	Cool	Hot
Positive	2.43	3.00	2.34	2.48
Negative	3.17	2.60	3.46	3.09

[a]Transformed shock intensity x duration.

positive evaluations ($p < 0.01$), but inhibited such behavior by subjects receiving negative evaluations ($p < 0.01$). In contrast, in the drink condition, high ambient temperatures failed to enhance aggression by subjects receiving positive evaluations ($p > 0.20$) and produced a reduction in aggression of only borderline significance ($0.10 > p > 0.05$) among those receiving negative assessments. Thus, consistent with our initial expectations, the influence of uncomfortably high temperatures upon subsequent aggression was substantially reduced — and in the

The Curvilinear Relationship: A Systematic Test

Not surprisingly, we viewed the findings of our lemonade study as quite encouraging. Taken as a whole, they were consistent with our suggestions that: (1) the influence of ambient temperature upon aggression is mediated by subjects' level of negative affect; and (2) the relationship between such reactions and aggression is curvilinear in nature. More specifically, when negative affect was reduced by the administration of cooling liquid refreshment, the impact of high ambient temperatures upon subjects' behavior was altered in the expected manner. Uncomfortable heat no longer inhibited aggression by subjects who had previously received a negative evaluation, and such conditions no longer facilitated aggression by individuals who had received positive feedback. Thus, as expected, their reactions seemed to have been shifted back along the curvilinear function we proposed.

Although these results were clearly consistent with our theoretical model, they did not, of course, provide direct evidence for its validity. Our next step, then, was that of subjecting these suggestions to more direct empirical test. The general strategy we adopted for accomplishing this task was quite straightforward. First, on the basis of both extensive pilot research and the findings of previous investigations (Byrne, 1971), we developed a set of experimental conditions which would enable us to vary subjects' level of negative affect over a relatively wide range of values. Then, in our main investigation, subjects in various experimental groups were exposed to these conditions, and the effects upon their level of aggression were observed (Bell & Baron, 1976).

The study we conducted, then, involved the systematic manipulation of three factors, all of which had been shown to strongly influence subjects' affective state: ambient temperature (cool or hot), type of evaluation from another person (positive or negative), and degree of attitude similarity to this same individual (low or high). The general procedures of the study were similar to those of our earlier experiments with the following exceptions. During the initial, *affect-induction* phase of the study, the subject and confederate each completed a brief 10-item attitude questionnaire. The subject's questionnaire was then given to the confederate, who was instructed to record his impression of his partner on a special form, the Interpersonal Judgment Scale (IJS) developed by Byrne (1971). After a few minutes' delay, both the attitude questionnaire completed by the confererate and his supposed ratings on the IJS were returned to the waiting subject, who was asked to examine these forms, and then to rate the confederate on another copy of the IJS. In reality, of course, both the confederate's replies to the attitude questionnaire and his ratings of the subject were varied in a systematic manner. In the *similar* condition, the confederate completed his own attitude questionnaire so as to suggest that he agreed with the subject's replies on 9 of the 10 items; in the *dissimilar* condition, he completed his form so as to indicate that he agreed on only one item. Further, in the *positive* evaluation condition he rated the subject in a very favorable manner, while in the *negative* evaluation condition, he provided highly unfavorable assessments.

Following these procedures, subjects completed a Personal Feelings Scale, on which they indicated their current feelings along six different dimensions: comfortable–uncomfortable, bad–good, high–low, sad–happy, pleasant–unpleasant, and negative–positive. Their responses to these items provided a measure of their overall affective state.

Once the Personal Feelings Scale had been completed, the investigation proceeded in the same manner as our earlier studies. That is, subjects were first provided with an opportunity to aggress against the confederate by means of electric shock, then completed a postexperimental questionnaire, and finally received a thorough debriefing. As in our previous investigations, the entire study was conducted either under comfortably cool (72–73°F) or uncomfortably hot (93–94°F) environmental conditions.

The major results of the experiment are represented in Fig. 4.6, where subjects' level of aggression against the confederate is plotted against their reported affective state. Examination of this figure suggests that the prediction of a curvilinear relationship between these two variables was strongly confirmed. As negative affect increased from very low levels in the case of the cool–positive, evaluation–similar attitudes (CPS) group through intermediate levels (e.g., the cool–negative, evaluation–dissimilar group), aggression increased. However, as negative feelings on the part of subjects continued to rise, aggression was actually reduced. The curvilinear nature of this function was confirmed by the results of a trend analysis performed upon these data. This analysis yielded a significant

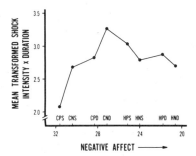

FIG. 4.6   Mean level of aggression (transformed shock intensity × duration) as a function of reported negative affect. (From Bell & Baron, 1976, fig. 1, p. 25.)

quadratic trend $(F = 8.41, df = 1/56, p < 0.007)$ with the test for deviations from quadratic trend nonsignificant $(F = 1.10)$. Thus, consistent with our theoretical model, aggression and negative affect appeared to be curvilinearly related.

In addition to the trend analysis described above, a 2 × 2 × 2 analysis of variance was also performed on the aggression data. The results of this analysis generally yielded findings consistent with those of our earlier studies. More specifically, both the interactions of temperature with type of evaluation $(F = 4.71, df = 1/56, p < 0.04)$ and temperature with attitude similarity $(F = 5.49, df = 1/56, p < 0.02)$ were significant. Examination of the appropriate means indicated that as was the case in our previous research, aggression was enhanced by high ambient temperatures when subjects received positive evaluations or learned that the confederate's attitudes were similar to their own, but was actually inhibited by such environmental conditions when they received negative evaluations from this person, or learned that his attitudes were quite dissimilar to their own. Thus, our earlier findings regarding the mediating impact of factors influencing subjects' affective state were confirmed once again.

Extending The Curvilinear Relationship:
The Effects Of Uncomfortable Cold

Our final attempt to examine the validity of the theoretical framework described earlier in the chapter involved a simple and straightforward prediction. If, as we suggested, the impact of ambient temperature upon aggression is mediated by individuals' level of negative affect, uncomfortably cold environmental conditions should produce effects on aggression similar to those induced by uncomfortably hot circumstances. More specifically, uncomfortable cold should enhance subsequent aggression under conditions in which subjects' level of negative affect is moderate or low (e.g., when they receive positive evaluations from the confederate), but should inhibit such behavior when their level of negative affect is relatively high (e.g., when they receive negative evaluations from this person).

In order to examine these predictions, we conducted a study (Bell & Baron, 1977) in which male subjects first wrote sketches about themselves and then received either positive or negative feedback from a male confederate in the man-

TABLE 4.3
Mean Level of Aggression[a] Delivered to the Confederate
by Subjects in Eight Experimental Groups

Personal Evaluation	Ambient Temperature			
	Cold	Cool	Warm	Hot
Positive	2.78	2.34	2.72	2.99
Negative	3.27	3.53	3.76	3.06

[a]Transformed shock intensity x duration.

ner previously described. Following these procedures, they were provided with an opportunity to aggress against this person in the usual manner (i.e., by means of electric shock). To determine whether uncomfortable cold would influence subsequent aggression in a manner similar to that of uncomfortable heat, temperatures during the entire session were varied so as to be either unpleasantly cold (63–65°F), comfortably cool (71–73°F), moderately warm (84–86°F), or uncomfortably hot (92–94°F).

The major results of the experiment are summarized in Table 4.3. As can be readily seen, the pattern of findings obtained was generally consistent with our predictions. Under conditions in which subjects received a negative evaluation from the confederate, aggression was inhibited both by uncomfortably cold and uncomfortably hot environmental conditions. However, under conditions in which subjects received a positive evaluation, aggression was facilitated by both environmental extremes. While these increments and decrements in aggression were significant ($p < 0.05$) in the case of the hot condition, they only approached significance in the case of the cold condition. Given the fact that temperatures in the former group departed from comfortable environmental circumstances to a greater degree than did those in the latter, however, this pattern of findings is not very surprising. In short, consistent with predictions derived from our theoretical model, unpleasantly low ambient temperatures exerted effects upon aggresion quite similar to those induced by uncomfortably high readings.

An Attempt At Generalization:
Horn-Honking At Intersections

Before concluding this discussion, one attempt at generalizing the findings of our laboratory research to more naturalistic field settings should be mentioned. In this investigation (Baron, 1976), we reasoned that exposure to uncomfortably warm environmental conditions (temperatures in the mid-80's F) might well influence the behavior of motorists in traffic situations. In particular, we reasoned that assuming no other sources of negative affect were present on the scene, motorists exposed to uncomfortably warm conditions would be more likely to honk their horns at another driver who delayed them for a brief period than motorists not exposed to such environmental conditions. This would be the case because in the absence of other sources of negative affect, unpleasantly warm ambient temperatures would shift subjects' behavior upward along the rising portion of the hypothesized curvilinear function relating negative affect to aggression.

In order to examine these predictions, conditions were arranged so that a male confederate failed to move his vehicle for fifteen seconds after the light turned green at selected intersections, thus delaying the driver behind him. These delays were enacted during the afternoon (2:30—4:00 P.M.) on several sunny weekdays during the months of June and July, so that temperatures in all cases were in the mid-80's ($M = 83.14°F$). In order to assess the effects of exposure to such environmental conditions upon horn-honking — a form of behavior found to be aggressive in other studies (Turner, Layton, & Simons, 1975) — the reactions of individuals driving air conditioned and nonair conditioned cars were compared.[5] Data concerning such reactions (i.e., horn-honking) were collected by two observers seated in a second car parked near the intersection. One of these individuals operated a portable tape recorder so as to obtain a permanent record of the frequency and of the frequency and latency of horn-honking, while the second noted other types of behavior (e.g., verbal comments, facial expressions, etc.) on a special form.

Since the study was designed to investigate several other questions as well, a number of different experimental conditions were included. However, those of most central interest in the present context were ones in which: (1) no other person was present on the scene (the *control* group); and (2) a female confederate dressed in conservative attire crossed the intersection, disappearing from sight before the light had turned green (the *distraction* group). The latency of horn—honking demonstrated by subjects in these groups is presented in Table 4.4, where it can be seen that exposure to uncomfortable environmental warmth produced the expected effects in both cases. That is, individuals in nonair conditioned cars honked at the confederate significantly sooner than those driving air conditioned vehicles. Thus, consistent with the findings of our laboratory research, and also in agreement with predictions derived from our theoretical

---

[5]The presence or absence of air conditioning was noted by the two observers as each subject approached the intersection and came to a stop behind the confederate's car. Autos possessing tinted glass and with the windows rolled up were classified as being air conditioned, while vehicles without tinted glass and with the windows rolled down were classified as being nonair conditioned. (Those few autos that possessed tinted glass but had the windows rolled down, or which lacked tinted glass but had the windows rolled up were not included in the study in order to avoid any ambiguity regarding the presence or absence of air conditioning equipment.)

TABLE 4.4
Mean Latency (Sec.) of Horn-Honking as a Function of
Experimental Treatment and Exposure to
Uncomfortably Warm Ambient Temperatures

	Condition	
	Control	Distraction
Not exposed to warm temperatures (air-conditioned cars)	10.68	13.13
Exposed to warm temperatures (non-air-conditioned cars)	7.19	7.99

model, exposure to unpleasantly warm temperatures enhanced aggression under the present conditions.

THE CURVILINEAR RELATIONSHIP: SOME IMPLICATIONS

Perhaps it is most appropriate to begin this concluding section by summarizing the results of the studies performed to investigate the accuracy of our theoretical framework. In the first of these experiments, conditions expected to lower sub- jects' level of negative affect were found to reduce the impact of high ambient temperatures upon their behavior in the predicted manner. In the second, direct evidence for the existence of a curvilinear relationship between negative affect and aggression was obtained. The third study revealed that uncomfortable cold exerted effects upon aggression highly similar to those induced by uncomfortable heat — an outcome also predicted by our theoretical model. Finally, a field in- vestigation produced results consistent with those of our laboratory experiments.

Considered together, the findings of these various studies seem to provide relatively strong support for our theoretical framework. Specifically, they sup- port the view that the impact of ambient temperature upon aggression is mediated by subjects' level of negative affect, and that this mediation, in turn, is underlain by a curvilinear relationship between negative affect and aggressive behavior. That is, up to some determinable point, aggression seems to become increasingly dominant in subjects' behavior hierarchy as negative affect rises. Beyond this point, however, the tendency to engage in such behavior seems to decrease as other responses incompatible with aggression (e.g., escaping from the extremely unpleasant situation; minimization of present discomfort) become increasingly prepotent (refer to Fig. 4.5). If further research offers additional confirmation of this curvilinear function, two important implications would appear to follow.

First, it would be expected that high ambient temperatures, which have been found to induce considerable negative affect among human adults (e.g., Griffitt, 1970; Griffitt & Veitch, 1971), may either facilitate or inhibit subsequent aggression depending upon where, along this function, subjects' level of negative affect happens to fall. If, as seems to have been the case in the negative evaluation conditions of our research, the level of such affect falls at or to the right of the inflection point on the affect—aggression function, further increments in such feelings produced by exposure to high ambient temperatures may lead to lowered aggression. However, if negative affect is less intense and falls to the left of this point — as may well have been the case in the positive evaluation condition of our research — increments in negative affect may serve to facilitate overt attacks against others. In short, increments in feelings of annoyance or discomfort induced by exposure to uncomfortably hot (or cold) environmental conditions may either facilitate or inhibit subsequent aggression: the precise effects produced will depend upon whether such conditions serve to shift subjects' reactions along ascending or descending portions of the affect—aggression function.

Second, and of somewhat greater importance, the existence of a curvilinear relationship between negative affect and aggression suggests that virtually any factor — environmental or social — that strongly influences subjects' affective state will influence aggression in a manner analogous to that of ambient temperature. That is, such factors may either increase or decrease aggressive behavior by inducing shifts along rising or falling portions of the curve. For example, such environmental conditions as crowding (Freedman, Heshka, & Levy, 1975), irritating noise (Geen & O'Neal, 1969; Glass & Singer, 1972; Konecni, 1975), or even unpleasant odors (e.g., Rotton, Frey, Barry, Milligan, & Fitzpatrick, 1978) may all facilitate aggression when moderate, but inhibit such behavior when extreme, or when presented in combination with other factors which also induce negative affect. Direct evidence regarding these suggestions can only be obtained through further empirical study in which several affect-inducing factors are varied simultaneously. However, our theoretical framework suggests that so long as these variables influence subjects' affective state in a negative direction, effects analogous to those produced by ambient temperature may well be observed (see Baron, 1977).

A Note On Collective Violence

Before concluding, we should comment briefly on the relevance of our findings to the "long hot summer" — the supposed facilitating effect of high ambient temperatures on riots, civil disorders, and similar occurrences. As we noted at the start of this chapter, many mass media descriptions of such events have suggested that they are due, at least in part, to the irritating influence of unpleasant heat. What, then, do the findings of our research suggest with respect to such proposals? Basically, they seem to point to three tentative conclusions.

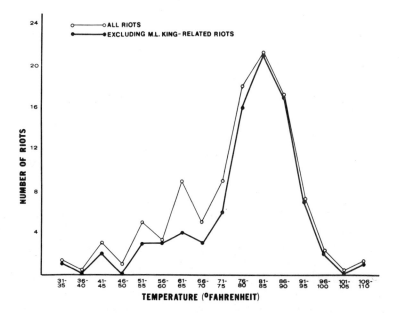

FIG. 4.7.   Frequency of collective violence (riots) as a function of ambient temperature.

First, the results of our studies indicate that while ambient temperature may indeed influence human aggression, the effects produced are far from simple or straightforward. Thus, it does not seem reasonable to expect that the incidence of collective violence will increase in a simple linear manner with increments in ambient temperature, as has frequently been proposed. Rather, on the basis of the hypothetical relationship between negative affect and aggression shown in Fig. 4.5, we would expect the link between these variables to be curvilinear in nature. And as can be seen in Fig. 4.7, we have recently gathered convincing evidence that this is indeed the case (Baron & Ransberger, 1978). That is, when the frequency of dangerous riots occurring in the years 1967–1971 is plotted against the ambient temperatures prevailing in the locations involved on the dates in question, a striking curvilinear relationship emerges.

Second, the complex nature of the relationship between ambient temperature and aggression points to the conclusion that the frequent occurrence of riots, looting, and similar events during the summer months (Goranson & King, 1970) does not stem directly or exclusively from the presence of uncomfortable heat during such periods. Rather, it appears that other factors, such as a greater number of people out on the streets, the longer hours of daylight, and the presence of teenagers home from school, may contribute to the stimulation of such events.

Finally, the results of our research and our theoretical model seem to explain why, under some conditions at least, high ambient temperatures may in fact impel individuals living in central city ghettos in the direction of collective violence. Such persons, we reason, are constantly exposed to many unpleasant, negative affect-inducing environmental factors (e.g., crowding, irritating noise, unpleasant smells, etc.). Thus, at first glance, the addition of high ambient temperatures to their surroundings might be expected to shift them in the direction of reduced rather than increased aggression, as minimization of discomfort or escape become increasingly dominant reactions. Unfortunately, however, such individuals often find escape from these unpleasant conditions quite impossible. With their most dominant responses blocked, therefore, they may well turn to other, slightly less prepotent forms of behavior. And given the strong provocations they have often endured at the hands of police, storekeepers, employers, and others, aggression may well turn out to be one such reaction. Further, as noted earlier, the presence of many people out on the street during summer "heat waves" may increase the probability that any quarrels or provocative incidents will develop into dangerous, violent episodes. For these reasons, even persons whose level of negative affect is already quite high may sometimes be propelled in the direction of collective violence by uncomfortable heat (see Fig. 4.8).

If this analysis is indeed correct, then one means of counteracting such effects is readily suggested: individuals subjected to such unpleasant environmental con-

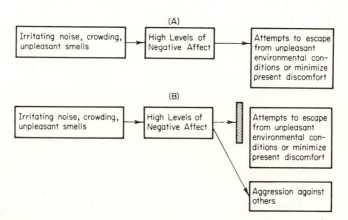

FIG. 4.8.   When, because of the presence of irritating noise, crowding, etc., the level of negative affect experienced by central-city residents is high, the addition of unpleasant heat may lead to strong attempts to minimize such discomfort (A). Under conditions where such actions are impossible, however, individuals may turn to other, less prepotent responses including aggression (B). It is for this reason that high ambient temperatures may sometimes facilitate the occurrence of collective violence.

ditions should be provided with means for minimizing or reducing their discomfort. Presumably, the presence of such alternative courses of action will serve to inhibit aggression, and prevent the outbreak of collective violence, at least in some situations. In short, the "long hot summer" may in fact be cooled by the construction of parks and swimming pools, or the installation of air conditioning in community centers and similar locations. However, the reasons for such beneficial effects, should they occur, may be far more complex than those originally proposed.

SUMMARY

It has often been contended that uncomfortably high ambient temperatures facilitate the occurrence of human aggression. Research concerning this possibility, however, suggests that the relationship between heat and aggression is far more complex than initially suspected. The results of several experiments indicate that high ambient temperatures may well facilitate subsequent aggression when no other sources of negative affect are present in the situation. However, they may actually serve to inhibit such reactions when other sources of negative affect (e.g., derogatory evaluations from another person) are present. Thus, the effects of ambient temperature upon aggression appear to be mediated by subjects' level of negative affect.

Additional research suggests that these mediating effects, in turn, are underlain by a more general curvilinear relationship between negative affect and aggression. Basically, it appears that up to some determinable point, aggression becomes increasingly dominant as negative affect — induced by high temperatures or any other social or environmental factor — rises. Beyond this point, however, the tendency to engage in aggression may decrease as other responses incompatible with such behavior (e.g., escaping from the aversive situation) become increasingly prepotent.

Consistent with this theoretical framework, the provision of a cooling drink has been found to reduce the impact of high ambient temperatures upon aggression in the predicted manner. Similarly, uncomfortably low temperatures have been found to produce effects quite similar to those induced by unpleasant heat. Finally, when subjects' level of negative affect is systematically varied through exposure to previously selected experimental conditions, a curvilinear relationship between degree of self-reported negative affect and aggression is in fact observed.

Existing evidence suggests that uncomfortably high ambient temperatures may well contribute to the occurrence of collective violence under some circumstances. However, the impact of such environmental conditions is far more complex than previously suspected, and uncomfortable heat by no means produces such effects in all cases. Thus, acceptance of any broad or sweeping generalization regarding the influence of ambient temperature upon aggression (e.g., the oft-cited "long hot summer" effect) seems unjustified at the present time.

ACKNOWLEDGMENTS

Portions of this research were supported by Grant GS-35276 from the National Science Foundation to the author. Sincere appreciation is expressed to Paul A. Bell whose able assistance proved invaluable in the conduction of several of the experiments reported.

REFERENCES

Bandura, A. Social learning theory of aggression. In J. F. Knutsen (Ed.), *Control of aggression: Implications from basic research.* Chicago: Aldine–Atherton, 1971.

Bandura, A. *Aggression: A social learning analysis.* Englewood Cliffs, N.J.: Prentice-Hall, 1973.

Baron, R. A. Aggression as a function of ambient temperature and prior anger arousal. *Journal of Personality and Social Psychology,* 1972, *21,* 183–189.

Baron, R. A. Threatened retaliation from the victim as an inhibitor of physical aggression. *Journal of Research in Personality,* 1973, *7,* 103–115.

Baron, R. A. The reduction of human aggression: A field study of the influence of incompatible reactions. *Journal of Applied Social Psychology,* 1976, *6,* 260–274.

Baron, R. A. *Human aggression.* New York: Plenum, 1977.

Baron, R. A., & Bell, P. A. Aggression and heat: Mediating effects of prior provocation and exposure to an aggressive model. *Journal of Personality and Social Psychology,* 1975, *31,* 825–832.

Baron, R. A., & Bell, P. A. Aggression and heat: The influence of ambient temperature, negative affect, and a cooling drink on physical aggression. *Journal of Personality and Social Psychology,* 1976, *33,* 245–255.

Baron, R. A., & Eggleston, R. J. Performance on the "aggression machine": Motivation to help or harm? *Psychonomic Science,* 1972, *26,* 321–322.

Baron, R. A., & Lawton, S. F. Environmental influences on aggression: The facilitation of modeling effects by high ambient temperatures. *Psychonomic Science,* 1972, *26,* 80–82.

Baron, R. A., & Ransberger, V. M. Ambient temperature and the occurrence of collective violence: The "long, hot summer" revisited. *Journal of Personality and Social Psychology,* 1978, *36,* 351–360.

Bell, P. A., & Baron, R. A. Aggression and heat: The mediating role of negative affect. *Journal of Applied Social Psychology,* 1976, *6,* 18–30.

Bell, P. A., & Baron, R. A. Aggression and ambient temperature: The facilitating and inhibiting effects of hot and cold environments. *Bulletin of the Psychonomic Society,* 1977, *9,* 443–445.

Berkowitz, L. The contagion of violence. In W. J. Arnold & M. M. Page (Eds.), *Nebraska Symposium on Motivation.* Lincoln, Neb.: University of Nebraska Press, 1970.

Berkowitz, L. Some determinants of impulsive aggression: Role of mediated associations with reinforcements for aggression. *Psychological Review,* 1974, *81,* 165–176.

Berkowitz, L., & Geen, R. G. Film violence and the cue properties of available targets. *Journal of Personality and Social Psychology,* 1966, *3,* 525–530.

Buss, A. H. *The psychology of aggression*. New York: Wiley, 1961.

Byrne, D. *The attraction paradigm*. New York: Academic Press, 1971.

Doob, A. N., & Wood, L. Catharsis and aggression: The effects of annoyance and retaliation on aggressive behavior. *Journal of Personality and Social Psychology*, 1972, *22*, 156–162.

Freedman, J. L., Heshka, S., & Levy, A. Population density and pathology. Is there a relationship? *Journal of Experimental Social Psychology*, 1975, *11*, 539–552.

Geen, R. G., & O'Neal, E. C. Activation of cue-elicited aggression by general arousal. *Journal of Personality and Social Psychology*, 1969, *11*, 289–292.

Glass, D. C., & Singer, J. E. *Urban stress*. New York: Academic Press, 1972.

Goranson, R. E., & King, D. *Rioting and daily temperature: Analysis of the U.S. riots in 1967*. Unpublished manuscript, York University, Ontario, Canada, 1970.

Griffitt, W. Environmental effects on interpersonal affective behavior: Ambient effective temperature and attraction. *Journal of Personality and Social Psychology*, 1970, *15*, 240–244.

Griffitt, W., & Veitch, R. Hot and crowded: Influence of population density and temperature on interpersonal affective behavior. *Journal of Personality and Social Psychology*, 1971, *17*, 92–98.

Konecni, V. J. The mediation of aggressive behavior: Arousal level versus anger and cognitive labeling. *Journal of Personality and Social Psychology*, 1975, *32*, 706–712.

Latané, B., Eckman, J., & Joy, V. Shared stress and interpersonal aggraction. *Journal of Experimental Social Psychology*, 1966, *2*, 80–94.

Provins, K. A., & Bell, C. R. Effects of heat stress on the performance of two tasks running concurrently. *Journal of Experimental Psychology*, 1970, *85*, 40–44.

Rotton, J., Frey, J., Barry, T., Milligan, M., & Fitzpatrick, M. Modeling, malodorous air pollution, and interpersonal aggression. *Journal of Applied Social Psychology*, 1978, in press.

Turner, C. W., Layton, J. F., & Simons, L. S. Naturalistic studies of aggressive behavior: Aggressive stimuli, victim visibility, and horn honking. *Journal of Personality and Social Psychology*, 1975, *31*, 1098–1107.

United States Riot Commision. *Report of the National Advisory Commission on Civil Disorders*. New York: Bantam Books, 1968.

5 Helpfulness in the Urban Environment

Charles Korte
University of St. Andrews
Scotland

INTRODUCTION

One of the yardsticks commonly used to mark the ebbing quality of life in our contemporary cities is the absence of mutual aid. Cruz, one of the key figures in Oscar Lewis' account of lower class life in Puerto Rico (Lewis, 1965), tells of one of her problems with moving into a San Juan housing project: "I hated to go out because it's hard to find your way back to this place even if you know the address. The first couple of times I got lost and I didn't dare ask anyone the way for fear they would fall on me and beat me" (p. 662). Her fears of physical violence may not be a pervasive problem of urban living, but common to many urbanites is the difficulty of finding informal support and aid from those about them. Residents of a middle-class, high-rise housing development on the outskirts of Amsterdam formed a volunteer service organization to offer assistance to other residents, e.g., cooking meals and shopping for a family when the mother was ill (Huismans & Korte, 1977). Even though social workers in the development were aware of considerable numbers of residents failing to receive precisely the type of aid offered by the volunteer group, there were very few people who requested assistance from the residents' organization. Such reticence to seek help may not seem surprising when one considers the many episodes reported in the press of persons whose appeals for help appeared to fall on deaf ears [e.g., Kitty Genovese (Rosenthal, 1964)]. The popular portrayal of urbanites as uncaring, withdrawn, impersonal and exploitative is reinforced by many scholarly analyses of the urban environment. Wirth (1938) argued that the size, density and population heterogeneity of the contemporary city generated a way of life that he termed "urbanism." Among other things, urbanism is a complex of traits which reflects the urbanite's adaptation to a situation in which social relationships are often transitory, role-defined, and superficial. Hence, according to Wirth, the urbanite shows a characteristic reserve, indifference and blasé attitude in the face of his fellow urbanites who largely remain strangers to him.

It is only recently that this view of urban social contact and mutual aid has been scrutinized in terms of both its generality and the validity of the alternative explanations available. In this review, an effort will be made to evaluate the current state of our understanding about the occurrence of helpfulness and mutual aid in an urban environment. Is a lack of helpfulness in fact a general characteristic of cities, and if so, why? It has been suggested that the urbanite's failure to offer aid is a result of urban "bombardment" − sights, sounds and "inputs" − and also of urban design and architecture. These two prominent *environmental* explanations of urban social behavior will be examined in detail in this paper. In addition, a case will be made for the generally unrecognized *cultural* limitations to the association between urbanization and deficient helpfulness. Finally, a simple integrative model will be offered within which the interaction between environmental features and behavioral patterns can perhaps best be conceptualized.

HELPFULNESS AND URBANIZATION

A relative infrequency of helpfulness in the urban environment can be expected from an analysis of the determinants of helpfulness as well as from an analysis of the characteristics of the urban environment. The growing literature on helping behavior has identified several deterrents to helpfulness which would appear to be more prominent or frequent in an urban environment. The occurrence of mutual aid is *diminished* by increased numbers of potential bystander "interveners" (Bickman, 1971; Darley & Latané, 1968; Korte, 1970; Schwartz & Clausen, 1970; for an exception, see Piliavin, Rodin, & Piliavin, 1969), racial dissimilarity between help-seeker and potential help-giver (Gaertner & Bickman, 1971; Wegner & Crano, 1975), time pressure (Darley & Batson, 1973), increased ease in avoiding people needing help (Staub, 1974), residential density (Bickman et al., 1973), and high levels of environmental stimulation or "input" (Korte, Ypma, & Toppen, 1975; Matthews & Cannon, 1975; Sherrod & Downs, 1974). Each of these factors would seem to be enhanced by urbanization, though direct evidence for such correlations is often lacking. It seems fair to observe that given the array of situational factors that inhibit helpfulness, one would expect the general impact of urbanization on the occurrence of helpfulness to be negative rather than positive, yet it is well to point out that urbanization is more than a collection of situational influences, a point that will be developed later on in the paper when a closer look is taken at the *explanations* for urbanization effects.

Theoretical analyses of urbanization and the urban environment also lead to an expectation of reduced levels of mutual aid between urbanites as opposed to their less urban counterparts. This effect has been attributed to a diversity of factors, the principal ones being role segmentation and the weakness of primary ties in the city (Wirth, 1938), the pace, tempo and monetary orientation of urban life (Simmel, 1950), urban architecture (Alexander, 1967; Newman, 1973), and the level of environmental inputs (Milgram, 1970). There is hence quite a convergence of popular thinking and social science theorizing that suggests a negative association between urbanization and mutual aid. We shall turn now to the evidence for this hypothesized relationship.

There is much anecdotal and case study evidence for the infrequency of mutual aid in an urban environment, but a search for *comparative* studies of the actual occurrence of mutual aid in urban versus nonurban settings shows very little evidence. For those few comparative studies that do exist, the principal research method has been the use of naturalistic measures that test individual responses to situations in which assistance is needed and thus allows one to compare the helpfulness of urbanites versus nonurbanites. This is a very clear-cut means of evaluating the hypothesis of urban unhelpfulness, though it is restricted to mutual aid between strangers rather than between friends and neighbors. Data on mutual aid between friends and neighbors basically are available only by means of self-report measures, which can be liable to distortion and misrepresentation. A very small number of such comparative studies have included items on mutual aid; more generally these studies are concerned with the level of sociability and social contact (see Korte, 1976a). But let us now examine those studies which compared helpfulness in locales with varying degrees of urbanization.

The studies on the helpfulness shown toward another person generally support the hypothesis of urban unhelpfulness. One measure researchers have used in this regard is the "wrong number" technique: persons are contacted on the telephone by a caller who first indicates that he has called a wrong number from a pay phone, then appeals to the listener for a small request, e.g., to relay an important message on to the intended party on the pretext that the caller has no more money to place the call again. Milgram (1970) compared the response to wrong number requests for people in Chicago, New York City and Philadelphia versus those living in small towns in Illinois, New York and Pennsylvania, and found greater helpfulness (though of unreported significance levels) in the small town residents. Similarly, Korte and Kerr (1975) found more helpfulness in response to a wrong number request among residents in small towns of eastern Massachusetts versus Boston. Another "mishap" that has been used by researchers as an indication of the level of helpfulness in a particular locale is the "lost letter" technique (see Milgram, Mann, & Harter, 1965). Stamped, addressed envelopes are left in various places so as to appear "lost" by persons intending to mail them. They are coded as to the location of their "drop," allowing for a comparison of the return rate between different locales (e.g., urban and nonurban). Studies using this measure show mixed results. Korte and Kerr (1975) "dropped" postcards bearing an important message (a request to meet the sender's train at a specific time and place) and found a higher return rate in Massachusetts small towns than in Boston (70% vs. 61%), though the difference did not reach statistical significance. Krupat and Coury (1975) found the return rate of letters lost in small towns throughout central New Jersey to be greater than in Manhattan; this difference appeared largely attributable to the density of people in the settings where the postcards were lost. With density controlled for, little variation in the response to the lost letter was attributable to the urban—nonurban dimension. Finally, Forbes and Gromoll (1971) report no difference in the return rate of lost letters between areas of differing levels of urbanization.

Latané's (1970) study of sidewalk helpfulness in New York City, measuring the response to requests, e.g., for directions and change, was replicated by Merrens (1973) in midwestern cities and small towns. His results showed greater helpfulness in the midwestern cities and towns, but no general difference *between* cities and towns in the Midwest. More dramatic measures of helpfulness have been used in research concerned with emergency intervention and, on a few occasions, these studies have compared the helpfulness of subjects from urban versus nonurban environments, with only weak support for the urban unhelpfulness hypothesis. Darley and Latané (1968) exposed subjects in a psychology experiment to an apparent laboratory accident, involving the collapse of another subject located in a different room. The speed with which subjects responded by taking steps to help the distressed person showed a significant inverse correlation with the size of the subject's home community: The smaller the community, the faster the response. Unfortunately, this finding was not replicated in two other studies by Schwartz and Clausen (1970) and Korte (1970), which found no correlation between giving assistance to another person in a laboratory "accident" and urban versus nonurban background. Weiner (1976) actually found laboratory subjects with urban backgrounds to be *more* helpful than rural background subjects in their response to a laboratory accident. It is important to note a possibly significant limitation to all of these results, which correlate laboratory helpfulness to the urban versus nonurban background of the subject. Differences in helpfulness as a function of background are expected on the assumption that growing up in one type of environment or the other has resulted in certain behavioral characteristics that persist beyond the environment of their origin. Yet if the behavioral characteristics are determined to some degree by the actual conditions of the immediate environment, then there is little reason to expect a persistence of that behavior in a completely different context (e.g., the psychological laboratory in a university setting). Perhaps particular patterns of social behavior *are* associated with the urban environment, but only when people, both urbanites and nonurbanites, are at that moment located in an urban environment.

A final collection of evidence relevant to the association between helpfulness and urbanization comes from measures which involve elements of trust and honesty in the offering of assistance. Milgram (1970) reported a comparison between New York City residents and residents of small towns outside of the city in their response to a stranger at the door. These "strangers," actually university students conducting the study, would ring the doorbell, explain that they had lost the address of a friend who lived nearby, and ask to use the telephone. Compared to the city residents, the small town residents were far more likely to offer the use of the telephone to the stranger (72% vs. 27%).

City and small town store clerks were studied by Korte and Kerr (1975) who examined their response to an "accidental" overpayment by customers for small purchases. The oversight was more frequently corrected by small town clerks in comparison to their urban counterparts (80% vs. 55%). City bank clerks were observed by Lowin, Holtes, Sandler, & Bornstein (1971) to make more frequent checks on the money paid in by customers than was true for small town clerks, a difference that may reflect greater suspicion on the part of the urban clerks. Finally, using a measure that may in part reflect a customer's helpfulness toward the store in which he or she is shopping, Gelfand, Hartman, Walder, & Page (1973) found that shoppers from more urban locales were less likely to report episodes of shoplifting than were nonurban shoppers.

Taken together, this small number of behavioral comparison of urban and nonurban helpfulness reveals a favorable verdict for the expected negative association between urbanization and helpfulness. Although some of the comparisons were inconclusive or showed no differences, there were no cases where helpfulness in the urban setting *exceeded* what had been obtained elsewhere. Although this evidence may clarify some of the speculations that have been made about the impact of an urban environment, it is only a preliminary step in this endeavor and one that has a number of limitations. It is worth considering two of the most important of these limitations, which are interrelated and point quite logically to the next stage of research in this field. Put simply, the limitations lie with: (1) the conceptualization of urbanization, which ignores crucial variations and complexities related to urban form, such as differences *within* a single urban environment and *between* urban environments in different cultures; and (2) the failure to identify the particular factors that are influencing the level of helpfulness and mutual aid. These two points are considered in turn.

Defining "urban" in terms of population size runs the risk of treating as equal things that may not be equal. The expectation of infrequent helpfulness in urban environments may be founded within limited sections of the total urban environment and may be inapplicable to other sections. Not all parts of the city are dense, noisy and dangerous, filled with high-rises and mobile, fast-paced individuals who live away from family and friendship networks. Several community studies claim to have found urban neighborhoods where mutual aid and cooperation flourish in a fashion that many people associate with small town life. Jacobs (1961) has depicted parts of New York City (Greenwich Village) and Boston (the North End) as high in the extent of helpful and friendly gestures that pass between neighbors, and the sense of safety that visitors to these districts have due to feelings that in a troublesome situation they would be supported by the local residents. Gans (1962) adds to the reputation of another Boston neighborhood in his characterization of the West End, a district that has since been destroyed as a result of urban development. The West End, according to Gans, had extensive interpersonal networks that provided considerable support to individuals in times of hardship and distress. Mutual aid was quite intensive and recognized by the residents as a feature lacking in many other sections of Boston. Urban environments frequently do have distinct districts which may be quite different in the considerateness and helpfulness which is shown toward other people. Such interurban variations might exceed those found between urban and nonurban environments and would be highly relevant to the identification of the particular factors influencing the occurrence of mutual aid and helpfulness. At the very least, such variations would illustrate the oversimplification involved in treating the urban environment as a homogeneous entity. An attempt to evaluate the significance of interurban differences in mutual aid was undertaken by Korte, Ypma, and Toppen (1975) in a study conducted in the Netherlands. Surprisingly, this study failed to confirm strong expectations which were held about the existence of interurban differences in the Netherlands' largest city, Amsterdam. A preliminary survey of Amsterdam residents was conducted to identify those districts with strong reputations for helpful and friendly social relations, both between residents and between residents and outsiders. Four neighborhoods were selected on this basis, two each at either end of the continuum (i.e., either very helpful and friendly or very unhelpful and unfriendly). Data were then collected in each of the four neighborhoods, using three measures of helpfulness: willingness to grant an interview to a Dutch university student, calling attention to a key someone else had dropped, and stopping to assist a person showing considerable difficulty finding his present location on a map. The results of this study were totally unexpected: no differences in helpfulness occurred at all between the two stereotypically different types of neighborhoods. These results were equally surprising to Amsterdam residents, especially since one of the neighborhoods (the Jordaan) had a widely known reputation for its warm, considerate, helpful atmosphere. It is hard to reconcile these results with the very convincing argument for the existence of important interurban differences in social behavior, though a single study in a single city is hardly conclusive evidence. Interurban differences might be more readily expected with measures that tap helpfulness between acquainted persons (e.g., friends and neighbors, rather than between the unacquainted, as was done in the Korte et al., 1975, study).

In addition to interurban variability, urban phenomena can also differ between different cultures. Considerable controversy has surrounded the question of how successfully accounts of urbanization effects, especially Wirth's (1938), have treated urbanization independently of any specific cultural forms of urbanization. Most accounts of urban social relations, including the character of mutual aid and helpfulness, seem to presume a universality of the social effects that are associated with an urban environment. But might urbanization incorporate cultural influences that could lead to considerably different outcomes, perhaps demonstrated by cross—cultural differences in urban social relations? This seems to be a very strong possibility, with both theoretical and empirical support. Goudsblom (1967), a Dutch sociologist, considered one aspect of urbanization in the Netherlands to be the emergence of a norm of "civility." He argued that the historical origins of a culture of civility in the Netherlands can be traced to the development of Dutch urban centers and the rise of a burgher class that came to dominate city life. Hence, Dutch urbanization may be conditioned by factors specific to that culture, a possibility which could easily apply to many other cultures. Several observers of Asian societies have commented on the differing quality of social behavior in Asian cities as compared to western ones. Hauser (1965) has informally reviewed four Asian cities — Rangoon, Bangkok, Djakarta, and Calcutta — for the presence of what in the West are regarded as "typical" urban traits (e.g., loneliness, superficiality and depersonalization). He concluded that none of these cities give evidence of such effects. Chinese society, according to Bloodworth (1966), makes a much greater distinction than most western societies between obligations toward relatives versus strangers. The mass of strangers encountered in an urban environment elicits no reactions of social responsibility from Chinese urbanities in moments when assistance is needed, an effect that could be misinterpreted without a proper appreciation of Chinese culture.

In support of these observations are a small collection of studies that have shown the inconsistent relation between urbanization and helpfulness across different cultures. No association was found between urbanization and helpfulness in the Netherlands study just cited by Korte et al. (1975). The three measures described — an interview request, a dropped key and a lost person — were administered in two major Dutch cities (Amsterdam and the Hague) as well as in four medium-sized towns in central Holland, with no differences occurring between cities and towns. The absence of any difference could be a confirmation of Goudsblom's (1967) suggestion of an urban civility effect present in the Netherlands or it could reflect any number of other factors present (e.g., small geographical size and population homogeneity). The more usual *negative* association between an urban background and helpfulness has been reported in laboratory studies carried out in Israel (Shapira & Madsen, 1969) and Colombia (Marin, Majia, & de Oberle, 1975). In both cases children were tested for the degree of cooperativeness shown toward another child in a game situation. Urban children in Israel and Colombia showed significantly less cooperation than children from more rural backgrounds. A somewhat different examination of helpfulness in urban environments was undertaken by Feldman (1968), who administered naturalistic measures of helpfulness in Paris, Athens and Boston. His design did not include a comparison of urban and nonurban settings, but it did test for the generality of a compatriot bias in urban helpfulness (i.e., whether urbanites are more willing to assist a compatriot who seeks help than they are to assist a foreigner).

The compatriot bias held for Paris and Boston, whereas in Athens a foreigner found more success in getting help than a native Greek, which Feldman attributed to the favorable image of the "outgroup" in Greek culture. Hence, from this small collection of studies it seems clear than numerous cultural factors do intervene between the urban environment to which people are exposed and the social behavior shown in those environments. It does not seem justifiable to treat urban phenomena as having a universal quality which permits broad generalizations about its effects. As with interurban variations, it appears crucial to identify cultural variations in the behavioral characteristics of urban environments, which can only strengthen our understanding of the particular ways in which the urban environment becomes associated with particular forms of social behavior.

A second limitation to the research that establishes a connection between urbanization and helpfulness is that it does not discriminate between the various factors that might be responsible for this connection. An urban environment differs from a less urban one in a multitude of ways, any one of which could influence the occurrence of social behavior such as helpfulness. Further progress in understanding the relationship between the urban environment and patterns of social behavior such as helpfulness requires *identifying* those features of the urban environment which may influence the occurrence of helpfulness and *evaluating* the explanatory value of each of these variables. Without further clarification of such relationships, it is not terribly illuminating to continue the accumulation of data on simply the existence or nonexistence of an association between urbanization and helpfulness. In addition, it is important to establish whether particular factors that are seen as urban and that might be related to helpfulness are, in fact, related to urbanization in the expected way. Some variables may seem to exert some influence on urban unhelpfulness, but if these variables are not ones on which more urban and less urban environments differ, then they are largely irrelevant to the explanation of any overall urban—nonurban differences in helping behavior. It is quite often very hard to determine whether some factor *does* vary systematically with urbanization and our everyday impressions of cities may not be a very reliable guide. One measure of density, the number of persons per room, is actually negatively correlated with population size (Duncan, 1957), whereas environmental "input" level, as measured in the Netherlands, has not shown the expected degree of increase with rises in population size (Korte et al., 1975). As an alternative to the strategy of looking for factors to explain a presumed difference in the level of helpfulness found in urban and nonurban settings, a more productive course might be to identify environmental influences on helpfulness, which would at least partially explain patterns of helpfulness. Such findings could then be applied to settings where that environmental feature was present, whether that be in cities versus towns, or in some particular parts of the urban environment and not in others.

Some of the most fruitful explanations for the occurrence of urban forms of social behavior have been, in fact, environmental ones that suggest a causal link between particular environmental characteristics that are usually seen as "urban" (e.g., density, input level, housing architecture), and resulting patterns of social behavior. This environmental determinism view has come under increasing attack, though it continues to find considerable support in empirical research. We shall now turn to a consideration of the case for attributing behavioral effects to two important features that seem fundamental to the urban environment: input level and urban design.

HELPFULNESS AND ENVIRONMENTAL INPUT LEVEL

To many observers, the urban trait of unconcern or noninvolvement is not surprising when one considers the constant stress, tumult and demands to which the urbanite is subjected. In fact, urbanites may even take a perverse pride in their ability to "tune out" all the activity and irritations (both human and nonhuman) that bombard them in our largest cities. The absence of this characteristic is often the mark of the small town visitor, who can be identified by attentiveness to all the bewildering events swirling around him. Does continual exposure to all the events and people in an urban environment result in a necessary adaptation, whereby all those events and people become less important, less noticed, less bothersome? Does the seasoned urbanite show less concern or responsiveness toward other people? Simmel (1950) was convinced of this and, in an important turn-of-the-century paper on urban mentality, argued for the important psychological consequences of the intensity of change and stimulation that occurs in the city. According to Simmel, the sheer quantity of stimulation from people and things in the city produces in the urbanite a reserve, indifference and even latent hostility toward his fellow urbanites.

A sharpened presentation of this view has been offered recently by Milgram (1970), who elaborated Simmel's idea of stimulation into a system's concept of "input overload." The urban environment can be depicted as a multitude of "inputs" (e.g., sights, sounds, and demands) that have the potential of drawing the urbanite's attention and response. Yet the capacity to deal with environmental inputs is limited and Milgram suggested that an urban environment quite readily exceeds this threshold point, producing "input overload". A common response to situations of input overload (e.g., by computers, telephone switchboards, busy offices) is to reduce the overload by various adaptations (e.g., ignoring inputs, screening inputs according to some criterion, or deflecting responsibility for an input on to another "system"). In a like manner, the urbanite's adaptation shows itself in oblivion to many environmental events, the decision not to respond to various requests, demands, or opportunities, and internalization of urban norms of behavior.

This "input overload hypothesis" suggests a very concrete explanation for how the urban environment affects helpfulness and is an explanation that should be amenable to experimental evaluation. A recent study conducted by the author, already cited (Korte et al., 1975), undertook to see if urban helpfulness was a function of "input overload". Testing Milgram's formulation revealed several complexities that may not at first be apparent. The basic complexity concerns the existence of *alternative* means by which the level of environmental inputs can affect the occurrence of helpfulness and other types of social behavior. The urbanite's adaptation to input overload may be long-term and/or it may be situational (and short-term). A long-term adaptation would be indicated by a chronic manner of helpfulness which reflects the *general* level of inputs in some locality but is not determined by situational or temporal variations in input level. Such an adaptation involves the emergence of behavioral norms and tactics of coping with everyday events that will develop to the degree that the stressfulness of the general environment, e.g., the city or the distict, "demands" it. Alternatively, or additionally, the urbanite may show a continuous accommodation to the input level of the immediate situation, becoming more or less responsive to environmental events as the input level decreases or increases. This variable responsiveness in turn could be mediated by different mechanisms, such as awareness, fatigue or decisional processes. A high input level may cause people to be less aware of situations and cues that indicate the need for help, or the high level may fatigue people and thereby influence people to decide to ignore some or all of the inputs in a situation, thus reducing helpfulness by another means. This of course does not exhaust the means by which input level might affect helpfulness in a direct and immediate way.

A clear-cut empirical test of input effects as mediated by *long-term* adjustments seems nearly impossible, as the variable of interest, a city's or district's characteristic input level, would be correlated with so many other potentially influential factors. Thus, in the Korte et al. (1975) study, it was decided to test for input effects only as they might occur on a continuous basis (i.e., variable input level resulting directly in variable helpfulness). It was recognized that this was a more stringent test of the "input overload" hypothesis, since it tests for only one of the ways by which input effects could be operating. An additional problem with the "input overload" hypothesis is the sheer impossibility of specifying the occurrence of *overload*, which depends in part on individual states and processes not easily accessible to investigation. A more manageable expression of the hypothesis is to predict effects as a function of the *increase* in environmental input level, realizing that it may only be differences across some critical, undefined threshold point that are instrumental to any effects obtained. The actual measurement of the environmental input level required some preliminary work, as no existing measures suitable to the broad definition of "inputs" could be found. The measure eventually developed (see Korte et al., 1975, for details) consisted of traffic noise data, counts of traffic and pedestrian density and a count of retail and commercial establishments. This index satisfactorily met tests of validity and reliability and was a key tool in establishing the quasi-experimental conditions in this study. The basic design consisted of comparing the helpfulness of pedestrians in closely adjacent sites which, as far as could be ascertained, differed only in their ratings on the environmental input measures. The sites were chosen so as to share the same flow of pedestrian traffic (hence ruling out any population differences), a control that appeared to have been successfully accomplished. Altogether, 10 different pairs of sites were used, which were located in six different towns and cities in the Netherlands.

The results, using the previously described naturalistic meausres of helpfulness, quite clearly supported the hypothesized role of input level in helpfulness. In the sites of lower input level, pedestrians were significantly more likely to grant a street interview (73% vs. 63%), to stop and help a person needing directions (6% vs. 1%), and showed a tendency toward greater assistance in response to a lost key (47% vs. 33%). This study adds strength, then, to the viability of attributing urban unhelpfulness to the influence of the input or bombardment level of the urban environment. What remains is to clarify *how* high levels of environmental input result in a reduction in helpfulness (i.e., whether another person's need for assistance is less noticed, considered less important, perceived as more bothersome, etc.). Additional work (Korte & Grant, 1976) has demonstrated that higher levels of environmental input do result in less awareness of environmental features. This study compared pedestrians in Dundee, Scotland between times when the setting was relatively free from traffic noise and times when traffic was much heavier. In the heavy traffic periods, pedestrians were found to notice less (other people and objects) about the environment they were passing through and were also found to differ in their visual behavior and walking speed. During heavy traffic periods, pedestrians spent more time looking straight ahead and were less likely to avert their gaze and scan to the left or right. Walking speed was also significantly faster during the periods of heavy traffic. These differences appear not to have been contaminated by differences in the purposes and activities of pedestrians (e.g., shopping vs. going to work) between the different periods of time when data were collected. These results confirm that awareness of one's immediate environment can be a casualty of input bombardment and hence, may in part explain the reduced helpfulness that results from this bombardment.

Further support for the detrimental effects of high input levels on helpfulness comes from studies by Matthews and Cannon (1975), Sherrod and Downs (1974), and Weiner (1976). In both laboratory and field settings, Matthews and Cannon (1975) found decreased helpfulness with increased levels of environmental noise. Subjects waiting for an experiment to begin were exposed to a small mishap (another student dropping a load of books) in a room with either ambient noise (48 dB.), low noise (65 dB.) or high noise (85 dB.). Help became far less likely as the room noise became greater: 72%, 67%, and 37%, respectively. A field replication of this study used a lawnmower in a suburban neighborhood as the noise generator. The helpfulness of pedestrians toward another person struggling with a pile of falling books differed considerably depending on whether the lawnmower was not running (50% helpfulness) or running noisily without a muffler (13% helpfulness). These results are very consistent with the Korte et al. (1975) study, showing again that as environmental bombardment goes up, helpfulness goes down. The *particular* means by which helpfulness was affected by the high noise level is important to consider.

A further experimental variation in the Matthews and Cannon (1975) study was used to test the hypothesis that reduced helpfulness in the high noise condition resulted from a lower awareness of environmental cues. The person needing help with the falling books was equipped half the time with a full-length arm cast, a cue which, if noticed, should increase the likelihood of helpfulness. In line with the researchers' hypothesis, this cue did increase helpfulness as expected in the low noise condition, but it had no effect on helpfulness during periods of high noise, suggesting that the cast simply wasn't noticed under these conditions. Of course other factors besides awareness could also be contributing to the reduction of helpfulness and, in addition, the failure of the arm cast to enhance helpfulness when the noise level was high can be interpreted in line with a study by Schaps (1972), which showed that as the costs for giving help increased, the dependency of the victim became less effective in eliciting a helpful response. Perhaps the "cost" of pausing in an irritating environment diminishes helpfulness regardless of the victim's degree of dependency.

Sherrod and Downs (1974) examined the aftereffects of several laboratory tasks performed under various levels of distraction. Subjects were approached at the completion of the experiment with an apparently unrelated request for assistance from another student. The results showed greatest helpfulness when the laboratory task had been subject to minimal distraction (low overload), least when overload was high, and an intermediate amount when overload was high but subjects felt that they could control the level of background distraction. Finally, Weiner (1976) added further support to the input overload hypothesis by finding that experimental subjects were less likely to assist another student injured in a staged accident under conditions of sensory bombardment versus low stimulus overload.

Hence, in the four studies to date, using a variety of research settings, helpfulness measures, and types of inputs, the input overload explanation of helpfulness has been supported. What then does this contribute to the search for an understanding of the urban unhelpfulness phenomenon? It is certainly an important step in the process of sorting out the relevance of the various urban factors that *might* play a crucial role in social behavior such as helpfulness. The social unresponsiveness of urbanites does appear to be in part attributable to the intensity of stimulation in their environment. The failure to respond to others needing assistance may occur at times through sheer inattentiveness to the surrounding environment. Yet this is probably the more trivial of input adaptation effects. The lack of helpfulness found in cities cannot be written off as simply a problem of attention. Urban unhelpfulness does not disappear as an effect when the helpfulness measure used guarantees attention. The more interesting and perhaps compelling means by which input overload leads to social withdrawal and noninvolvement have yet to be verified. These other means would include psychological states that result from input overload and lead to less helpfulness (e.g., tension and irritation) and social processes that may result from conditions of chronic and persistent input overload (e.g., emergence of noninvolvement norms and group inhibition).

As promising as the input overload explanation of urban effects appears to be, it is not without its weaknesses. As already indicated, neither Simmel's (1950) nor Milgram's (1970) account specifies the precise way in which input level leads to a change in social behavior. This paper has suggested some of the different possible mechanisms that mediate overload effects and that have yet to be evaluated. Also unspecified is the *screening system* which urbanites apply to the incoming flow of events, demands, noises, etc. Clearly the urbanites inattentiveness is in some sense an intelligent one, reflecting a semiconscious monitoring system or else a series of decisions. The input overload hypothesis would gain tremendously in usefulness if we could understand more about screening systems which have the complexity needed for coping with an urban environment. Milgram (1970) recognized this problem and suggested that at the extreme, urbanites admit inputs from friends, but not from strangers, and admit inputs only if they are relevant to personal need satisfaction. The methodology of environmental perception studies (e.g., Lynch, 1960 and Lynch and Rivkin, 1959) would seem to be well suited to gaining an understanding of environmental "screening."

Another criticism of the input overload explanation arises when one considers the *extent* of input "problems" in an urban environment. For many urbanites, especially those who are at least moderately well off, bombardment by the environment is a contained and perhaps infrequent phenomena. If home, work and leisure occur in settings of some peacefulness, it may only be the time spent in public (e.g., shopping and commuting) that subjects the urbanite to overload. It may be the home environment that is of greatest significance to individual lives and it appears quite likely to be the one place in an urban environment that is least likely to be overloaded. What is perhaps the best measure of overload for the home environment, the number of people per room in the home, ironically shows rural environments to be *more* overloaded than urban ones (Duncan, 1957). Yet the city is not a bed of roses and many urbanites may spend a considerable portion of their days cramped into crowded apartments or straining against deadlines, ringing telephones, sirens and queues. The important point is that we in fact know very little about the nature of environmental parameters such as input level. The development of measuring tools, such as input level measures in Korte et al. (1975), will facilitate a start toward some solution to this problem.

A final criticism of the importance of input overload to urban social behavior is the limited allowance it makes for other human characteristics (Fischer, 1974, 1976). This argument considers overload adaption to be a limited account of what people do in an urban environment. Individuals often act as information-seekers, striving to find novelty and change in their environments, even urban ones. In addition, an urbanite's social behavior is influenced by many more things than just environmental parameters; culture, social class and individual personality provide a crucial context for the occurrence of social behavior such as helpfulness. These are all important points relevant to an understanding of urban social behavior, yet in fairness to the input overload account (Milgram, 1970), it is clear that overload adaption was conceived to include social processes beyond the level of individual behavior (e.g., the emergence of urban norms) and that overload adaptation was only seen as part of the totality of forces operating to produce the forms of social behavior that we find in an urban environment.

Environmental input level then is one of the environmental features that appear to be important in producing the low level of helpfulness found in cities. A second explanation lays the blame on city design and architecture. Do we build buildings that inadvertently diminish the occurrence of mutual aid and support between city residents? We turn now to a look at this possibility.

HELPFULNESS AND URBAN DESIGN

Urban design and architecture involve variations in the urban environment at many different levels of scale, from the macroscopic (e.g., site plans and building type) to the microscopic (e.g., the design of rooms and placement of walls). There is little question that in design and architecture, the city *looks* different from the small town or village, though hard evidence is lacking that would specify the particular dimensions along which urban and nonurban environments differ. Certainly one of the architectural symbols of the contemporary city is the high-rise office or apartment building and much has been written about the possible social and psychological consequences of this type of environment. Unfortunately, the empirical evidence available on these questions is extremely limited and there are considerable methodology difficulties in determining the effects of a design variable independently of other correlated factors. Yet it is possible to identify the particular arguments that can be made for implicating urban design in the determination of urban behavior and, in particular, helpfulness between urbanites.

Mutual aid and helpfulness may depend upon the existence of proprietory attitudes and territorial behavior on the part of city residents. To the degree that environmental design influences these variables, it may then also influence the level of urban helpfulness. The primary champions of this position have been Jacobs (1961) and Newman (1973). Jacobs argued that the key ingredient to a helpful and supportive atmosphere is ultimately a diversity in spatial use, a mix of different functions (residential, commercial, recreational, etc.) in any particular locale. This mix produces an active street life during nearly all parts of the day, consisting of residents, shoppers, shop-keepers and people "on the town" at night, in contrast to single-function areas that show a cyclical pattern of high activity and desertion (e.g., theater, housing or business districts). This continual active street life, according to Jacobs, guarantees the presence of "sidewalk supervisors," local people or even visitors who will take a responsible attitude toward the happenings in the area. Jacobs cites shop-keepers and store owners as especially valuable in the maintenance of safety and mutual aid; new urban residential developments quite often lack the small local shops and sidewalk activity that generate a helpful corps of sidewalk supervisors. A somewhat more microscopic analysis of architectural variables that may influence social responsibility and involvement has been put forward by Newman (1973). Newman attempted to link urban architecture to crime prevention in a way that involves the assumption of a link between urban residential design and social behavior. Newman's argument goes as follows. Architectural features of an urban residential environment influence the degree to which residents can perceive and control activity that occurs within their residential space. When monitoring and control are made relatively easy, residents will exhibit proprietory attitudes toward this space and adopt policing measures. This both reduces the success of criminal intrusion and, more importantly, reduces the image of the housing project as a vulnerable target for criminal activity. Space that fosters such proprietory attitudes and behavior has been termed "defensible space" by Newman, who lists four architectural features that encourage defensibility:

1. markers that define the territorial domain of residents;
2. windows that allow residents to survey exterior and interior public areas;
3. building forms that reduce the stigma of a housing development as being set apart from the surrounding area; and
4. locations in compatible areas that do not offer continual threats.

The analyses of Jacobs and Newman are both principally concerned with the determinants of informal patterns of crime deterrence that develop through the residents' own efforts, yet it seems fair to extend their ideas to the occurrence of helpfulness and mutual aid. Residents whose neighborhood has an active street life, reflecting a diversity of activity and whose housing space shows a defensible quality, may be expected to show a more responsible and protective attitude toward the local area and the other people who live there. The basic explanatory mechanisms in Jacobs' account seem to be self-interest and social norms: the "helpers" have a vested interest in keeping the neighborhood safe from harm by those who would threaten others and damage property. This example and the existence of continual face-to-face community contact leads to a shared norm of social responsibility toward dangerous or threatening public episodes. Jacob's positive view of an active, busy and well-populated environment seems diametrically opposed to the view that sees this high level of environmental inputs as inhibiting social contact and helpfulness. It may be critical to Jacobs' analysis that she stresses life that is active, with people having local identities and commitments. Hence, the regularity and familiarity of the routines and happenings in the environment may mitigate the more harmful effects of input overload. Whatever mechanisms may be involved in the relation between social behavior and spatial diversity, Jacobs' view is a hard one to evaluate empirically. Jacobs cites anecdotal evidence to support her analysis, but a multitude of possibly relevant variables are involved in her contrast between highly diversified, small-scale neighborhoods and high-rise housing projects, making it difficult to determine which are the critical factors. It would appear quite difficult to design research that would identify the behavioral consequences of spatial diversity and street activity and no research has yet emerged directly on this point. Jacobs' argument does have an intuitive appeal to our stereotypes of different urban neighborhoods, which suggests the fruitfulness of further efforts to find behavioral differences between urban neighborhoods in spite of a previously cited failure in this regard (Korte et al., 1975).

The architectural features of concern to Newman are far more specific and hence, should allow for a more clear-cut test of his defensible space hypothesis. Newman has analyzed urban crime statistics for public housing in New York City and reported some correlations with design and location variables in a way consistent with his hypothesis. Crime rates were found to increase with building height, from 9 felonies per thousand population in three story buildings to 20 felonies in buildings over 12 stories; in addition, crime was more likely to occur in the interior public spaces of a building as a direct function of building height. Newman argued that the defensibility of space, especially interior public space, becomes more difficult in higher buildings, where space is harder to monitor (e.g., in elevators, stairways, and entrances). No direct evidence is available to support our extension of Newman's argument that helpfulness and mutual aid are lower when the residential space is less defensible. Newman does cite a dramatic example of a New York City housing project that was altered to increase its defensible space qualities, with the result that residents took a more active role in caring for the grounds of the project.

It is hard to rule out the possibility that behavioral effects resulting from a modification of the environment are due to heightened morale produced by the special treatment that the environment is receiving. Because a contrast between existing environments entails equally troublesome problems (e.g., great numbers of intercorrelated variables), it appears that the effects of both defensible space and diversity of spatial use will have to be tested using many different alternative methodologies, with multiple measures and indicators, in order to establish sufficient confidence by finding a consistency across different research approaches. Another way to examine Jacobs' and Newman's analyses is to take a close look at the one environment where they both make clear statements about the negative behavioral consequences to be expected. This environment is the high-rise apartment building, which will be considered at a later point in the paper.

Architecture and design may also diminish helpfulness and mutual aid in the urban environment by failing to provide other spatial elements which facilitate social contact between urban residents. A number of studies have demonstrated the significance of spatial proximity for the development of informal social relations between neighbors (Festinger, Schachter, & Back, 1950; Kuper, 1953; Nahemow & Lawton, 1975; Whyte, 1956). Although urban residential architecture may offer a person many close at hand neighbors, it may arrange the residential space so that informal contact with these neighbors is discouraged. Large apartment buildings that route all residents through a single entrance-lobby-elevator path severely tax the residents' ability to distinguish fellow residents from visitors and intruders. Even when a neighbor in an apartment building has become a familiar figure, there can be difficulties stemming from the lack of any semiprivate "conversational space" where spontaneous contact is likely to occur between apartment dwellers. The corridor of an apartment building, where residents will often meet going to and from home, is often treated as a place appropriate only for a superficial exchange of greetings, whereas the problems of achieving privacy in an apartment building often increase the intimacy signified by an invitation into a neighbor's apartment, hence reducing the helpfulness of this space as a locale for the development of neighborly contact. In contrast, the occupants of detached homes are supplied with much better space for informal neighborly contact (e.g., yards, porches, and driveways, which can lay the base for the subsequent occurrence of mutual aid and support; see Reed, 1974).

Alexander (1967) has strongly suggested that current urban design makes it extremely difficult for residents to have enduring intimate friendships with other people. Spontaneous "dropping-in" between friends, which according to Alexander is essential to the development of an intimate relationship, is made difficult by the problems of reaching a friend's place with speed and ease, and by the urbanite's aversion to social visits and intrusions, a feeling that results from urban stress. Alexander offered a radical solution by means of an innovative residential design which he felt would encourage "dropping-in" between friends who would otherwise have only a limited relationship characterized by infrequent, prearranged get-togethers. This environment would have high levels of density, with detached houses standing close to the street and partially open to view from passing cars and pedestrians. Residents would be more exposed and open to possible contact with others, while at the same time having private areas within their homes for retreat and solitude. Alexander's proposal is highly provocative and has yet to be tested in a real environment. Yet it suggests additional architectural features that may be hypothesized to facilitiate the occurrence of mutual aid and helpfulness between urban residents.

If there is any effect on urban helpfulness attributable to the various design and architectural features described previously, then one should certainly expect to find a very weak level of help-giving and mutual aid among dwellers of high-rise apartment buildings that exhibit so many of these features. The evidence on helpfulness in high-rise settings is limited, but basically supports the expectation of diminished helpfulness in these environments. A recent study (Huismans & Korte, 1977) examined the frequency of mutual aid in the Amsterdam high-rise housing development (referred to earlier) that has a low reputation for neighborly help-giving. A large sample (222) of residents was interviewed about recent occurrences of mutual aid and their attitudes toward seeking help from others. Over the past 6 months, residents recalled an average of 1.1 occasions when they received household-related help from others (e.g., assistance with projects, babysitting, helping with a personal problem), with *no* occasions reported by over 40% of the respondents. This help came from neighbors (versus friends, relatives, etc.) only 30% of the time. Using a list of 12 different types of neighborly assistance, respondents checked on the average 3.3 items from the list as types of help that they had offered to others over the past 12 months. Respondents were also asked which different people they would think of when help was needed. Neighbors were the first persons mentioned for slightly less than a quarter of the time (24.3%), while 45% of the respondents gave no mention of neighbors at all.

These results suggest a very low level of mutual aid between people who would seem to have rather close contact, though the figures are hard to interpret without any baseline comparison. One kind of comparison that has been reported is that which looks at the experience of people moving from low-rise to high-rise environments. Consideration of helpfulness and mutual aid was given in two such studies by Young and Willmott (1962) and Jephcott (1971), who examined the move from old tenement housing to new high-rise apartments in London and Glasgow respectively. Both studies found, as a consequence of the move, an increase in isolation and loneliness and a decrease in neighborliness and mutual aid. These differences also present problems of interpretation, as the move entailed more changes than simply a new type of building (e.g., departure from old friends and a shift from a settled community to an entirely new one).

The most reliable test of the impact of the high-rise environment per se on helpfulness comes from three studies which included helpfulness measures within an analysis which compared residents who were in quite similar circumstances except for building type, which differed between high- and low-rise forms. For two of these studies, support for high-rise unhelpfulness was found. Stevenson,

Martin and O'Neill (1967) carried out an extensive survey of the inhabitants of a public housing development in Melbourne, Australia. This project consisted of 374 housing units, contained in either a high-rise housing block (20 stories) or one of several low-rise apartment buildings (4 stories). The interviews revealed a considerably greater amount of helpfulness and friendliness between the low-rise residents as compared to those in the high-rise. Three-quarters of the low-rise respondents reported that they had made real friendships in the housing project compared to the less than half that reported this in the high-rise sample. More respondents in the low-rise (84% vs. 59% for the high-rise) said they gave and received help by doing one another's shopping, borrowing things or taking care of a sick neighbor.

A comparison of student residence halls was carried out by Bickman, Teger, Gabriele, McLaughlin, Berger, & Sunaday (1973), who used a combination of behavioral and interview measures. The "lost letter" measure, described earlier, was applied to dormitories at the University of Massachusetts and Smith College, which were either high-rise (22 stories), medium-rise (4 to 7 stories), or low-rise (2 to 4 stories). The return rate of letters was highly related to building type, with rates of 63%, 87%, and 100%, respectively. Several items in the questionnaire administered to students living in these dormitories were concerned with aspects of helpfulness. Students in the high-rise dormitories were most likely to say they would ignore any stranger they found wandering through their dormitory (53% versus 40% and 23% for medium- and low-rise, respectively), and least likely to say they would report a broken window (33% versus 60% and 82%). Their helpfulness was intermediate to the medium- and low-rise students on two additional questions — willingness to pick up a pile of candy wrappers left in the hallway and willingness to loan the use of their rooms to someone else. On both of these questions the most helpful students were those in the low-rise dormitories. The interpretation of these differences is complicated by several contaminating factors present in the study. The dormitories differed in density as well as height and, in addition, the high- and medium-rise dormitories were located at one school (University of Massachusetts), while the low-rise sample came from the other (Smith College). Hence, population and density effects are viable alternative explanations for the differences in helpfulness that occurred.

The presence of contaminating factors is a fundamental and persistent problem in any effort to evaluate the effects of specific environmental features. This is why the strategy of multiple methodologies must be stressed in this area of research. Any single environmental variable may be correlated with other variables that are present in some settings but not in others. If a consistent relationship is found between the environmental variable of interest and some behavioral effect and the studies have been carried out across many settings that *differ* in terms of the various contaminating variables that are present, then it is more likely that the variable that is constant throughout these settings is responsible for the effect than that any one of a number of different alternative explanations is responsible.

A final study that compared residents of different types of apartment buildings found no differences in their neighborliness or willingness to approach neighbors for help. This survey, by Ashton (1976), took place in several public housing projects in Dundee, Scotland that had three principle types of housing: 15–17 story high-rises, 4–6 story medium-rises, and 2-story connected town houses (usually 4 or 6 in a unit). Respondents from these three different types of housing did not differ on those questionnaire items relevant to helpfulness and mutual aid: how well neighbors were known and how likely it was for a neighbor to be named as a source of help.

Considering all the evidence available on the behavior of high-rise residents, as uneven as it is in usefulness and reliability, it does seem to be the case that helpfulness is lower in high-rise settings. This tentative finding is important, though the data do not differentiate between the different explanations available for a relationship between residential design and social behavior. Indefensible space, lack of spatial diversity, spatial barriers to informal chats and get-togethers and numerous other factors may all play some role in determining the level of mutual aid and helpfulness found in high-rises or, more generally, in an urban environment. Each of these variables has yet to be subjected to an adequate test, but clear tests are difficult to devise. Yet there is some promise in the consistency that has been found between the various analyses of the behavioral effects of urban environmental features and the data collected so far. Those effects for which data are available are greatly outnumbered by effects for which we have no information, which leaves the role of design and architecture in urban social behavior still in a state of considerable uncertainty.

So far, the key to urban unhelpfulness has been sought in the various features of the urban environment, an approach that regards these features as capable of shaping and influencing behavioral patterns such as helpfulness. Yet serious reservations have been raised about the validity of attributing behavioral patterns to environmental influences (i.e., accepting environmental determinism). These reservations apply very much to the issues that have been of major concern in this paper. The final section of the paper considers this problem and suggests a rather simple model of environment–behavior interaction that seems to best fit the available data.

ENVIRONMENTAL DETERMINISM
AND ENVIRONMENTAL SELECTION

The major problem with an environmental deterministic view of urban social behavior is that urbanites do not just adapt to their environments, they also select them, modify them, and move away from them. In so far as there is an element of *choice* in occupying a particular environment, there may be a tendency for a particular type of person to choose a particular type of environment or for a person to choose an environment that is seen as compatible with a certain pattern of behavior. This selection of particular environments by people might in itself explain the association of a particular pattern of behavior with a particular type of environment. For example, if individuals seeking a withdrawn, highly private life free from neighborly contact are selectively drawn toward high-rise apartments, then any lack of helpfulness evident in this setting may not perhaps be a result of the environmental properties of the setting.

Evidence that apparent environmental effects may be due to environmental selection has been offered by Gans (1967), who studied persons moving to a new suburban community outside Philadelphia. He did find changes in social behavior as a result of the move (more active social life, more family-centered activities, more privacy and freedom of action), but these changes were actually premove aspirations that the new residents were seeking in their move to a new environment. This example illustrates the complexity of the means by which environmental selection can account for particular environment—behavior relationships. Selection may operate in accordance with environmental factors that are believed by potential residents to be instrumental to the achievement or frustration of a preferred life style (i.e., an environment is chosen or rejected *because* it is seen as having a particular impact on a person's behavior and life style). Hence, environmental selection may operate in a way that assumes the operation of environmental determinism, at least in the eyes of the selectors. Whether the environment—behavior associations that result from this are to be viewed as genuine environmental effects or as self-fulfilling prophecies is an open question. Environmental selection also results in environment—behavior associations in a slightly different way, when people occupying a particular environment bring with them characteristics that distinguish them from people less likely to be found in that setting. For example, if high-rise apartment buildings contain an unusually high portion of children, then damage and maintenance problems may reflect this population characteristic rather than the inherent effects of the residential environment.

The importance of environmental selection seems undeniable in the occurrence of particular forms of social behavior in certain kinds of environments, which makes untenable any explanatory model that assumes only environmental determinism. Yet, this realization should not ignore the fact that the environment *does* exert an independent influence on social behavior. This is evident in much of the research reviewed in this paper and has been confirmed in studies in which environmental selection is inoperative and hence untenable as an alternative explanation (e.g., in which persons were assigned randomly to residential environments; see Festinger, Schachter, & Back, 1950; and Valins & Baum, 1973).

What seems required by the data, then, is a combined *adaptation-selection* model of environmental effects that incorporates the combined processes of *adaptation* to particular environmental features and *selection* of particular environments by particular individuals. Hence, an association between an envir-

onmental form and a behavioral pattern is viewed as arising in one or more of
the following ways: Individuals bring established behavior patterns to the
environments that they occupy; they bring aspirations and expectations about
new behavior patterns to be realized in a given environment, and they react and
adapt to environments with changes in their own behavior. This more complete
account of environment–behavior relations is quite similar to Michelson's (1976)
model of intersystem congruence, which posits the evolution of an optimal
fit between the environmental and behavioral systems, where accommodation
occurs by changes in *either* of the two systems. The importent job ahead is to
determine the relative importance or predominance of adaptation and selection
processes, to specify if possible the relevance of each to particular environment–
behavior patterns. This can be approached as an empirical question and best be
answered by longitudinal studies of the persistence and change (intended as well
as unintended) of behavioral patterns across different environments. Research
planned by the author (Korte, 1976b) has been designed to examine the separate
roles played by adaptation and selection in the patterns of social behavior that
occur in different types of residential environments. This research will identify
changes in social behavior and life style that accompany changes in a person's
residential environment. Then, from the pre- and post-move data, it will be
possible to determine whether these changes were personal aspirations implicated in the decision to move and hence better understood in terms of environmental *selection*; or whether these changes were unanticipated (or anticipated,
but not part of one's aspirations) and hence, reflecting *adaptation* to environmental influences.

What is expected to be central to the operation of selection processes are
the environmental perceptions about the desirability of particular residential
settings and the presumed impact of particular environmental features. Of course,
even when there is some choice involved in selecting a particular environment,
this selection is dictated by more than the perceived desirability of a place and,
for many people, there is often no real choice to begin with. Clearly, the
explanatory value of selection processes for environment–behavior associations
becomes more likely when there is personal choice (with few constraints on a
person's choice of environments) or impersonal choice (with external factors,
e.g., economic, that influence the type of persons likely to occupy a particular
environment).

The degree to which selection or adaptation are responsible for establishing
a particular behavioral pattern in some type of environment is of considerable
practical importance to planners and designers. The effectiveness of environmental modification as an instrument of social intervention or "behavior
engineering" is quite enhanced if behavioral patterns are to some degree environmental adaptations, whereas it is quite limited where the proper explanation of
"environmental effects" lies with selection processes. Environmental adaptation,
indicating that behavior patterns respond directly to variations in the form of

the physical environment, tells the planner and architect that some solution to various urban problems can be found by discovering the *particular* environmental form that shapes and influences behavioral patterns in the desired way. This has, in fact, been a guiding assumption among many workers in urban planning and design (Korte, 1976b).

If, on the other hand, it is the case that behavior patterns occurring in association with particular environmental features result not from adaptation but from *selection*, then the policy implications are quite different. In this case, the essential issues for social policy become the origin and change of particular environmental reputations, both good and bad, as well as environmental aspirations, and the identification of barriers to a greater choice in environmental selection. Adaptation and selection need not be viewed as alternative explanations for environment–behavior relations, but will probably emerge as having particular areas of applicability in terms of our understanding of certain behavior patterns.

It must also be stressed that there is still no certainty that consistent and predictable environment–behavior relationships are the rule rather than the exception. Behavioral patterns may prove eventually to be only weakly associated with environmental variables, though this is a conclusion that would greatly confound our common sense. Whatever the outcome, advances in our understanding of the interplay between environmental and behavioral patterns is essential for any endeavor to create environments that are compatible with human needs.

REFERENCES

Alexander, C. The city as a mechanism for sustaining human contact. In W. Ewald (ed.), *Environment for man*. Bloomington, Ind.: Indiana University Press, 1967.

Ashton, A. *Type of housing and social interaction*. Unpublished Master's thesis, St. Andrews University, Scotland, 1976.

Bickman, L. The effect of another bystander's ability to help on bystander intervention in an emergency. *Journal of Experimental Social Psychology,* 1971, *7,* 367–379.

Bickman, L., Teger, A., Gabriele, T., McLaughlin, C., Berger, M., & Sunaday, E. Dormitory density and helping behaviour. *Environment and Behavior,* 1973, *5,* 465–490.

Bloodworth, D. *The Chinese looking glass.* New York: Farras, Straus, Giroux, 1966.

Darley, J., & Latané, B. Bystander intervention into emergencies: Diffusion of responsibility. *Journal of Personality and Social Psychology,* 1968, *8,* 377–383.

Darley, J., & Batson, D. From Jerusalem to Jericho: A study of situational and dispositional variables in helping behavior. *Journal of Personality and Social Psychology,* 1973, *27,* 100–108.

Duncan, O. D. Community size and the rural urban continuum. In P. K. Hatt & A.J. Reiss, Jr. (Eds.) *Cities and society.* New York: Free Press, 1957.

Feldman, R. Response to compatriot and foreigner who seek assistance. *Journal of Personality and Social Psychology,* 1968, *10,* 202–214.

Festinger, L., Schacter, S., & Back, K. *Social pressures in informal groups.* New York: Harper & Bros., 1950.

Fischer, C. *Sociological comments on psychological approaches to urbanization.* Unpublished manuscript, University of California, Berkeley, 1974.

Fischer, C. *The urban experience.* New York: Harcourt, Brace, Jovanovich, 1976.

Forbes, G. B., & Gromoll, H. F. The lost-letter technique as a measure of social variables: Some explatory findings. *Social Forces,* 1971, *50,* 113–115.

Gaertner, S., & Bickman, L. The effects of race on the elicitation of helping behavior: The wrong number technique. *Journal of Personality and Social Psychology,* 1971, *20,* 218–222.

Gans, H. *The urban villagers.* New York: Free Press, 1962.

Gans, H. *The Levittowners.* New York: Pantheon Books, 1967.

Gelfand, D., Hartman, D., Walder, P., & Page, B. Who reports shoplifters? A field experimental study. *Journal of Personality and Social Psychology,* 1973, *25,* 276–285.

Goudsblom, J. *Dutch society.* New York: Random House, 1967.

Hauser, P. Application of the ideal-type constructs to the metropolis in the economically less-advanced area. In P. Hauser & L. Schnore (Eds.), *The study of urbanization.* New York: Wiley, 1965.

Huismans, S., & Korte, C. *Seeking help in a Dutch high rise.* Unpublished manuscript, The Free University of Amsterdam, 1977.

Jacobs, J. *The death and life of great American cities.* New York: Vintage Books, 1961.

Jephcott, P. *Homes in high flats.* Edinburgh: Oliver & Boyd, 1971.

Korte, C. Effects of individual responsibility and group communication on help-giving in an emergency. *Human Relations,* 1970, *24,* 149–159.

Korte, C. *The effects of an urban environment on social behavior.* Unpublished manuscript, St. Andrews University, 1976.(a)

Korte, C. *Urban residential housing: Preferences, perceptions and social psychological consequences.* Unpublished manuscript, St. Andrews University, 1976.(b)

Korte, C., & Grant, R. *Traffic noise and environmental awareness.* Unpublished manuscript, St. Andrews University, 1976.

Korte, C., & Kerr, N. Responses to altruistic opportunities under urban and rural conditions. *Journal of Social Psychology,* 1975, *95,* 183–184.

Korte, C., Ypma, I., & Toppen, A. Helpfulness in Dutch society as a function of urbanization and environmental input level. *Journal of Personality and Social Psychology,* 1975, *32,* 996–1003.

Krupat, E., & Coury, M. *The lost letter technique and helping: An urban–non-urban comparison.* Paper presented at American Psychological Association Convention, Chicago, September 1975.

Kuper, L. Blue print for living together. In L. Kuper (Ed.), *Living in towns.* London: The Crasset Press, 1953.

Latané, B. Field studies in altruistic compliance. *Representative Research in Social Psychology,* 1970, *1,* 49–61.

Lewis, O. *La vida.* New York: Random House, 1965.

Lowin, A., Holtes, J., Sandler, B., & Bornstein, M. The pace of life and sensitivity to time in urban and rural settings: A preliminary study. *Journal of Social Psychology,* 1971, *83,* 247–253.

Lynch, K. *The image of the city.* Cambridge, Mass.: MIT Press, 1960.

Lynch, K., & Rivkin, M. A walk around the block. *Landscape,* 1959, *8,* 24–34.

Matthews, K. E., & Canon, L. K. Environmental noise level as a determinant of helping behaviour. *Journal of Personality and Social Psychology,* 1975, *32,* 571–577.

Marin, G., Majia, D., & de Oberle, C. Cooperation as a function of place of residence in Colombian children. *Journal of Social Psychology,* 1975, *95,* 127–129.

Merrens, M. Nonemergency helping behaviour in various sized communities. *Journal of Social Psychology,* 1973, *90,* 327–328.

Michelson, W. *Man and his urban environment.* Reading, Mass.: Addison-Wesley, 1976.

Milgram, S. The experience of living in cities. *Science,* 1970, *167,* 1461–1468.

Milgram, S., Mann, L., & Harter, S. The lost letter technique: A tool of social research. *Public Opinion Quarterly,* 1965, *29,* 437–438.

Nahemow, L., & Lawton, M. Similarity and propinquity in friendship formation. *Journal of Personality and Social Psychology,* 1975, *32,* 205–213.

Newman, O. *Defensible space.* New York: Collier Books, 1973.

Piliavin, I., Rodin, J., & Piliavin, J. Good semaritanism: An underground phenomenon. *Journal of Personality and Social Psychology,* 1969, *13,* 289–299.

Reed, P. Situated interaction: Normative and non-normative bases of social behavior in two urban residential settings. *Urban Life and Culture,* 1974, *2,* 460–487.

Rosenthal, A. *Thirty-eight witnesses.* New York: McGraw-Hill, 1964.

Schaps, E. Cost, dependency and helping. *Journal of Personality and Social Psychology,* 1972, *21,* 74–78.

Schwartz, S., & Clausen, D. Responsibility, norms and helping in an emergency. *Journal of Personality and Social Psychology,* 1970, *16,* 299–310.

Shapira, A., & Madsen, M. Cooperative and competitive behavior of kibbutz and urban children in Israel. *Child Development,* 1969, *40,* 609–617.

Sherrod, D., & Downs, R. Environmental determinants of altruism: The effects of stimulus overload and perceived control on helping. *Journal of Experimental Social Psychology,* 1974, *10,* 468–479.

Simmel, G. In Kurt Wolff (Ed.), *The sociology of Georg Simmel.* New York: Free Press, 1950.

Staub, E. Helping a distressed person: Social, personality and stimulus determinants. In L. Berkowitz (Ed.), *Advances in experimental social psychology* (Vol. 7). New York: Academic Press, 1974.

Stevenson, A., Martin, E., & O'Neill, J. *High living, a study of family life in flats.* Australia: University of Melbourne Press, 1967.

Valins, S., & Baum, A. Residential group size, social interaction and crowding. *Environment and Behavior,* 1973, *5,* 421–439.

Wegner, D., & Crano, W. Racial factors in helping behavior: An unobtrusive field experiment. *Journal of Personality and Social Psychology,* 1975, *32,* 901–905.

Weiner, S. Altruism, ambiance and action: The effects of rural and urban rearing on helping behavior. *Journal of Personality and Social Psychology,* 1976, *34,* 112–124.

Whyte, W. H., Jr. *The organization man.* New York: Simon & Schuster, 1956.

Wirth, L. Urbanism as a way of life. *American Journal of Sociology,* 1938, *44,* 1–24.

Young, M., & Willmott, P. *Family and kinship in east London.* New York: Pelican Books, 1962.

6 In Defense of the Crowding Construct

Daniel Stokols
University of California, Irvine

INTRODUCTION

The study of crowding and behavior is currently one of the fastest growing areas of psychological research. The recent appearance of several books on human spatial behavior (e.g., Altman, 1975; Baum & Epstein, 1978; Esser, 1971; Freedman, 1975; Sommer, 1969) and the swelling of scientific journals with articles on crowding attest to the rapid expansion of this research domain over the past decade.[1] The rise of interest in crowding is largely attributable to a growing concern in contemporary society over problems such as overpopulation, urbanization and pollution, and parallel research developments as epitomized by Calhoun's (1962) report of the devastating impact of population density on laboratory animals.

It is not the intent of this chapter to review the voluminous research literature on crowding (comprehensive reviews are provided by Altman, 1975, Schopler & Stokols, 1976, and Baum & Epstein, 1978), but rather to examine two divergent theoretical orientations reflected in this literature. The first defines crowding as a condition of the environment, namely high density or spatial restriction (cf. Booth, 1975, Freedman, 1975; Griffitt & Veitch, 1971). The second conceptualizes crowding as a motivational state involving the need for more space (Stokols, 1972a), the desire for increased privacy (Altman, 1975), or for reduced stimulation (Desor, 1972; Esser, 1972; Valins & Baum, 1973).

There has been a good deal of debate recently among the proponents of physicalistic and psychological approaches to crowding research (cf. A. Patterson, 1976). The first group contends that psychological definitions of crowd-

---

[1] Sundstrom (1978) cites 83 studies of human crowding and behavior, about half of which were completed between 1974 and 1976.

ing are essentially superfluous and serve only to confuse the relationship between density and behavior (e.g., Freedman, 1975; Griffitt, 1974). The second group, on the other hand, asserts that the conceptualization of crowding as a motivational construct permits an identification of personal and situational factors that mediate the impact of high density, or interpersonal proximity, on people (e.g., Altman, 1975; Baum, Harpin, & Valins, 1975; Loo, 1973; M. Patterson, 1976; Stokols, 1972a; Worchel & Teddlie, 1976).

The confrontation among these alternative perspectives on crowding has important implications both for future research on environment and behavior, and for the development of community-design strategies aimed at minimizing the potentially undesirable effects of population density. Quite simply, physicalistic and psychological analyses of crowding offer very different conclusions about the impact of high density on people, and the policy implications of these analyses are divergent as well. In view of the rapid development of crowding research, it seems important for researchers in this area to give pause and to examine the relative utility of alternative theoretical perspectives. Such an assessment might shed light on unresolved conceptual issues, and reveal critical directions for future research. At the same time, it would behoove architects, urban designers, government officials, and other participants in the planning process to evaluate competing assumptions about high density quite carefully before acting on them prematurely to the possible detriment of their communities.

Before considering the specific arguments for and against alternative theories of crowding, it might be useful to place this discussion within a broader historical and substantive context. The debate surrounding the conceptualization of crowding as a psychological state rather than an environmental condition is rooted in a classic controversy waged several decades ago by proponents of stimulus–response ("S–R" or "radical behaviorist") and mediational ("S–O–R") theories of human behavior. On the one hand, S–R theorists emphasized the direct linkages between environmental conditions and behavior while disavowing any reference to mental or organismic processes (cf. Skinner, 1953; Watson, 1913). On the other hand, mediational theorists argued that the relationship between stimuli and responses could not be predicted accurately without reference to intervening, cognitive or emotional processes that, in effect, mediate the impact of the environment on behavior (cf. Hull, 1943; Rotter, 1954; Spence, 1948; Tolman, 1938). These processes were referred to as *hypothetical* or *intervening constructs* (MacCorquodale & Meehl, 1948), for the reason that they supplied theoretically derived connections between specific S and R variables, thereby helping the researcher to account for empirically observed correlations among environmental and behavioral events.

Anyone who is familiar with Lewin's (1935) famous equation, Behavior = f (Person and Environment), may regard the current discussion as an unnecessary rehashing of an old and already-resolved debate. After all, the utility of intervening constructs in psychological research would seem to be a moot issue—one that is taken for granted by modern-day adherents of "interactionism." The most recent articulations of the interactionist perspective by Bowers (1973), Bem and Allen (1974), and Magnusson and Endler (1977) offer an abundance of theoretical and empirical support for the assumption that human behavior can be more fully understood as a joint product of situational *and* intrapersonal factors, than as the result of either set of factors alone.[2]

Yet the appropriate role of intervening constructs in behavioral research is an issue that has not been resolved completely, at least within the realm of environmental and ecological psychology. The renewed debate on this issue perhaps can best be explained by considering some of the unique features of contemporary research on environment and behavior.[3] First, unlike traditional areas of psychological research, ecological and environmental psychology are centrally concerned with the effects of the large-scale physical environment on the behavior of individuals and groups. In the more established subareas of psychology (e.g., cognitive, social, developmental, clinical, and physiological psychology), the behavioral implications of the built and natural environment have been largely ignored.

A second important feature of the environment-and-behavior field is its community-problems orientation. This orientation emphasizes the utilization of behavioral science theories and research in developing guidelines for social planning and urban design. Until recently, most experimental psychologists regarded the analysis of complex environmental problems as peripheral to the concerns of psychological science.

The explicit concern of environment-behavioral research with the analysis and design of the molar physical environment has prompted some environmental psychologists to warn against an overreliance on intervening constructs in the study of environment and behavior. In a provocative article, entitled "The Environment is not in the Head!", Wohlwill (1974) contends that there has been a "subjectivist bias" in many areas of environmental research;[4] this bias is reflected in "the dual tendency to define environmental variables in phenomenological or personalistic terms, rather than in terms of objective physical dimensions, and to emphasize the contribution of factors based in the individual to the study of environment—behavior relations, at the expense of environmental determinants per se [p. 166]." From Wohlwill's perspective, researchers

---

[2]See also the discussions of trait-centered and situationist models of behavior presented by Allport (1937, 1966), Mischel (1968, 1973), and Murray (1938).

[3]For more thorough analyses of the environment-and-behavior field and its unique features, see Altman (1975), Barker (1968), Craik (1973), Ittelson, Proshansky, Rivlin, and Winkel (1974), Wohlwill (1970), and Stokols (1976).

[4]Additional critiques of the environment-and-behavior field in terms of its subjectivist bias have been presented by Cone and Hayes (1976) and by Willems (1977).

interested in the behavioral impact of existing environments and in the optimal design of future settings should be more concerned with the direct effects of the physical environment on behavior than with the rather elusive (often unmeasurable) psychological processes that allegedly mediate these effects. Although he does not deny the value of intervening constructs for certain types of psychological research, Wolhwill does argue that they have been used too extensively and inappropriately by environmental researchers. In his words, "unless we can show that there are major differences in the way various individuals respond to the same environmental variables, it does not seem profitable to focus on perceptions, hypotheses or other internally-based constructs as the *determining* variables [p. 169]."

The role of intervening constructs in environmental research can be questioned on other grounds, as well. The theoretical utility of constructs derives from the fact that they specify causal linkages between environmental and response variables that can be submitted to empirical test under controlled, experimental conditions. Yet, recent conceptualizations of environmental psychology question the suitability of hypothetico–deductive models and experimental methodologies for the study of environment–behavior relationships. Proshansky (1973, 1976a, 1976b), for example, emphasizes the cyclical and dynamic nature of human-environment transactions. Not only does the environment affect behavior but people, in turn, play an active role in determining the structure and quality of their surroundings. According to Proshansky, these bi-directional relationships are not accessible to short-term laboratory studies, nor are they explainable in terms of one-way causal processes—the typical target of experimental research in the behavioral sciences.

Proshansky's view of environmental psychology poses several theoretical and methodological imperatives. Most importantly, physical environments must be understood as complex systems of mutual–causal processes whose intricacies can be charted only through unobstrusive, naturalistic research that maintains the "absolute integrity" of behavior–setting events (1976a, pp. 305–306). From this perspective, the utility of hypothetical or intervening constructs appears to be questionable, at best; for the more abstract and deductive our theories are, the more removed they become from the complex realities of naturalistic settings.

The preceding discussion provides a backdrop for examining construct-oriented analyses of crowding in more depth. In the following section, the alleged advantages and major criticisms of the crowding construct are reviewed, and its value as a basis for future research and public policy is assessed. Despite the foregoing reservations about using intervening constructs in environmental research, it is argued that an increased reliance on these deductive, theoretical tools will enhance rather than hinder our investigation of environment–behavior relationships. The contributions of the crowding construct to an understanding of high-density environments, and the ways in which these settings can be designed so as to minimize social interference and stress, are discussed as evidence for a "proconstruct" orientation in environmental psychology.

THE CROWDING CONSTRUCT: PRO AND CON

The use of intervening variables in the construction of psychological theories was first discussed by Tolman (1938) and later elaborated upon by Hull (1943a, 1943b) and Spence (1944, 1948). According to these theorists, the major function of intervening constructs is to aid in the discovery of empirical laws that designate enduring relationships between environmental conditions (E) and patterns of behavior (B): $B = f(E)$; or $E \rightarrow B$.

The existence of such a law presupposes that: (1) all relevant environmental variables are known; and (2) the nature of all functional relations between environmental and behavioral variables have been ascertained. To the extent that these conditions can be met through empirical investigation alone, the introduction of intervening constructs into the $E-B$ equation is unnecessary. For example, if a specific condition of the environment, E (e.g., high density), is observed invariably to elicit a particular response, B (e.g., aggression), then all relevant variables in the equation are presumed to be known, and B can be represented as a direct function of E.

Human behavior, however, is notoriously complex and variable even under the most static of environmental conditions. Thus, high density (E_1) has been observed to elicit aggression (B_1) in certain experiments (e.g., Freedman, Levy, Buchanan, & Price, 1972); withdrawal from social interaction (B_2) in other studies (e.g., Loo, 1972; McGrew, 1970; Price, 1971); increased attraction and affiliation (B_3) in some studies (cf. Freedman, 1975); and no response differences (B_0) in still others (cf. Sundstrom, 1978). It is in relation to such phenomena, where invariant E-B relationships are not readily discerned through direct observation, that intervening constructs (e.g., crowding) can be utilized to deduce the conditions under which $B_0, B_1, B_2, B_3, \ldots$, or B_n, will occur in conjunction with E_1.

The crowding construct evolved as a logical culmination of early research in which repeated attempts were made to identify a stable relationship between density and behavior, of the following form:

High density $\rightarrow$ Negative behavioral effects; or
High density $\rightarrow$ Neutral or positive behavioral effects

The accumulation of contradictory findings from numerous studies made it clear that the relationship between density and behavior is a good deal more complex than that predicted by either of these equations. That is, the effects of density on human behavior might be either favorable *or* unfavorable depending on other, nonspatial factors present in the situation.

Thus, an alternative formulation was proposed:[5]

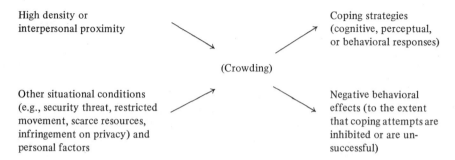

High density or interpersonal proximity → (Crowding) → Coping strategies (cognitive, perceptual, or behavioral responses)

Other situational conditions (e.g., security threat, restricted movement, scarce resources, infringement on privacy) and personal factors → (Crowding) → Negative behavioral effects (to the extent that coping attempts are inhibited or are unsuccessful)

Crowding was defined as a motivational state directed toward the alleviation of perceived spatial restriction (Stokols, 1972a), infringement of privacy (Altman, 1975; Proshansky, Ittelson, & Rivlin, 1970), or excessive stimulation (Desor, 1972; Esser, 1971; Valins & Baum, 1973). The experience of crowding was thought to arise from conditions of high density (or interpersonal proximity) *only* in the context of certain personal and situational factors that sensitize individuals to the potential inconveniences of proximity with others. And on the behavioral side of the equation, at least three patterns of response were hypothesized: cognitive, perceptual, and behavioral modes of reducing the salience of perceived crowding (cf. Stokols, 1972b). To the extent that these coping strategies are unsuccessful, physiological and behavioral impairments were expected to occur.

By defining crowding as the need for more space, privacy, or solitude, it was possible to deduce a variety of circumstances that might heighten or reduce this need in a particular situation. For example, a person might wish to obtain more space as a means of keeping threatening others at a distance; performing activities that require large, open areas; or avoiding noise and other kinds of stimuli created by the concentration of many people in a small area. A major advantage of the crowding construct, then, was that it facilitated a more precise delineation of the density–behavior relationship, and made it possible to specify in advance what otherwise could be established only through a prolonged and relatively random series of empirical observations (i.e., the nonspatial determinants of crowding intensity).

A number of investigators, however, have questioned the utility of the crowding construct. Freedman and others (e.g., Griffitt, 1974) have argued consistently that "*crowding* should be understood always as referring to the physical situation of high density, not to an internal feeling," and that it is the former that

---

[5]The diagrammatic representation of the crowding construct, presented here, is highly oversimplified and does not convey the sequential or homeostatic features of the crowding models discussed by Altman (1975), Stokols (1972b), and Sundstrom (1978).

must be studied rather than the latter (Freedman, 1975, pp. 11, 115). To date, three major criticisms of the crowding construct have been presented. These are as follows:

1. The crowding construct has prompted an inappropriate and premature shift in the focus of research from the effects of density on behavior to the effects of "perceived crowding" on behavior (cf. Griffitt, 1974). This argument is reminiscent of Brunswik's (1943) criticism of Lewin's (1936, 1943) field theory in terms of its "encapsulation," or overemphasis on intervening subjective states without due regard for the environmental antecedents of overt behavior.

2. The perception of crowding, which is defined as stressful and is presumed to promote negative behavioral effects, is not always accompanied by stress and behavioral impairments (cf. Griffitt, 1974).

3. To the extent that negative environmental conditions exist, correspondingly negative behavioral reactions will occur regardless of the level of density present in the situation. This position is most clearly reflected in Freedman's (1975) "density—intensity" notion, which suggests that proximity with other people merely intensifies the prevailing quality of any given situation. If a situation is pleasant to begin with (e.g., involves nice people, plenty of food and drink), density will make it better. And conversely, an inherently unpleasant situation (e.g., presence of nasty people, scarcity of resources) will be worsened by conditions of high density. From this perspective, it is unnecessary to invoke a construct of crowding to explain the effects of density on behavior.

Although these arguments touch upon some important issues relating to the use of intervening constructs in the behavioral sciences, they do not mitigate the value of the crowding construct as a basis for research on density and behavior. Justification for this "proconstruct" view is presented below in the form of replies to the above criticisms.

First, the argument that the crowding construct has led to an overemphasis on intervening states and an underemphasis on environmental and response variables is more a criticism of improper use of the construct than of the construct itself. As noted earlier, the function of constructs is to suggest hypothetical connections between environmental and behavioral dimensions, thereby assisting the researcher in the discovery of significant $E-B$ regularities. The ultimate focus of the discovery process must be on the assessment and verification of the proposed $E-B$ linkages, rather than on the measurement of hypothesized intervening states of the organism.[6] Thus, proponents of the crowding construct

---

[6]In this regard, Hull (1943a) has noted that "symbolic constructs can have nothing more than a rather dubious expository utility unless they are anchored to observable and measurable conditions on both the antecedent and consequent sides [of the E—B equation] [p. 281]."

would agree with Griffitt's (1974) contention that an overemphasis on the measurement of felt crowding, in isolation from the more essential process of assessing the linkages between hypothesized antecedents and consequences of crowding, reflects a superficial and unproductive approach to the study of human crowding.

It should be emphasized, however, that direct assessments of the physiological, perceptual, and cognitive concomitants of crowding are not inappropriate as long as such measures are eventually related, in an empirical manner, to corresponding environmental antecedents and behavioral consequences; or to the extent that physiological, perceptual, and cognitive states themselves can be viewed as theoretically relevant responses to environmental conditions associated with the experience of crowding.[7]

In response to the second criticism of the crowding construct, it can be argued that the frequent lack of association between subjective reports of crowding and overt manifestations of stress reflect the lack of refinement in current measures of crowding rather than the inadequacy of the crowding construct. For example, where questionnaire scales are used to assess "crowding," subjects' responses may confound both the environmental (observed crowdedness or density of the setting) and experiential (felt crowding) connotations of the term. Negative behavioral effects would not be expected to accompany reports of crowding to the extent that such reports reflected only the former meaning of the term. Therefore, in order to determine more reliably whether the experience of crowding actually promotes stress and negative behavioral consequences, it is necessary to employ multiple measures which converge on the hypothesized concomitants (e.g., physiological, cognitive, perceptual, overt-behavioral) of this experience.[8]

A related point is that crowding experiences may vary in intensity depending upon relevant situational parameters (cf. Stokols, 1976). It seems reasonable to assume that the intensity of crowding, as well as the direction of the individual's response to it, would depend upon his/her assessment of the potential problems of having too little space in a particular situation. In some cases, the person might decide to tolerate a certain amount of crowding in order to obtain other rewards in the situation. Here, reports of crowding would be associated with little evidence of stress. But in other cases, the individual might decide that certain density-related problems, if not alleviated, would lead to very serious costs. In

---

[7]See also Spence's (1944) discussion of "neurophysiological theories."

[8]A number of other methodological issues must be examined more closely by crowding researchers, including the problem of demand characteristics (Orne, 1962). The use of extremely small rooms in many laboratory experiments often may provide subjects with cues concerning the experimenter's interest in crowding.

such instances, the stressful concomitants of unrelieved crowding would tend to be more pronounced.

The third argument against the crowding construct is essentially that negative behavioral effects, when they do occur in high-density situations, are attributable to nonspatial problems in the setting (e.g., lack of resources, ongoing hostility) rather than to high density itself. Although such problems might be accentuated by high density, they will not be caused by it and therefore, the occurrence of behavioral impairments can be predicted directly from nonspatial factors and without reference to a hypothetical state of crowding.

The conclusion that density exerts negligible effects of its own on behavior is premature in view of recent experimental evidence indicating that high density or close interpersonal distance, with other factors such as group size held constant, can heighten physiological arousal (cf. Epstein & Aiello, 1974; Evans, 1975; Middlemist, Knowles, & Matter, 1976) and can induce both immediate and delayed (poststressor) task performance deficits (Evans, 1975; Paulus, Annis, Seta, Schkade, & Matthews, 1976; Sherrod, 1974; Worchel & Teddlie, 1976). Considering these findings in conjunction with earlier reports that high density had no effect on levels of arousal or task performance (e.g., Freedman, Klevansky, & Ehrlich, 1971; Ross, Layton, Erickson, & Schopler, 1973; Stokols, Rall, Pinner, & Schopler, 1973), the argument can be made that further refinement of the crowding construct, rather than its abandonment, is required to permit a more precise specification of the conditions under which high density will or will not increase arousal and impair task performance.

Similarly, a refinement of the crowding construct might help to account for currently contradictory evidence in relation to Freedman's (1975) density–intensity hypothesis. Whereas Freedman and Schiffenbauer and Schiavo (1976) report data consistent with the notion that high density merely intensifies the effects of nonspatial factors in a setting, other findings suggest that high density can exert independent behavioral effects, such as goal-blocking or overload (Sundstrom, 1978) to transform a previously pleasant or neutral situation into an unpleasant one (Emiley, 1974; Keating & Snowball, 1974). In light of these findings, it is conceivable that the inconveniences sometimes associated with high density might become more problematic where people have high rather than low (or no) expectations about the favorableness of the situation, due to the frustration arising from violated expectancies [see also Thibaut & Kelley's (1959) comparison-level theory of social behavior].

On balance, then, the criticisms of the crowding construct discussed above do not undermine the value of psychological approaches to crowding but, rather, suggest ways in which these approaches can be made more useful in the future. Previous research has demonstrated convincingly that human reactions to high density are quite variable. The main value of psychological analyses of crowding is that they offer a basis for understanding the diverse effects of density on behavior in terms of personal needs and situational factors. The utility of these analyses will be more fully realized to the extent that future research shifts its focus from the measurement of perceived crowding, in isolation from specific environmental and behavioral events, to an identification of situational factors that determine the salience of spatial needs and the intensity of behavioral attempts to satisfy those needs.

THE CROWDING CONSTRUCT AS AN ENVIRONMENTAL DESIGN TOOL

We have examined some of the major arguments for and against the crowding construct. In this section, we will consider the broader significance of the crowding-construct debate for future research on environment and behavior, and for the development of environmental design criteria.

As noted earlier, the use of intervening constructs in psychological research is predicated on at least two basic assumptions: (1) that human behavior can be understood more fully as a function of both environmental and intrapersonal variables, than as a product of either set of factors considered alone; and (2) that the scientific search for causal relationships between environmental and behavioral events is valuable from a practical as well as a theoretical standpoint. The second assumption implies that the environment-behavioral relationships identified through experimental research offer a basis for predicting behavior in nonexperimental (naturalistic) settings and, ultimately, for designing environments that are congruent with the needs and preferred activities of their users. To what extent are these "interactionist" and "hypothetico–deductive" assumptions justified in the context of crowding research, as well as in other areas of environmental psychology?

The crowding research discussed in the preceding section provides strong support for the first of the foregoing two assumptions. In general, the findings from this research reveal that people's reactions to high density are jointly determined by a variety of personal and situational factors, such as personality characteristics (Baron, Mandel, Adams, & Griffen, 1976; Cozby, 1973; Dooley, 1974; Schopler & Walton, 1974), feelings toward others in the situation (M. Patterson, 1976; Rall, Stokols, & Russo, 1976; Stokols, Rall, Pinner, & Schopler, 1973; Stokols & Resnick, 1975; Sundstrom & Altman, 1976), and the individual's perception of control over the environment in which crowding occurs (Baldassare, 1976; Baum & Valins, 1977; Rodin, 1976; Sherrod, 1974). Considering the striking variability of human response to high density reflected in these studies, the adoption of an interactionist perspective on crowding seems especially warranted. This conclusion is consistent with Wohlwill's (1974) observation that intervening constructs are of greatest theoretical utility when used in relation to environmental variables whose effects on different people are not uniform.

Additional evidence for the utility of an interactionist perspective in environmental research is provided by recent investigations of human response to noise (Glass & Singer, 1972; Cohen, Glass, & Singer, 1973; and Chapter 1, by Cohen, of this volume). A well-established finding from this research is that cognitive factors, such as the perception of being able to predict or escape from exposure to noise, are more crucial in determining the severity of noise-induced behavioral impairments, than the amplitude of the noise itself.

Although previous experimental studies have successfully identified functional relationships between environmental, psychological, and behavioral variables, the generalizability (or "external validity"; cf. Campbell & Stanley, 1963) of these relationships to naturalistic settings has been questioned by certain researchers. Proshansky (1973, 1976a, b), for example, contends that the environment-behavioral linkages observed within highly controlled laboratory situations are not at all representative of human behavior in complex, naturalistic settings.

Proshansky's assertion is based on a crucial assumption: that experimental and nonexperimental settings are not comparable. The former are viewed essentially as artificial and oversimplified representations of the latter. In experimental situations, for example, specific environmental variables can be isolated (through randomization and control groups) and their independent effects on behavior can be examined. In naturalistic settings, however, a complex network of interdependent environmental conditions affects behavior. Thus, it is difficult to isolate single determinants of behavior and to arrive at generalizations about environment—behavioral relationships based on observations within a particular setting, since each setting is comprised of a unique collage of physical and social attributes.

Moreover, the linkages between environmental and behavioral variables, suggested by intervening constructs and documented through experimental research, are basically unidirectional. That is, environmental conditions are construed as independent variables that instigate behavioral responses. The relationships between physical and behavioral events in naturalistic settings, however, are cyclical and multi-directional. Not only does the environment affect behavior — the individual, in turn, has the capacity to modify or rearrange the environment in accordance with personal goals and needs. Proshansky, therefore, regards the one-way causal relations among environmental and response variables, derived through experimentation, as irrelevant to an understanding of human behavior in naturalistic settings.

Proshansky's arguments are useful in alerting us to the complexity of human—environment transactions and the uniqueness of different behavior settings. His contention that environment—behavioral regularities cannot be generalized from experimental to nonexperimental situations, however, seems overly pessimistic, because it can be argued that the two kinds of settings are sometimes quite comparable. Specifically, the behavioral effects of environmental variables, isolated under experimental conditions, may be highly similar to those observed in naturalistic settings. The crucial problem is to identify a set of dimensions on which situations can be meaningfully compared. A knowledge of such dimensions would permit a categorization of settings in terms of their key similarities and dissimilarities, and an assessment of the relative potency of environmental variables within different situations.

A potentially important dimension on which settings might be categorized is suggested by the research on noise and density, mentioned earlier. Several laboratory studies have shown that people are most vulnerable to the negative effects of noise and high density when they perceive themselves as being unable to exercise control over physical and social features of the environment (e.g., Glass & Singer, 1972; Sherrod, 1974; Stokols & Resnick, 1975). More recently, these findings have been replicated in a number of field studies (cf. Cohen, Glass, & Phillips, in press; Sherrod & Cohen, 1976). In one study, children who were continually exposed to traffic noise in their apartments showed a greater impairment of auditory discrimination and reading ability than those who had less exposure to the noise (Cohen, Glass, & Singer, 1973). And in other studies, the potentially detrimental effects of exposure to high density (e.g., medical complaints, impaired task performance) were shown to be particularly pronounced among low-control or low-status groups, such as prison inmates (D'Atri, 1975; McCain, Cox, & Paulus, 1976), children (Booth, 1975; Booth & Johnson, 1975; Rodin, 1976), and persons confined for long periods to naval vessels (Dean, Pugh, & Gunderson, 1975). On the whole, these studies suggest that the dimension of occupants' perceived or actual control over the environment offers a basis for categorizing diverse situations, and for generalizing experimental findings to certain types of naturalistic settings.

To date a comprehensive taxonomy of environments has not been developed.[9] The dimension of environmental controllability does, however, suggest a preliminary dichotomy of environments that may be useful in assessing the practical utility of construct-oriented research. According to this dichotomy, certain settings are characterized by "environmental-optimization processes" (Stokols, 1977, 1978). These processes refer to individuals' attempts to interpret, respond to, modify, and evaluate their environments in accordance with personal goals and needs. Settings in which optimization occurs not only reflect the impact of the environment on its occupants, but also their reciprocal influence on the shape and quality of their surroundings [see Fig. 6.1 (a)]. In contrast, other settings are characterized more by adaptation than by optimization processes. Adaptation processes primarily reflect people's attempts to cope with existing environmental conditions rather than their ability to modify them according to

[9]The proposed dichotomy of situations is, of course, overly simplistic. For purposes of the present discussion, though, it offers a potentially important criterion (i.e., the level of occupants' control over their environment) for assessing the external validity of construct-oriented research. For more extensive discussions regarding the development of environmental taxonomies, see Altman (1975), Frederiksen (1972), Insel and Moos (1974), Price and Blashfield (1975), and Stokols (1976).

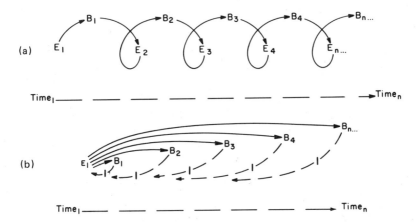

FIG. 6.1. (a) Human—environment optimization processes. The relationship between environment and behavior is depicted as a series of cycles in which people not only are affected (B_1) by environmental conditions at a particular point in time (E_1) but also modify the setting according to their preferences, thereby creating a new context (E_2) for subsequent behavior (B_2).[10] This cyclical pattern of human—environment transactions would be most typical of those settings in which people are able to exercise maximum control over environmental conditions. (b) Adaptation processes. As depicted in this diagram, adaptation involves a set of processes whereby an individual's or group's behavior over different points in time is controlled by relatively inflexible environmental conditions. The inability to modify situational constraints according to personal or group goals is represented by the blocked, broken arrows leading from behavioral states at times$_{1-n}$, toward the unyielding environmental conditions (E_1). This predominantly, one-way pattern of human—environment relations would be most representative of situations in which occupants are unable to exert control over the physical and social features of their setting.

personal preferences.[11] (Adaptation attempts may be more or less successful depending upon the severity of environmental conditions and the individual's coping abilities.) The essential difference between the two prototypical settings, then, is that the level of occupants' control over various aspects of the environment is more restricted in the latter than in the former [see Fig. 6.1 (b)]. Con-

---

[10]The cyclical and optimizing nature of human—environment transactions has been discussed in more detail by Altman (1975), Proshansky (1973), Smith and Klein (1976), Stokols (1977, 1978), and Wohlwill (1974).

[11]In this discussion, adaptation processes are viewed as behavioral, cognitive, or physiological adjustments to existing environmental conditions (cf. Dubos, 1965). Human—environment optimization refers to a more active, goal-oriented process whereby individuals not only adapt to the existing situation but also opt to maintain or modify certain aspects of their milieu in accordance with specified criteria of environmental quality. Thus, the optimization concept subsumes the processes by which people adapt to their surroundings but places an equal emphasis on man's reciprocal control over the environment.

sequently, the impact of environmental variables on behavior would tend to be more pronounced and enduring in the latter situations.[12]

An interesting implication of the proposed dichotomy is that experimental situations, in which the impact of the environment on behavior is emphasized, are more analogous to settings typified by adaptation rather than optimization processes. This parallel between certain experimental and nonexperimental settings serves to illustrate an important point. That is, the practical utility of environmental research can be enhanced through the development of criteria for judging the external validity of experimental hypotheses.[13] As one example, the proposed dichotomy suggests that predictions about the negative effects of high density, derived from the crowding construct, will be most generalizable to those settings in which individuals are unable to exercise control over various aspects of their environment; that is, where environment—behavior relationships are more unidirectional $(E \rightarrow B)$ than reciprocal $(E \rightleftarrows B)$.[14]

---

[12]Although this discussion has emphasized the similarities between environmental controllability and environmental optimization, several important differences between these concepts should be noted. First, the concept of control typically has been used in environmental research to refer to the individual's actual or perceived control over a particular aspect of the environment, such as noise (Glass & Singer, 1972), high density (Rodin, 1976), or architectural design (Sherrod & Cohen, 1976). Optimization, on the other hand, refers to the ways in which people orient toward, operate on, and respond to the molar environment in terms of the variety of goals and activities associated with a particular setting. Thus, optimization processes could relate to several different dimensions of environmental control, all of which might vary in their relative importance to users of the setting. Also, optimization processes reflect cycles of human—environment transaction involving different modes or phases (e.g., interpretation, evaluation, operation, response), whereas the control concept is used more narrowly to refer to actual or perceived states of environment—behavior congruence (cf. Michelson, 1976). The relationships between environmental control, congruence, and optimization are discussed more fully in Stokols (1977).

[13]The dimension of environmental controllability offers one of many possible criteria for judging the comparability between experimental and nonexperimental situations. Others might include the personality, cultural, and demographic characteristics of populations in the two types of settings. See Campbell and Stanely (1963) for a more comprehensive discussion of external validity criteria.

[14]This is not to say that experimental situations in which subjects have low control over the environment are necessarily comparable to naturalistic settings occupied by low-control or low-status groups. Subjects' lack of control over high density or noise in a laboratory experiment, for example, may not be analogous to the inability of residents in an apartment complex to regulate their exposure to environmental stressors over a prolonged period of time. A longitudinal field experiment conducted in the latter setting generally would have higher external validity (vis-a-vis similar situations) than a laboratory representation of it. Even so, generalizing from field experiments to similar naturalistic settings would be inappropriate in certain instances due to the numerous dimensions (in addition to environmental controllability) on which different settings and their respective occupants vary.

To summarize, the practical advantages of intervening constructs, such as crowding and environmental controllability, are twofold. First, they specify which groups, in what settings, will be most vulnerable to the negative effects of high density, noise, and other environmental stressors. This level of specificity is certainly an improvement over earlier deterministic theories of environment and behavior. Such theories are epitomized by the classical sociological analyses of urbanism (e.g., Simmel, 1950; Wirth, 1938) in which the effects of urban density and population size are viewed as invariably deterimental to the well-being of city residents, regardless of their personal and socioeconomic attributes.

A second advantage of intervening constructs is that they suggest several possible strategies for minimizing the stressful consequences of conditions such as high density in present and future environments. To the extent that urban planners can predict where people will be least able to avoid prolonged exposure to high density, they can take steps to design such settings in ways that enable occupants to reduce the behavioral interferences, privacy infringements, and overstimulation often associated with conditions of limited space. For instance, the partitioning of dwelling space so as to provide an adequate number of separate rooms and the incorporation of ample soundproofing materials may be more beneficial to families living in low-income housing units than the provision of additional square-footage per apartment. And in a different context, the confusion and constraints associated with urban traffic jams might be alleviated partially by incorporating traffic-metering devices on heavily used highways.

Our ability to assess the generalizability of research findings and the relative appropriateness of alternative design interventions within various settings should improve to the extent that we develop more refined systems for classifying situations. Future research along these lines must develop methods for measuring not only the actual controllability or behavioral *congruence* (Michelson, 1976) of settings but also their *salience* or psychological importance to users (Stokols, 1978). The impact of environmental constraints (or lack of congruence) is likely to be greater where occupants are emotionally invested in the setting than where they are psychologically detached from it (cf. Stokols, 1976, 1978). Also, the concepts of environmental control and congruence must be more fully dimensionalized to permit a consideration of different kinds of control (e.g., over physical versus social dimensions of the environment) and their relative importance to occupants of particular settings.

In conclusion, the evidence reviewed in this chapter argues strongly for continued use of intervening constructs in future research on density and behavior. Furthermore, the theoretical and practical advantages of psychological perspectives on crowding illustrate the utility of construct-oriented research within the environment-and-behavior field as a whole.

REFERENCES

Allport, G. *Personality: A psychological interpretation.* New York: Holt, 1937.

Allport, G. Traits revisited. *American Psychologist,* 1966, *21,* 1–10.

Altman, I. *The environment and social behavior: Privacy, personal space, territory and crowding.* Monterey, Calif.: Brooks/Cole, 1975.

Altman, I. Crowding: Historical and contemporary trends in crowding research. In A. Baum & Y. Epstein (Eds.), *Human response to crowding.* Hillsdale, N.J.: Lawrence Erlbaum Associates, 1978.

Baldassare, M. Residential density, household crowding, and social networks. In C. Fischer, M. Baldassare, K. Gerson, R. Jackson, L. Jones, & C. Stueve (Eds.) *Networks and places.* New York: Free Press, 1976.

Barker, R. *Ecological psychology: Concepts and methods for studying the environment of human behavior.* Stanford, Calif.: Stanford University Press, 1968.

Baron, R., Mandel, D., Adams, C., & Griffen, L. Effects of social density in university residential environments. *Journal of Personality and Social Psychology,* 1976, *34,* 434–446.

Baum, A., & Epstein, Y. (Eds.) *Human response to crowding.* Hillsdale, N.J.: Lawrence Erlbaum Associates, 1978.

Baum, A., Harpin, R. E., & Valins, S. The role of group phenomena in the experience of crowding. *Environment and Behavior,* 1975, *7,* 185–198.

Baum, A., & Valins, S. *The social psychology of crowding: Studies of the effects of residential group size.* Hillsdale, N.J.: Lawrence Erlbaum Associates, 1977.

Bem, D. J., & Allen, A. On predicting some of the people some of the time: The search for cross-situational consistencies in behavior. *Psychological Review,* 1974, *81,* 506–520.

Booth, A. *Final report: Urban crowding project.* Paper presented to the Ministry of State of Urban Affairs, Toronto, Canada, 1975.

Booth, A., & Johnson, D. R. The effect of crowding on child health and development. *American Behavioral Scientist,* 1975, *18,* 736–749.

Bowers, K. S. Situationism in psychology: An analysis and a critique. *Psychological Review,* 1973, *80,* 307–336.

Brunswik, E. Organismic achievement and environmental probability. *Psychological Review,* 1943, *50,* 255–272.

Calhoun, J. Population density and social pathology. *Scientific American,* 1962, *206,* 139–148.

Campbell, D. T., & Stanley, J. C. Experimental and quasi-experimental design for research on teaching. In N. L. Gage (Ed.), *Handbook of research on teaching.* Chicago: Rand McNally, 1963.

Cohen, S., Glass, D. C., & Phillips, S. Environment and Health. In H. E. Freeman, S. Levine, & L. G. Reeder (Eds.), *Handbook of medical sociology.* Englewood Cliffs, N.J.: Prentice-Hall, in press.

Cohen, S., Glass, D. C., & Singer, J. E. Apartment noise, auditory discrimination and reading ability in children. *Journal of Experimental Social Psychology,* 1973, *9,* 407–422.

Cone, J. D., & Hayes, S. C. *The submerged discipline of environmental psychology.* Paper presented at the annual conference of the Midwestern Association for Behavioral Analysis, Chicago, April 1976.

Cozby, F. Effects of density, activity, and personality on environmental preferences. *Journal of Research in Personality,* 1973, *7,* 45–60.

Craik, K. Environmental psychology. *Annual Review of Psychology,* 1973, *24,* 403–422.

D'Atri, D. Psychophysiological responses to crowding. *Environment and Behavior,* 1975, *7,* 237–252.

Dean, L., Pugh, W., & Gunderson, E. K. Spatial and perceptual components of crowding: Effects on health and satisfaction. *Environment and Behavior*, 1975, *7*, 225–236.

Desor, J. Toward a psychological theory of crowding. *Journal of Personality and Social Psychology*, 1972, *21*, 79–83.

Dooley, B. *Crowding stress: The effects of social density on men with 'close' or 'far' personal space*. Unpublished doctoral dissertation, University of California, Los Angeles, 1974.

Dubos, R. *Man adapting*. New Haven, Conn.: Yale University Press, 1965.

Emiley, S. *The effects of crowding and interpersonal attraction on affective responses, task performance, and verbal behavior*. Paper presented at the Annual Convention of the American Psychological Association, New Orleans, August 1974.

Epstein, Y., & Aiello, J. *Effects of crowding on electrodermal activity*. Paper presented at the annual Convention of the American Psychological Association, New Orleans, August 1974.

Esser, A. *Behavior and environment*. New York: Plenum Press, 1971.

Esser, A. A biosocial perspective on crowding. In J. Wohlwill & D. Carson (Eds.), *Environment and the social sciences: Perspectives and applications*. Washington, D.C.: American Psychological Association, 1972.

Evans, G. *Behavioral and physiological consequences of crowding in humans*. Unpublished doctoral dissertation, University of Massachusetts, Amherst, 1975.

Frederiksen, N. Toward a taxonomy of situations. *American Psychologist*, 1972, *27*, 114–123.

Freedman, J. *Crowding and behavior*. San Francisco: Freeman, 1975.

Freedman, J., Klevansky, S., & Ehrlich, P. The effects of crowding on human task performance. *Journal of Applied Social Psychology*, 1971, *1*, 7–25.

Freedman, J., Levy, A., Buchanan, R., & Price, J. Crowding and human aggressiveness. *Journal of Experimental Social Psychology*, 1972, *8*, 526–548.

Glass, D., & Singer, J. *Urban stress*. New York: Academic Press, 1972.

Griffitt, W. *Density, "crowding," and attraction: What are the relationships?* Paper presented at the Annual Convention of the American Psychological Association, New Orleans, August 1974.

Griffitt, W., & Veitch, R. Influence of population density on interpersonal affective behavior. *Journal of Personality and Social Psychology*, 1971, *17*, 92–98.

Hull, C. The problem of intervening variables in molar behavior theory. *Psychological Review*, 1943, *50*, 273–291. (a)

Hull, C. *Principles of behavior*. New York: Appleton-Century, 1943. (b)

Insel, P., & Moos, R. Psychological environments: Expanding the scope of human ecology. *American Psychologist*, 1974, *29*, 179–188.

Ittelson, W., Proshansky, H., Rivlin, L., & Winkel, G. *An introduction to environmental psychology*. New York: Holt, Rinehart & Winston, 1974.

Keating, J., & Snowball, H. *The effects of crowding and depersonalization on the perception of group atmosphere*. Unpublished manuscript, University of Washington, Seattle, 1974.

Lewin, K. *A dynamic theory of personality*. New York: McGraw-Hill, 1935.

Lewin, K. [*Principles of topological psychology*] (F. Heider & G. Heider, trans.). New York: McGraw-Hill, 1936.

Lewin, K. Defining the "field at a given time." *Psychological Review*, 1943, *50*, 292–310.

Loo, C. The effects of spatial density on the social behavior of children. *Journal of Applied Social Psychology*, 1972, *2*, 372–381.

Loo, C. Important issues in researching the effects of crowding on humans. *Representative Research in Social Psychology*, 1973, *4*, 219–226.

MacCorquodale, K., & Meehl, P. E. On a distinction between hypothetical constructs and intervening variables. *Psychological Review*, 1948, *55*, 95–107.

Magnusson, D., & Endler, N. S. (Eds.). *Personality at the crossroads: Current issues in interactional psychology.* Hillsdale, N.J.: Lawrence Erlbaum Associates, 1977.

McCain, G., Cox, V. C., & Paulus, P. B. The relationship between illness complaints and degree of crowding in a prison environment. *Environment and Behavior*, 1976, *8*, 283–290.

McGrew, P. Social and spatial density effects on spacing behavior in preschool children. *Journal of Child Psychology and Psychiatry*, 1970, *11*, 198–205.

Michelson, W. *Man and his urban environment: A sociological approach* (2nd ed.). Reading, Mass.: Addison-Wesley, 1976.

Middlemist, R., Knowles, E., & Matter, C. Personal space invasion in the lavatory: Suggestive evidence for arousal. *Journal of Personality and Social Psychology*, 1976, *33*, 541–546.

Mischel, W. *Personality and assessment.* New York: Wiley, 1968.

Mischel, W. Toward a cognitive social learning reconceptualization of personality. *Psychological Review*, 1973, *80*, 252–283.

Murray, H. *Explorations in personality.* New York: Oxford University Press, 1938.

Orne, M. T. On the social psychology of the psychological experiment: With particular reference to demand characteristics and their implications. *American Psychologist*, 1962, *17*, 776–783.

Patterson, A. Crowding: It ain't necessarily so. *Contemporary Psychology*, 1976, *21*, 530–531.

Patterson, M. L. An arousal model for interpersonal intimacy. *Psychological Review*, 1976, *83*, 235–245.

Paulus, P., Annis, A., Seta, J., Schkade, J., & Matthews, R. Density does affect task performance. *Journal of Personality and Social Psychology*, 1976, *34*, 248–253.

Price, J. *The effects of crowding on the social behavior of children.* Unpublished doctoral dissertation, Columbia University, 1971.

Price, R., & Blashfield, R. Explorations in the taxonomy of behavior settings: Analysis of dimensions and classifications of settings. *American Journal of Community Psychology*, 1975, *3*, 335–351.

Proshansky, H. Theoretical issues in "Environmental Psychology." *Representative Research in Social Psychology*, 1973, *4*, 193–207.

Proshansky, H. Environmental psychology and the real world. *American Psychologist*, 1976, *31*, 303–310. (a)

Proshansky, H. Comment on environmental and social psychology. *Personality and Social Psychology Bulletin*, 1976, *2*, 359–363. (b)

Proshansky, H., Ittelson, W., & Rivlin, L. Freedom of choice and behavior in a physical setting. In H. Proshansky, W. Ittelson, & L. Rivlin (Eds.), *Environmental psychology: Man and his physical setting.* New York: Holt, Rinehart & Winston, 1970.

Rall, M., Stokols, D., & Russo, R. *Spatial adjustments in response to anticipated crowding.* Paper presented at the annual meeting of the Eastern Psychological Association, New York, April 1976.

Rodin, J. Density, perceived choice and response to controllable and uncontrollable outcomes. *Journal of Experimental Social Psychology* 1976, *12*, 564–78.

Ross, M., Layton, B., Erickson, B., & Schopler, J. Affect, facial regard, and reactions to crowding. *Journal of Personality and Social Psychology*, 1973, *28*, 69–76.

Rotter, J. B. *Social learning and clinical psychology.* Englewood Cliffs, N.J.: Prentice-Hall, 1954.

Schiffenbauer, A., & Schiavo, S. Physical distance and attraction: An intensification effect. *Journal of Experimental Social Psychology*, 1976, *12*, 274–282.

Schopler, J., & Stokols, D. *A psychological approach to human crowding.* Morristown, N.J.: General Learning Press Modular Studies, 1976.

Schopler, J., & Walton, M. *The effects of expected structure, expected enjoyment and participants' internality–externality upon feelings of being crowded.* Unpublished manuscript, University of North Carolina, Chapel Hill, 1974.

Sherrod, D. R. Crowding, perceived control and behavioral aftereffects. *Journal of Applied Social Psychology,* 1974, *4,* 171–186.

Sherrod, D. R., & Cohen, S. *Density, personal control and design.* Paper presented at the seventh annual Environmental Design Research Association Conference, Vancouver, British Columbia, Canada, May 1976.

Simmel, G. The metropolis and mental life. In K. Wolff (trans. and Ed.), *The sociology of Georg Simmel.* New York: Free Press, 1950.

Skinner, B. F. *Science and human behavior.* New York: Macmillan, 1953.

Smith, T., & Klein, G. L. *Causal implications of the environment: Distorting clock-time affects mood.* Paper presented at Annual Convention of American Psychological Association, Washington, D.C., September 1976.

Sommer, R. *Personal space: The behavioral basis of design.* Englewood Cliffs, N.J.: Prentice-Hall, 1969.

Spence, K. W. The nature of theory construction in contemporary psychology. *Psychological Review,* 1944, *51,* 47–68.

Spence, K. W. The postulates and methods of 'behaviorism'. *Psychological Review,* 1948, *55,* 67–78.

Stokols, D. On the distinction between density and crowding: Some implications for future research. *Psychological Review,* 1972, *79,* 275–277. (a)

Stokols, D. A social–psychological model of human crowding phenomena. *Journal of the American Institute of Planners,* 1972, *38,* 72–84. (b)

Stokols, D. The experience of crowding in primary and secondary environments. *Environment and Behavior,* 1976, *8,* 49–86.

Stokols, D. Origins and directions of environment-behavioral research. In D. Stokols (Ed.), *Perspectives on environment and behavior: Theory, research, and applications.* New York: Plenum Press, 1977.

Stokols, D. Environmental psychology. *Annual Review of Psychology,* 1978, *29,* 253–95.

Stokols, D., Rall, M., Pinner, B., and Schopler, J. Physical, social and personal determinants of the perception of crowding. *Environment and Behavior,* 1973, *5,* 87–115.

Stokols, D., & Resnick, S. *An experimental assessment of neutral and personal crowding experiences.* Paper presented at the Southeastern Psychological Association Convention, Atlanta, Georgia, April 1975.

Sundstrom, E. Crowding as a sequential process: Review of research on the effects of population density on humans. In A. Baum & Y. Epstein (Eds.), *Human response to crowding.* Hillsdale, N.J.: Lawrence Erlbaum Associates, 1978.

Sundstrom, E., & Altman, I. Interpersonal relationships and personal space: Research review and theoretical model. *Human Ecology,* 1976, *4,* 47–67.

Thibaut, J., & Kelley, H. *The social psychology of groups.* New York: Wiley, 1959.

Tolman, E. The determiners of behavior at a choice point. *Psychological Review,* 1938, *45,* 1–41.

Valins, S., & Baum, A. Residential group size, social interaction, and crowding. *Environment and Behavior,* 1973, *5,* 421–439.

Watson, J. B. Psychology as the behaviorist views it. *Psychological Review,* 1913, *20,* 159–177.

Willems, E. P. Behavioral ecology. In D. Stokols (Ed.), *Perspectives on environment and behavior: Theory, research, and applications.* New York: Plenum Press, 1977.

Wirth, L. Urbanism as a way of life. *The American Journal of Sociology,* 1938, *44,* 1–24.
Wohlwill, J. The emerging discipline of environmental psychology. *American Psychologist,* 1970, *25,* 303–312.
Wohlwill, J. The environment is not in the head! In W. F. E. Preiser (Ed.), *Environmental design research* (Vol. 2) Fourth Annual Conference of the Environmental Design Research Association. Stroudsburg, Pa.: Dowden, Hutchinson & Ross, 1974.
Worchel, S., & Teddlie, C. Factors affecting the experience of crowding: A two factor theory. *Journal of Personality and Social Psychology,* 1976, *34,* 30–40.

7

Sociological Comments on Psychological Approaches to Urban Life[1]

Claude S. Fischer
University of California, Berkeley

INTRODUCTION

This volume is one more sign of a surging wave of interest among professional psychologists in the social psychology of urban life. Spurred by public attention to urban problems, the need of urban designers for guidance, and developments in the study of spatial behavior, many psychologists have turned from the laboratory to the street in an effort to understand the personal consequences of living in cities. Urban sociology, the discipline for which I presume to speak, has been concerned with the issue for decades but, unfortunately, in recent years, only as a minor interest. It is heartening to see the thought and research that psychologists are currently putting into this problem. At the same time that this work is welcomed, some reservations must be raised. I present them — and I hope they are received — as constructive criticisms, consideration of which will enable both psychologists and sociologists to make advances in the study of the social psychological aspects of urban life.

My comments are divided into two parts: first, a critique of contemporary psychological approaches to understanding the city's effects on individuals; and second, an outline of what insights a sociological perspective might provide. In each section, I am concerned with three quite general considerations: models of man (by which I mean "person"), models of the urban environment, and models of man-in-the-urban environment.

[1] An earlier version of this paper was presented to a conference on *Psychological Consequences of Urbanization: The Case of Nomadic Sedentarization*, University of California, Los Angeles, December 1974.

PSYCHOLOGICAL APPROACHES

Models of Man

If there is any legitimate division of conceptual labor between the disciplines of psychology and sociology, it is that the former develops models of man and the latter, models of society. This responsibility makes it all the more distressing and ironic that much, even most, of the writing on the consequences of urbanization by psychologists and others who are psychologically oriented seems to rely on embarrassingly elementary models of man. One suspects (as Mark Baldassare has suggested in a personal communication) that these models have been selected because they are *au courant*, the "latest thing," and not necessarily because they are the most appropriate to understanding urban life. Yet, at the same time there are available older but more sophisticated models. And the overly simplistic assumptions about man can yield overly simplistic theories about urban man. Three models appear to lie behind most of the current psychological literature on urbanization:

1. *The Territorial Animal:* Man is a territory and/or a personal space-defending organism. Violations of territory or space produce internal reactions (e.g., "stress") and/or behavioral reactions (e.g., aggression). It is this model that lies behind John Calhoun's extrapolations from rat pens to human cities and Edward Hall's warning that crowding in cities is more lethal than the hydrogen bomb. And this view has been adopted, implicitly or explicitly, by many psychologists.

The notion of territoriality — really more biological than psychological — is of dubious utility, it turns out, among many animals and especially among higher primates (see, e.g., Alland, 1972; Montagu, 1968). The notion of "personal space," I would argue, has been greatly oversimplified. One can certainly show behavioral correlates of interpersonal distances, but such correlations do not necessarily imply that the spatial metaphor, or the "bubble" metaphor, best captures the phenomena. Indeed, the tremendous variations in distancing behaviors and reactions that occur across different cultures, times, situations, personalities, and dyadic combinations suggest that nonverbal communication best labels this phenomenon and that there is little *sui generis* social significance to space itself. In any case, recognition, at least, of such variability would yield a suitably more complex model (see, e.g., Baldassare & Feller, 1975; Fischer, Baldassare, & Ofshe, 1975). Yet many people who apply this theoretical perspective of man as territorial animal to the topic of urbanization seemingly rest content with images of people as rudimentary organisms. The dominant principle of the human beings in these descriptions appears to be intrusion—reaction, just like the stickleback.

2. *The Passive Sensor:* According to this model, most influentially presented to psychologists by Stanley Milgram (1970) in his *Science* article on "The exper-

ience of living in cities," the critical feature of urban man is that he receives and processes sensory input. When the intensity of sensations becomes too great to process, the "overload" (man as electrical wiring?) produces internal reactions (e.g., stress) and/or behavioral adaptations (e.g., withdrawal).

As in the case of spatial behavior, one can demonstrate these sorts of reactions or circuit-breaking responses in the appropriate laboratory or field setting. For example, people subjected to noise can have difficulty concentrating on a problem; people at a congested intersection may not wish to pause there to please an experimenter; subjects irritated by one experiment may not wish to volunteer for another experiment; or people who have much work to do are likely to work fast (Glass & Singer, 1972; Korte, Ypma, & Toppen, 1975; Lowin, Holtes, Sandler, & Bornstein, 1971; Sherrod & Downs, 1971).

However, the issue is not whether something like "overload" can be isolated and demonstrated, but whether this suffices for a psychological model of man; whether it is legitimate to conclude that these results define "urban stress," "urban incivility," "the pace of urban life" or otherwise define urban ways of life. Is it not obvious that people, including urban people, do a lot more than stand around being bombarded by stimuli? Is not man as thinker, lover, and so on also relevant to this question? Man as a passive sensor is a very partial model. Indeed, consider an exactly contrary model: man as sensation- and information-seeker.

This is a quite plausible model; sensation-seeking is the essence of theories of human hedonism (e.g., Freudianism); information-seeking is stressed by dissonance, attribution, and rational-maximizer psychological theories. Man-as-information-seeker *benefits* from high-stimulation and high-information environments. Such milieus would permit him or her to optimize the various calculations or psychic processes in which he or she is engaged. He or she would seek out such milieus and be "starved" in low-sensation settings. As far as overload is concerned, it may be easily avoidable, or it may be accepted as a necessary cost outweighed by the advantages of information. Whatever the value of my information-seeking "model," it is apparent that the passive sensor model is woefully incomplete.

3. *The Preference-Holder:* It sometimes appears that the behavioral sciences will never recover from the introduction of factor analysis. As a user of the technique, I am too well aware that it is one of that seductive set that faithfully echoes the researcher's prejudices. An investigator convinced that feelings about ball-point pens form a major dimension of people's Meanings of Life need only include several items measuring such feelings in a questionnaire battery in order to "discover," sure enough, that ball-point pens are a major "factor" in the Meaning of Life. Factor analysis is also one of those methods, low on cost and effort but high on complex output, that tends to lead theory rather than to follow it. The point is that the popular technique of developing attitudes-toward-the-environment scales is, I suspect, of questionable utility, in general. And,

specifically, it seems to tell us little about man in the urban setting. At best, it implies that people are preference-holders.

This "environmental psychology" has shown us that people have "cognitive maps" of their environments that vary according to the person's physical and social location and that people vary in their preferences for specific environments. But what this field has not shown us, as far as I can tell, is whether all this makes much of a difference in people's reactions or behaviors and whether it makes more difference than factors such as access to resources, compatible neighbors, and other less esoteric considerations. If the environmental reality fits the preference, they are happy; if not, they are "strained" and likely to move. This work gives us little handle on the psychological effects of any given environment, because it is largely atheoretical, essentially descriptive, and not explanatory.

It seems remarkable, given the sophisticated models of man to be found in psychology, that they have been so little used. General theories, such as social learning, cognitive, decision-making, field, and exchange, as well as specific ones, such as attribution, social comparison, and dissonance, are abundant. Each provides a useful model of man to be applied to this problem. But, with rare exceptions, such as Stokol's use of reactance theory, the psychology of urbanization rests on simplistic models.[2]

Models of the Urban Environment

Models of man aside, my more important comments concern the models of the urban environment that appear in the psychological literature. Much of this literature is explicitly addressed to the consequences of variations in the microenvironment. And those theoretically interested in the macroenvironment usually do their research in a microenvironment (e.g., Freedman's, 1975, crowd-

---

[2]The survey of psychological approaches to urbanism in this chapter is hardly complete. Two more approaches deserve at least brief comment: Barker's (Barker & Gump, 1964) and Wicker's (1973) works on "behavior settings" are encouraging in the sociological elements they include. The concern with under- or overmanning is quite structural and is related to division of labor. I must admit to some reservations in the use of "behavior settings" as units of analysis. Sociologically, it seems bizarre to treat ends of corridors or separate rooms as significant entities when units such as groups, economic classes, businesses, and the like, exist.

Some of the ideas concerning bystander intervention and diffusion of responsibility have also been applied to urban life. The analysis is that individuals do not concern themselves with others in cities because of the crowds to which responsibility can be shifted. Whether accurate or not as an empirical description, this approach is also quite fragmentary. The assisting of strangers in need is but a small fraction of the urban experience, and concern for blame and guilt is but a small part of human activity.

ing experiments). At that level — microenvironments such as rooms, streets, or corridors — both the theoretical and the empirical work may be apropos and excellent. But what boggles the mind of the urban sociologist is the leap from micro- to macroenvironment. It seems that many psychologists think either that a city is a dense laboratory room magnified a millionfold or that it is a setting of a million dense laboratory rooms (for an extended critique of such attempts to make microlevel work relevant to cities, see Baldassare & Fischer, 1976; Fischer et al., 1975). Consider two variations:

1. *The City as Crowd:* Psychologies of urbanism based on the concept of density usually depict the city as a huge crowd or a setting of many instances of crowding. It is no doubt true that urban persons are more likely to encounter crowds than are people in the countryside. But, if crowding is to serve as the critical factor in a psychological theory of urban life (or, in technical terms, as the operational, causal attribute of the independent variable), it should be *highly* related to urban residence. It is not. The subway-at-rush-hour image of urban life is not typical; rather, it is atypical of reality. It ignores so much of city life, including the housewife alone at home in a residential district, the commuters who drive their own cars to spacious offices, and pensioners in their own apartments on deserted side streets. Quiet, residential avenues are more typical of even our largest metropolitan areas than is 42nd Street in Manhattan. This crowd model of cities also ignores the facts that: (1) within-residence densities are generally *lower* in urban than nonurban areas; and, (2) even persons who do encounter crowds usually have but episodic and brief encounters. At best, the crowd may be one of many features of urbanization. It is hardly adequate as *the* model of the city.

2. *The Sensuous Environment:* Similarly popular is a model of the city as the complex, heterogeneous, and sensuous environment. The essence of the city is, in this view, a ceaseless onslaught of sensations and a taxing perceptual complexity. As in the previous instance, this model raises a dramatic part of a phenomenon to the position of characterizing the whole. The grounds for doing so have been only impressionistic, anecdotal, and rhetorical. There is just as much reason to characterize the city (as has been done by architects and others concerned with improving the visual features of cities) by the perceptual *monotony* of apartment dwellers' air shafts and deserted hallways. And, as in the previous case, we are provided with but the vaguest notions of community differences in this variable. Is the weekly market of a rural village less sensuous than an urbanite's weekly trip to the supermarket? How much? What does seem clear is that, as with crowds, sensory stimulation may be a concomitant of urbanism but seems hardly adequate as a defining characteristic of urbanism.

These conceptualizations, and others like them (e.g., the architectured environment, the cognitively mapped environment), are certainly reasonable, although hardly comprehensive, when applied to small settings: apartments, airport lounges, and the like. In these cases, one is trying to explain social behavior in a small setting by the immediate features of that setting. The astounding thing to sociologists is to see these models applied to cities. It is quite a leap to go, as some psychologists do, from describing a laboratory experiment to speculating about city life.

A city is far more than an environment of crowds or sensations. At minimum, it is a permanent settlement with a large population. Depending on the sociologist, it may also be defined as dense, heterogeneous, nonagricultural, politically autonomous, and so forth. Consider all the elements of "city" or "urban" in this image: houses, streets, jobs, economic structures, cultural history, and much more.

Let us assume that "urban" is defined simply in terms of population size. For some psychologists, the implications at the individual level of community size are crowds, density, and sensations. For the sociologist, the implications at the structural level of size are more vast and more complex. They include one or more of the following:

— Changes in the economic system, such as a shift from primary to secondary and tertiary industries;
— Political changes, such as the rise of administrative bureaucracies;
— An increase in centralized communication and coordination activities, not only of the community but also of its hinterland;
— Increase in differentiation, such as the division of labor, and spatial segregation;
— Increased heterogeneity (of races, religions, social classes, and so on);
— Corresponding decreases in social consensus; and
— Increases in knowledge-creation, -storage, and -transmission.

Most sociologists would place increasing crowds and sensory experiences rather low, perhaps as correlates or hardly critical traits, on a list such as this (which can easily be expanded). If sociologists directed their attention to individual consequences, I suspect most would point to items in the foregoing list as clues to those consequences, rather than to interpersonal "press" or perceptual complexity.[3] Considerations such as these make psychological models of urbanization sociologically insubstantial.

Consider two recent studies in this vein. I chose them as examples not because they are poor studies but because they are relatively good ones. Bornstein and Bornstein (1976) recently attracted national media attention by finding, in a varied sample of American and foreign places, that people seem to walk faster

---

[3]Simmel (1905), of course, was one sociologist who did stress the perceptual elements of the city. I think he overdid it. It should also be remembered that his classic essay actually dealt mostly with the consequences of a money economy.

in the larger towns. Aside from possible methodological problems,[4] a sociologist is struck by their rather simplistic explanation — that the correlation is a result of crowding and overstimulation. The researchers sought "functionally parallel sites" by comparing single commercial streets from each town to one another. An urban ecologist would point out that such places are not very "functionally parallel," because (1) kinds of commercial activities vary by size of community (e.g., whereas Jerusalem is a city of many economic functions, Netanya is a beach and tourist resort); and (2) the connection of such a street to its environment varies by community size. In a small town, it may be the only nonresidential street in the community; in a metropolis, it is likely to be near other commercial streets and near office buildings. In the latter case, the street will often be used simply as a thoroughfare. An urban demographer would point out that population types vary by community size in terms of age, ethnicity, and economic position, among other things. There is a world of difference between an elderly pensioner strolling down the main street of his small town and a young office-worker dashing to a large-city store during her lunch hour — a difference that has little to do with "overload." In spite of all this and more, the Bornsteins *may* still be right about there being an inherent difference in walking speeds, but their interpretation does show much naiveté about the city as a *social* form.

Korte et al. (1975) recently reported a study conducted in the Netherlands of helpfulness in public settings. This study is probably the best-designed and most carefully conducted in the "Milgram" line. Essentially, they found no differences by size of community in people's willingness to help a stranger. Yet even this negative result can be questioned; there may have been uncontrolled differences that created "suppressor effects." A sociologist is compelled to wonder what the subjects in each place were like, where they were going, what they were doing, and so on. For example, Amsterdamers may have been unusually helpful because friendliness to strangers supports the tourist trade. In spite of their sophistication, Korte et al. also fall prey to simplifying the city. Unlike other researchers, they generally restrict their inferences just to urban—rural differences in public behavior toward strangers, but the temptation to infer to urban life *in toto* is great, and readers will no doubt succumb to it.

Because of their simple models of the city, psychologists trying to understand urban life pick problems to study that are unrepresentative of urbanites' general lives. (Very little of city life involves confronting Kitty Genovese-like crises.) And they pick features of the urban setting that are unrepresentative of the whole (for a detailed account of both the physical and social settings for individuals in the city, see Fischer, 1976).

---

[4]For example, the sample of communities was largely fortuitous, so the extent of generalizability is unknown. And, subjects were selected only from those walking "alone and unencumbered," a criterion that may well be correlated with community size.

Models of Man-in-the-Urban Environment

My loudest complaint goes beyond models of the urban environment to models of man-in-the-urban environment. Reading some essays on the psychological consequences of urban life, one can only imagine the city-dweller to be standing alone, socially naked, amidst the vast buildings, multitudes, and sensations of the megalopolis, much like a ship-wrecked sailor in a hurricane. The drama of this image just barely matches that presented by, say, Zimbardo (1969) in his description of urban "deindividuation, impulse and chaos." To be sure, one *can* find instances of the lone individual versus the city, but such instances are definitely rare and unrepresentative of urban life.

One finds little recognition in these essays of the fact that the everyday life of urbanites involves a family, friends, a job, many casual acquaintances, and the like — in short, a whole set of "social networks" that directly encompass their lives and that permit the megalopolis to impinge on them only indirectly (more on this later). Social psychologists, whose discipline includes the study of socialization, small group dynamics, and interpersonal influence, should be the first to reject a person-in-the-situation model that treats the individual as an isolated and autonomous actor.

Yet what implicit causal model can we find in these studies and essays? It is a simple experimental laboratory model of the human organism: a lone individual being subjected to impinging stimuli to which he or she reacts. The stimuli vary: noise, odor, flashing signals, the presence of others, social signals, and so on. And the measured responses are usually acquiescence, avoidance, or aggression. *Stimulus and response.* There are no intervening variables in these models — no cognitive factors such as purpose (what is the individual trying to *do* in that situation?), or understanding (how does the individual *perceive* the situation?), or learning (what has been the individual's *experience* in that situation?), or belief (what is the individual's cultural *expectation* about the situation?); and there are no social variables, such as group membership (age, sex, race, social class, etc.), social relations (involvement in a discussion, going to an appointment, etc.), or social climate (character of the neighborhood, crime rate, intergroup tension, etc.).

This too-simple model can lead to some naively ivory-tower explanations for events. A New Yorker rushing home after work may avoid a solicitor, not because the commuter is "overloaded," but because he knows the chances are good that if he stops the solicitor will hit him up for a few dollars and make him miss his train; the commuter may also ignore a drunk, not necessarily because he is callous, but because he wouldn't know what to do anyway, and there are people whose job it is to handle those problems; the commuter may rush by store windows, not because he has had a surfeit of stimuli, but because he has to meet some friends and get to an early show in time; and at home this New Yorker may be reluctant to open his twelfth floor apartment door to a stranger, not because he has become "withdrawn," but because this morning's *Daily News* had a headline about a similar Good Samaritan being clubbed to death. Now, these are the mundane but gritty, real aspects of the *social* environment of city residents. At least a consideration of them would make environmental psychologist's discussions of "stimulus—reaction" seem less "airy-fairy."

The lone-psyche-in-an-overstimulated-environment model harkens back to a similar crude environmental determinism in sociology. Aspects of the physical setting (e.g., density, housing condition, climate, crowding, location, and the like) were thought to, in some unclear way, directly produce social forms (e.g., delinquency, family disorganization, dementia, etc.). The environment directly "impacted" on individuals and groups. This is a poor way to understand man in the environment. As Louis Wirth (1945) wrote: "Physical factors, while by no means negligible in their influence upon social life and psychological phenomena, are at best conditioning factors offering the possibilities and setting the limits for social and psychological existence and development. In other words, they set the stage for man, the actor [p. 177]." And more important still is the fact that, on that stage, each actor has a set of socially taught purposes, a set of social commitments and relations, and acts in a play full of other *people* — not just other props.

These comments present some of the doubts I have about certain work in the area of the psychology of urbanism. In the remainder of this chapter, I present some sociological views that will, I hope, be useful to psychological researchers in the field.

SOCIOLOGICAL APPROACHES

Models of Man

Developing models of man has certainly not been sociology's strong point. In fact, one is occasionally embarrassed by the psychology that appears in its journals: often naive, often a hodge-podge of pop-Freudianism. Nevertheless, there appear to be some defensible and useful models implicit in the urban literature:

1. *Man as a Rational and Capable Decision-Maker:* Holding a set of values he wishes to maximize, he makes choices among the alternatives presented by the city so as to optimize his returns. Variations in behavior are attributed largely to variations in structured opportunities and constraints (e.g., variations in home ownership in the United States have relatively little to do with variations in environmental preferences and have a whole lot to do with money).

2. *Man as a Social Animal:* A person's experiences and his behaviors are shaped by those with whom he is intimately involved. If the social milieu in

which he lives holds together, he holds together; if it breaks down, he breaks down. This means that we ought to be interested in how communities and neighborhoods influence individuals' access to people and the character of their ongoing, significant social relations (on the issues of choice and constraint and of social networks, see Fischer, Jackson, Stueve, Gerson, Jones, & Baldassare, 1977).

Models of the Urban Environment

Sociological models of the urban environment were discussed earlier. They stress characteristics at the structural level — the economy, the polity, the class sytem, and the like. Probably the most significant and general characteristic of urbanism at this level is "structural differentiation." According to the classic sociological argument presented by Emile Durkheim (1893/1933) and elaborated by the "Chicago School," increasing population size together with increasing interaction lead people to specialize in many ways: economic specialization in terms of industries and jobs; areal specialization in terms of districts and neighborhoods; institutional specialization in terms of new oganizations; social specialization in terms of social relations and associations; and cultural specialization in terms of variations in beliefs and values (see Hawley, 1971). The city is, according to this view, the structurally differentiated environment. What are the personal, experimental manifestations of this environment, according to the standard sociological approach? I think that there are two major answers:

1. Cities present to individuals a different social structure of opportunities and constraints than do smaller communities. Primary in importance among the opportunities are economic ones. Cities provide a greater array of potential jobs (usually at better pay) than do small communities. Other structural opportunities include varieties of places to live, places to play, people to meet, things to buy, etc. Among the constraints are the by-products of congestion such as pollution, limited housing space, the reduction of individual influence in the political system, and the like. The fundamental point is that the city presents a different economic (both production and consumption), political, housing, and interpersonal structure within which individuals must act.

2. One of the opportunities the urban environment presents to the individual is a wide array of "social worlds," or subcultures — both those to which he belongs and those that he confronts. In the city, it becomes possible for a person to form a social network from very particular and special people. And thus we have the development of artistic communities, drug communities, communities of prostitutes, of tax lawyers, and so on and so forth. People's lives become encompassed by such social worlds. At the same time, individuals must confront persons in "foreign" milieus: Hardhats encounter hippies; wealthy matrons cannot help but notice pimps and dealers of the "superfly" style; third-generation

Italians rub elbows with Hassidic rabbis, etc. In these ways, the differentiation of urban life both encompasses and confronts the city dweller.

Models of Man-In-The-Urban Environment

Given these models of man and of the urban environment, the link between the two is simply described. On the one hand, individuals experience the urban environment through their positions in the social structure and through their personal social networks. On the other hand, they act upon that environment through their structural positions and social contacts (for discussions of the utility of network analysis for understanding man in the urban setting, see Fischer, 1975a; Fischer et al., 1977).

With regard to experiences, the effects of community size depend largely on how size impinges on the person's structural position (i.e., on how size affects the economic and social structure). Does it provide a better job, higher pay, a range of housing choices, a physically dangerous neighborhood, and the like? The archetypal farm boy who has found a good job in the city has been strongly affected — but indirectly so. Further, the effects of size on the individual will depend on how his social milieu is affected. Does he have a new circle of work associates; what is his relation to his neighbors, to his family; how are his intimates affected by urban social structure (are they in better jobs, or are they joining a wierd sect, for example)? In sum, people experience the city not nakedly but through thick social fabric. The strength of the fabric will vary from person to person and may vary from place to place; that's a topic for study. But one must attend to the importance of the fabric.

Similarly, people act through their structural positions and social networks. They use their jobs, their citizenship, their memberships in ethnic, neighborhood, and interest groups to achieve personal or political ends. And they use friends, kin, and work associates to find jobs and professional assistance, learn about housing opportunities, pull political strings, comfort them in crisis, or applaud them in success. In sum, people do not grapple barehanded with the city, but instead employ a complex myriad of social connections. That is a realistic picture of man-in-the-urban environment.

Sociological Theories

These models — of man, of the urban environment, of man-in-the-urban environment — lie behind most sociological treatments of the consequences of urbanization. Stated in this manner, however, all this sounds quite abstract. Therefore, I illustrate my point by briefly describing a few sociological theories of urbanism.

The first is an economic analysis. Though varied in many presentations, the argument is essentially that cities are efficient economic systems (density and proximity lower costs) and act as economic coordinators for large hinterlands.

The larger a community is, the greater the wealth it produces. It also produces more specialized division of labor, particularly by supporting white-collar, professional, and bureaucratic work. Concomitant with this development is an increased differentiation and elongation of the class structure. The individual consequences of urbanism, for this school, should be sought among the psychological consequences of holding certain jobs, belonging to certain sharply defined classes, and earning certain levels of income.

The most well-known sociological theory of urbanism is that expounded by Louis Wirth.[5] He explicitly treated psychological consequences — largely negative ones — but the thrust of his analysis is that those consequences result from changes in the social structure. His argument was that the multifaceted structural differentiation of urbanism (occupational, institutional, spatial, etc.) prevents normative consensus at the community level and also weakens small, primary groups by narrowly specializing them, usurping their functions, and luring their members away. (For example, jobs take people from their families most of the day; voluntary associations and public recreation do so at night; and services — from restaurants to public welfare — render families less necessary.) The consequence is weaker social integration. And the psychological effect of this is alienation, disengagement, and aberrant behavior.

I have used much the same set of sociological concepts to make a contrary argument: that population size permits the development and strengthening of many and specialized subcultures. The larger the population, the greater the chances of a group reaching the "critical mass" necessary to become a functioning, cohesive "community." People can be at least as psychologically integrated in these subcultures as they can be in rural towns. Although there may be little community-wide normative consensus because of conflict between these subcultures, there does exist a range of cohesive social worlds (Fischer, 1975b, 1976).

Finally, I should note what is probably the most current popular position in sociology: that the small, social worlds within which people live are so resilient and powerful as to be largely impervious to factors like size and density; and that they are essentially similar in large and small communities. Thus, there are *no* psychological consequences of urbanization. (There may be spurious correlations between urbanism and social psychological traits because of urban–rural differences in class, ethnic, or life-cycle distributions. Once these are controlled, however, differences should disappear.) The weight of the current evidence tends to confirm *this* theory.[6]

---

[5]Wirth's paper, "Urbanism as a way of life," is reprinted in virtually every urban sociology reader. An exegesis appears in Fischer (1972).

[6]The most definitive statement of this position is by Herbert Gans in "Urbanism and suburbanism as ways of life: A re-evaluation of definitions," which is widely reprinted [e.g., in R. Gutman & D. Popenoe (Eds.), *Neighborhood, city, metropolis.* New York: Random House, 1970].

There are, of course, other theories — ones that stress political or cultural processes, for example — but my effort here has simply been to point out the ways in which sociologists employ the models I described earlier.

The essential moral of my discourse is clear. From a sociological perspective, psychological approaches to urbanization often make an egregious error. In both theories and methods, they treat the consequences of urbanism as if they involved only a simple psyche confronting an immense stimulus. Both ends of that equation — the model of man and the model of the city — are unrealistic. More important still, the intervening elements — social structure and social groups — are missing from this formulation. From my standpoint, the chances of understanding the psychological consequences of urbanism are greater if we first examine urbanism's social consequences than if we persist in assuming that people encounter their cities as autonomous and isolated individuals.

ACKNOWLEDGMENTS

This work was supported in part by the Institute of Urban and Regional Development, Berkeley. Mark Baldassare provided important comments on earlier drafts.

REFERENCES

Alland, A. *The human imperative*. New York: Columbia University Press, 1972.

Baldassare, M., & Feller, S. Cultural variations in personal space. *Ethos,* Winter 1975, *3,* 481–503.

Baldassare, M., & Fischer, C. S. The relevance of crowding studies to urban life. In D. Stokols (Ed.), *Perspectives on environment and behavior*. New York: Plenum Press, 1976.

Barker, R. G., & Gump, P. V. *Big school, small school*. Stanford, Calif.: Stanford University Press, 1964.

Bornstein, M. H., & Bornstein, H. G. The pace of life. *Nature*, February 19, 1976, pp. 557–559.

Durkheim, E. [*Division of labor*] (G. Simpson, trans.). New York: Free Press, 1933. (Originally published, 1893.)

Fischer, C. S. Urbanism as a way of life: A review and an agenda. *Sociological Methods and Research*, 1972, *1,* 187–242.

Fischer, C. S. The study of urban community and personality. *Annual Review of Sociology,* 1975, *1,* 67–89. (a)

Fischer, C. S. Towards a subcultural theory of urbanism. *American Journal of Sociology,* 1975, *80,* 1139–1141. (b)

Fischer, C. S. *The urban experience*. New York: Harcourt, Brace, Jovanovich, 1976.

Fischer, C. S., Baldassare, M., & Ofshe, R. J. Crowding studies and urban life: A critical review. *Journal of the American Institute of Planners*, 1975, *31,* 406–418.

Fischer, C. S., Jackson, R. M., Stueve, C. A., Gerson, K., Jones, L., & Baldassare, M. *Networks and places*. New York: Free Press, 1977.

Freedman, J. L. *Crowding and behavior*. San Francisco: Freeman, 1975.

Glass, D., & Singer, J. *Urban stress*. New York: Academic Press, 1972.

Hawley, A. *Urban society*. New York: Ronald Press, 1971.

Korte, C., Ypma, E., & Toppen, A. Helpfulness in Dutch society as a function of urbanization and environmental input level. *Journal of Personality and Social Psychology*, 1975, *32*, 996–1003.

Lowin, A., Holtes, J., Sandler, B., & Bornstein, M. The pace of life and sensitivity to time in urban and rural settings. *Journal of Social Psychology*, 1971, *83*, 247–253.

Milgram, S. The experience of living in cities. *Science*, 1970, *167*, 1461–1468.

Montagu, M. F. A. (Eds.). *Man and aggression*. New York: Oxford, 1968.

Sherrod, D., & Downs, R. Environmental determinants of altruism. *Journal of Experimental Social Psychology*, 1974, *10*, 468–479.

Simmel, G. The metropolis and mental life. In R. Sennet (Ed.), *Classic essays on the culture of cities*. New York: Appleton-Century-Crofts, 1969. (Originally published, 1905.)

Wicker, A. W. Undermanning theory and research. *Representative Research in Social Psychology*, 1973, *4*, 185–206.

Wirth, L. Human ecology. In R. Sennet (Ed.), *Classic essays on the culture of cities*. New York: Appleton-Century-Crofts, 1969. (Originally published, 1945.)

Zimbardo, P. G. The human choice: Individuation, reason, and order versus deindividuation, impulse, and chaos. In W. Arnold & D. Levine (Eds.), *Nebraska Symposium on Motivation*. Lincoln, Neb.: University of Nebraska Press, 1969.

8 Personal Control as a Mediator of Crowding

Reuben M. Baron
University of Connecticut

Judith Rodin
Yale University

INTRODUCTION

Although the term *crowding* is frequently used as synonomous with high density, there appears to be ample justification for distinguishing between these terms (Stokols, 1972). People may experience crowding when their goals are blocked by the mere presence of other people even if there is sufficient physical space for all (e.g., Stokols, 1976), and they may feel uncrowded even when sharing a restricted amount of space (Freedman, 1975). To understand these and other apparently contradictory findings with regard to density and crowding (Altman, 1975; Proshansky, Ittelson, & Rivlin, 1976; Sundstrom, 1978), we suggest the following basic proposition: Crowding effects are assumed to occur whenever high spatial or social density leads to a loss of personal control regarding (1) the selection of importantly valued actions or goals, (2) the means by which they are attained, and/or (3) the actual attainment of these valued options. The introduction of control as a major mediator of stress effects in high density allows us to bring density within the same conceptual purview as other *potential* environmental stressors such as noise (Glass & Singer, 1972), which have important effects on the health and behavior of organisms.[1]

---

[1] It is recognized, following Averill (1973) and Weiss (1968, 1971) that there are situations in which the apparent exercise of control can increase rather than decrease stress — for example, situations in which the exercise of control is not accompanied by discriminative feedback concerning the effectiveness of the control response in eliminating an aversive stimulus (cf. Weiss', 1971, experimental critique of Brady's executive monkey research). However, in such situations, it is doubtful that perceptions of control will remain high at any level of awareness over time.

The present paper first reevaluates current conceptual analyses of psychological control and then extends them. Next, a control-crowding model is presented that is designed to view crowding not as a single state but as a multistage process involving: (1) the instigation of arousal–stress effects as a function of the implications of density for processes of attention and control; (2) attempts by the person to utilize various attentional, cognitive, and behavioral mechanisms to ameliorate or eliminate environment-control incompatibilities; and (3) the consequences of particular coping strategies for subsequent adjustments to the physical and social environment. Specifically, this elaborated control model of crowding will be used to explain and predict how and when diverse instigating conditions, including architecturally mediated reductions in unit space, interpersonal encounters of various types and levels, and variations in group size, create crowding stress. This model distinguishes between the impact of density on attention–arousal processes and its impact on response capability–control processes. After we specify the course that coping is likely to take within each of these different types of crowding-stress situations, we compared the present model to other current approaches to crowding.

BASIC CONCEPTS

Personal Control

We define personal control as the ability to establish a correspondence between intent and the environmental consequences of one's actions. There are important theoretical and heuristic reasons for treating personal control as the hypothetical construct of relevance rather than using alternative formulations such as *perceived* control (i.e., phenomenal awareness of control as measured by verbal self-report) or *behavioral* control (i.e., exercising a control-relevant response). Personal control is preferred over behavioral control, because it has been shown repeatedly that a person's belief that he has control, even in the absence of actually exercising control, will bestow many of the same benefits (Geer & Maisel, 1972; Glass & Singer, 1972). Lefcourt (1973) has referred to this phenomenon as the "illusion of control." On the other hand, there is research that suggests: (1) that perceived choice does not necessarily increase with objective increases in the number of choice alternatives (Averill, 1973; Harvey & Johnston, 1973); and (2) that objectively enhanced control may have benefits even in the absence of increments in self-reported control (Langer & Rodin, 1976; Rodin & Langer, 1976).

From these studies one may conclude that explicit awareness of the availability of control is a sufficient but not a necessary condition for control to exist as a psychologically relevant event. Specifically, it is proposed that control may be perceived or cognized at a tacit level of awareness (Turvey, 1977); that is, to paraphrase Polyani (1958), we may know more of control than we can say. It is assumed, however, that although control is sometimes not represented at the level of explicit verbal awareness, it can still be operative as a psychologically relevant process (see Erdelyi's, 1974, and Shiffrin & Schneider's, 1977, analyses of the conditions under which selective responding may occur without awareness). Thus, it is not necessary to demonstrate that subjects explicitly label a set of stimulus conditions as enhancing or diminishing their control. The important criterion is that organisms make a control-relevant response to appropriate stimulus conditions. Subsequently, they may become aware of their exercise of control (e.g., by observing their own responses) or continue to make control-relevant adjustments while remaining unaware of the eliciting conditions. Indeed, Nisbett and Wilson (1977) suggest that people are frequently unaware of the situational variables that have determined a particular response and that when they are called upon to explain that response, they often give the most normative or plausible explanation rather than the correct one. Thus control need not be in central awareness to guide action (Turvey, 1977).

It appears possible to establish clear criteria for the existence of a control-response pattern and/or set without resort to verbal self-reports. One can assess, for example, whether there are characteristic differences in aspects of information processing and/or patterns of action when the person is exercising control. Specifically, control appears to be operative when there is reliable covariation between environmental opportunities to establish contingent control over outcomes and operant response patterns (Seligman, Maier, & Solomon, 1967) and when the level of perceptual organization manifests an orderly shift from small to larger units (Newtson, 1976).[2]

Types of Control

In the interest of solving more general conceptual and operational problems in establishing control as a psychologically relevant event, we have postponed an important set of differentiations between outcome and decision control. Although previous attempts to differentiate these concepts have focused on differences in sets of beliefs (e.g., Steiner, 1970), we treat both decision freedom and outcome control in terms broad enough to encompass instances where control may exist at either an explicit or tacit level. At the level of explicit verbal awareness, such *decision freedom* translates to a person's belief that he

_____

[2]Newtson (1976) proposes that unpredictability of events generates a more fine-grain unitization that shifts to a more molar unitization when mastery over the situation is achieved and responding becomes more automatic.

rather than other people or circumstances selects both the goals sought and the means to obtain them (Steiner, 1970).

Where one has reason to believe that decision freedom is experienced at a tacit rather than explicit level, one can infer the existence of high decision freedom from a configuration of: (1) unconflicted decisions (e.g., low decision time); (2) relative absence of postdecision regret [e.g., no devaluation of chosen alternative occurs (Festinger, 1964)]; and (3) lack of signs of reactance [e.g., the person does not seek to increase or change his range of alternative (Brehm, 1966)]. Directly within the present mode of analysis, one might describe a high freedom of choice situation as one where one's means and ends are substantially self — as opposed to externally — determined. Such self-defined alternatives need not be easily accessible phenomenally.

The essence of *outcome control* lies in the person's knowledge that there is a reliable impact of what one does on what one gets. As noted earlier, such knowledge may or may not involve conscience awareness. At the level of direct awareness, outcome control involves a person's belief that he can influence the value and range of outcomes that accrue to him (Crandall, 1975; Steiner, 1970). At the level of tacit awareness, outcome control is expected to be relevant when action—outcome covariation occurs under suitable conditions of environmental opportunity [e.g., predictable sequences of stimulus events occur (Geer & Maisel, 1972)].[3] Retrospective accounts of personal causality that converge with these operations would further demonstrate the operation of outcome control as a psychologically relevant event but would not be necessary. With regard to the covariation criterion, it may be noted that although we typically seek a pattern of covariation over time (Kelley, 1972), it is possible for a person to infer that he has control with only a limited number of trials, or indeed a single trial, under certain conditions. Specifically, a person may act as if he has control over outcomes after only a single trial if an action he takes generates a highly distinctive outcome (i.e., a unique effect likely to be associated with this act). For example, if when a person bangs his fist on a table, a cup flies in the air, he is likely to perceive control over the movement of the cup. Similarly, if in an interpersonal encounter a person makes an outrageous request and the other person complies immediately, he will likely subsequently act as if he can control this other person. Thus it might be argued that one can trade distinctiveness and frequency of occurrence as criteria for the presence of control, because they both imply that the actor is the origin of effects (DeCharms, 1968).

---

[3]Although predictability is implicated in the process of achieving outcome control, it has a distinct set of environmental properties. Thus, whereas the predictability of events is a prerequisite for the exercise of outcome control (Seligman, 1975), it is possible for a person to be able to predict the occurrence of events without being able to exercise behavioral control over them (Averill, 1973; Geer & Maisel, 1972; Pervin, 1963). In the present context, predictability may vary with regard to the nature, probability, and timing of stimuli.

Using changes in personal control, as defined above, as the crucial mediating process, we first demonstrate how the effects of high density may be understood and predicted a priori. Second, we attempt to demonstrate that other descriptions of crowding effects may be seen as specific features of this more general explanatory model. Third, we attempt to provide a psychological analysis of crowding stress that may be applied to any potential environmental stressor.

Attributions, Crowding, and Control

There appear to be a number of good reasons for believing that attributional processes are often implicated in reactions to high density. First, attributions can function to increase or decrease perceptions of control (Kelley, 1972; Weick, 1970). Second, attributions are most likely to occur when the actual course of environmental events does not follow a sequence that is expected (Kelley, 1972). Certain types of density situations (described later), particularly those involving various types of intrusive environmental events, are likely to be of this character (Edney, 1975).

It should be noted, however, that attributions may enter the crowding-stress process at a number of different points, leading to very different outcomes. First attributions may be directly tied to the *instigation* of crowding stress. In this instance, a reduction in unit space will arouse qualitatively different types of crowding problems depending on whether a social or physical environmental attribution is made.[4] Recent work by Worchel and Teddlie (1976) directly supports the assumption that the range and intensity of negative consequences produced by personal space invasions (i.e., loss of boundary control) may vary as a function of whether a social or physical attribution is made. Further, because people often attribute blame for uncontrollable negative outcomes to other persons (Drabek & Quarantelli, 1967; Shaw & Skolnick, 1971), it is likely that when numerosity makes other people salient sources for such labeling, attributions of feelings of crowding and interpersonal hostility will occur.

Another function of attributional processes involves its role in the coping process. First, attributions may function as *coping mechanisms*, which can give subjects increased or reduced feelings of control depending on the particular attribution that is made (Weick, 1970). For example, a particular event may be reappraised as less threatening if attributed to an unstable, as opposed to a stable, parameter of high density. In addition, attributions may direct the choice of other coping mechanisms. For example, attributions to social features of the

---

[4]Moreover, as we attempt to demonstrate later, the relative prepotence of internal architectural, as opposed to social, constraints is likely to affect the sequencing of the foregoing stages. For example, direct coping responses may begin earlier and last longer when loss of control is attributed to the social environment.

situation (the behavior of others) should increase the probability of reactance, group formation, or deindividuation. These are all responses to, and attempts to modify, the nature and quality of the social stimulation. On the other hand, attributions to the physical setting may lead to behavior directed toward objects (e.g., moving the furniture, or defacing the walls in the extreme case).

In line with the present view of the role of awareness, it should be noted that the processes affecting attributional labeling need not be assumed to be conscious. Specifically, a person may focus on different causal loci for the loss of control because of differences in the perceptual salience of environmental arrangements. Taylor (1975) has suggested that the person's focus of attention will be an important determinant of the source of his attributions. Thus factors such as the press of another's body, the blocking of one's view, or the obtrusiveness of an arrangement of furniture are likely to produce cues that can become major sources of one's causal attributions even though the person may not be aware of their usage. Finally, according to the present view, it is possible for a total sequence of successful or unsuccessful coping to emerge without attributions having any direct role in the coping process. Here, attributions may only serve to give an ex post facto coherence to one's actions (Nisbett & Wilson, 1977).

Density

Recent research has progressed to the point where varying aspects of spatial density (variations in unit space per person holding group size constant), social density (number of persons occupying a fixed area of space), and immediacy of contact (e.g., likelihood of physical touching) have been operationally unconfounded (cf. Paulus, Annis, Seta, Schkade, & Mathews, 1976). Attempts to provide a conceptual basis for when different parameters of density will produce similar and different effects, however, have either not been attempted (Sundstrom, 1978), have had an ad hoc character (Marshall & Heslin, 1975), or have been largely descriptive (Baum & Koman, 1976). We believe that one important advantage of the current control model is that it provides the basis for a unified conceptual analysis of the physical and social features of density.

The first difference between physically and socially mediated density is that social stimuli are often immediately scanned in attributional terms and thus may have greater perceptual salience than physical stimuli. This suggests that increased social density will be analyzed more closely and perhaps earlier for its control-relevant implications than increases in purely physical density. Consequently, with reductions in room size, attributional processes may be likely to arise only after unsuccessful attempts have been made to control representative outcomes in the setting. If the foregoing line of reasoning is correct, it might be expected that: (1) it will be more difficult to link crowding stress to internal design features than to group size differences; and (2) effects of room size will emerge only when group size cues are not perceptually salient. There are several studies that, taken together, can be reinterpreted in this way.

First, a number of experiments have demonstrated that either when group size was held constant but large, or when room size and group size were independently varied, variations in unit space available did not produce negative reactions over a variety of measures (Freedman, Klevansky, & Ehrlich, 1971; Marshall & Heslin, 1975; Sundstrom, 1975; Worchel & Teddlie, 1976). However, when group size was small (Baum & Koman, 1976), or reduced in salience as the result of a large interaction distance (Worchel & Teddlie, 1976), there were spatial-density effects. With a large interaction distance, subjects in the small room complained more about feeling uncomfortable, ill at ease, confused, and crowded than subjects in the large room. With a small interaction distance or large groups, these investigators found no effects of physical density. Taken together, the Baum & Koman and the Worchel and Teddlie studies appear to support the assertion that social stimuli have greater perceptual salience than physical stimuli. Unless there are special environmental arrangements involved that dampen the salience of interpersonal factors, these factors are likely to dominate the arousal and labeling of crowding stress.

Although the perceptual salience of restrictions in spatial density may be a priori weaker than social density, we can suggest at least two further reasons why the role of room size has failed to be demonstrated in current studies of crowding. First, *experimental* treatments involving reductions in room size have sometimes inadvertently eliminated potential implications for personal control. For example, in the course of avoiding distraction effects from task activities, a number of recent studies of the effects of room size have had the subjects perform no activity at all in the setting where physical density was manipulated (e.g., Aiello, Epstein, & Karlin, 1975). A second problem in detecting room-size effects centers around whether subjects have been offered coping responses sensitive to the problems that reductions in room size may create. Thus the fact that Baum and his associates have been among the few investigators to demonstrate an effect of room size on behavior may be related to the fact that Baum's program may be the only one in which subjects have consistently been offered adaptive responses specifically appropriate to dealing with variations in spatial density (e.g., selecting seating arrangements). Unfortunately, Baum's experiments thus far have relied on anticipated, as opposed to experienced, density. We believe, however, that effects of spatial manipulations might be obtained more readily if measures relevant to these manipulations, such as Baum and Koman (1976) used, were employed.

A second difference between the social and spatial density is that increased social density affects the *amount* of information to be processed, whereas spatial density may not. Specifically, the larger the group size, the greater the potential information-processing load on the individual. By contrast, the amount of unit space available is assumed to affect the *rate* of processing. It does so by increasing the salience or immediacy of all aspects of the environment. That is, the more salient the elements, the greater the rate of information processing (Rapoport, 1975), presumably because salient elements are more difficult to process selectively over time. It is assumed that the effects of group size on processing rate depend on whether or not increases in group size occur in a constant or variable area – that is, whether unit space is also affected.

Environmental Potential

The foregoing analysis highlights a problem that has made it difficult to interpret many crowding studies. Specifically, because density is a multidimensional phenomenon, it is important to decompose it into its essential components. Amount and rate of information to be processed, features of density related to its direct stimulus properties, must be differentiated from the higher-order properties of density that involve the implications of density for means—ends sequences (supports and constraints; see Chein, 1954). Thus it is proposed that any density change potentially effects a wide range of environmental properties. Taken together, the general stimulus features and the factors that facilitate or hinder goal attainment constitute the environmental potential (EP) of any significant change in the properties of environment. The implications of these distinctions for clarifying the meaning of crowding stress are directly elaborated in the following section.

THE GENERAL NATURE OF
CROWDING EFFECTS

Attention—Arousal Versus Crowding Stress

The present conceptualization distinguishes between the impact of density on attention—arousal processes and its impact on response capability—control processes. It will be proposed that the term *crowding stress* be reserved for situations in which increases in density have clear relevance for decision freedom and/or outcome control.

Density and Attentional Processes. The amount of attention or vigilance required in any setting is influenced by several parameters of density. These include the number of stimulus features to be processed and the predictability of stimulus events, factors that are both likely to be parameters of group-size variations. A further parameter of importance is the rate at which stimuli have to be processed (a potential property of both variations in room size and physical immediacy of contact). Specifically, conditions of density that require a person to monitor environmental events closely and continuously at a high rate per unit of time are likely to produce a mobilization of attention that is highly arousing physiologically. Such arousal, however, is not viewed as indicative of "true" stress unless decisional or outcome control are impaired (see below). Operationally, stress and simple (direct) stimulus-based arousal may be distinguished by the form of the arousal function. Specifically, arousal based primarily on stimulus complexity-type factors is assumed to adapt out relatively quickly. Control-based arousal is assumed to be more long-term and more likely to interfere with ongoing activities [e.g., result in deficits in task performance (see Hamilton, 1975; Sarason, 1975)].

Response Capability, Control, and Stress.   Density parameters not only have an impact on attention—arousal processes, they also constitute environmental supports or barriers that have implications for a person's response capabilities. In terms of the present formulation, the critical antecedents of response capability are assumed to be decision freedom and outcome control. As in the case of attentional processes, we do not assume that a person's appraisal of response capabilities is necessarily readily accessible at a verbal level. Further, with regard to outcome control, we distinguish two types of mechanisms: *onset control*, which affects the ability to delay, avoid, or initiate contact with environmental challenges: and *offset control*, which determines the person's ability to terminate contact with a potential stressor. In a later section, we discuss the heuristic value of this distinction.

Now let us consider crowding stress itself. Stimulated by McGrath's (1970) analysis of the general properties of stress as a psychological phenomenon, we assume that crowding stress arises when density induces a threat to response capability either by radically changing the availability of means and means (supports for decision freedom) or by threatening one's ability to *attain* desired outcomes, given a change in the availability of means and ends. This formulation of stress in terms of control helps to specify the psychological implications of Selye's (1973) proposal that the essence of stress is the intensity of the demand for readjustment.

The person's recognition that control is threatened need not occur at a conscious level for stress to occur (Lazarus, 1968). What is crucial, however, is the assumption that the anticipation of a loss of control created by various parameters of density (e.g., group size, interpersonal proximity, etc.) is sufficient in and of itself to induce an initial stress reaction. Strong evidence supporting this assumption in regard to density may be found in a recent series of studies carried out by Baum and his associates (Baum & Greenberg, 1975; Baum & Koman, 1976). These studies demonstrate that the mere anticipation of being part of a large, as opposed to a small, group is sufficient to produce experiential discomfort and instrumental coping aimed at increasing interpersonal distance.

It is important to note at this point that within the present mode of thinking, it is possible for changes in density to have independent effects on attentional

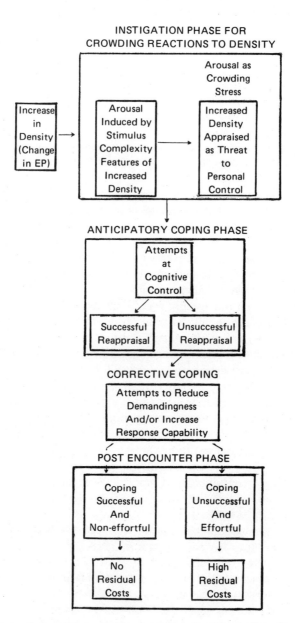

INSTIGATION PHASE FOR
CROWDING REACTIONS TO DENSITY

Arousal as
Crowding
Stress

| Increase in Density (Change in EP) | Arousal Induced by Stimulus Complexity Features of Increased Density | Increased Density Appraised as Threat to Personal Control |

ANTICIPATORY COPING PHASE

Attempts at Cognitive Control

| Successful Reappraisal | Unsuccessful Reappraisal |

CORRECTIVE COPING

Attempts to Reduce Demandingness And/or Increase Response Capability

POST ENCOUNTER PHASE

| Coping Successful And Non-effortful | Coping Unsuccessful And Effortful |
| No Residual Costs | High Residual Costs |

FIG. 8.1. Sequential–temporal processes in extreme crowding stress. The phases of instigation and coping depicted represent a highly stressful sequence of events for which coping is ineffective at each successive phase. In order to simplify the visual layout of this "flow chart," feedback loops that would allow for "stop" or "exit" messages are omitted.

and control-based arousal processes. It is the failure to understand this fact that has led to misunderstandings concerning the nature of relationships among density, attentional arousal, and crowding stress. This point can be made clearer by example: Consider a situation in which a second secretary is added to an office whose original size is then doubled. Here unit space may not change significantly, but crowding stress would be aroused to the extent that loss of privacy lowers one's response capability; that is, a reduction has occurred in the person's freedom of choice [for the purposes of this example, we are ignoring the increases in arousal likely to be created by the mere presence of another person (e.g., Zajonc, 1965)]. In another instance, increases in social density may increase attentional arousal simply by increasing the complexity of information processing. This rise in social density may also result in an increase in control over positive outcomes (e.g., the presence of additional people provides a potential increase in resource availability, which may be perceived as facilitating problem-solving ability), a situation that overall may be characterized by an increase in attentional arousal, an increase in control, and no necessary instigation of initial crowding stress reactions. However, if social density also lowers outcome control, we should find increases in attention—arousal processes *along with* signs of crowding stress arousal such as the instigation of negative mood states and at least momentary impairments in ongoing tasks and/or interpersonal activities.

In sum, changes in environmental potential are assumed to instigate a cycle of reactions that move from direct arousal based on stimulus-complexity/attentional-dynamic to more long-term arousal effects which implicate threats to control. With regard to these long-term effects, increases in density are assumed to generate a series of reactions which include anticipatory, actual encounter and postencounter coping processes.

This general sequence is presented in a "flow chart" form in Fig. 8.1. It should be noted that the sequence of events depicted in Fig. 8.1 describes an extreme case in which coping at each stage is largely ineffective. In actuality, there are a number of points where the stress reaction can be short-circuited or eliminated. Thus high density is assumed to produce effects other than attentional arousal only when an appraisal of response capability indicates a possible loss of control. Furthermore, when anticipatory coping is successful (e.g., when attributional reappraisal provides cognitive control), stress reduction reactions are assumed to be terminated. Finally, when corrective coping is successful and relatively noneffortful, no delayed costs are expected.

Rather than treat these phases in general terms, we will "flesh them out" in terms of the operation of specific parameters of density. Furthermore, this delineation of coping processes will be carried out in the context of a typology of crowding stress derived from the present analysis of the features of control-relevant processes.

A TYPOLOGY FOR THE INSTIGATION OF CROWDING STRESS

We now turn to an in-depth specification of how the present framework can be used to differentiate among the most commonly described antecedents of crowding stress. Such an approach allows us to treat conditions such as decrements in room size, invasions of personal space and territory, and increases in group size, as distinct in terms of the particular readjustment problems created and as conceptually related in terms of the higher-order general relevance of a personal-control framework.

Diminished Space Unaccompanied by Social Intrusion

Decision Freedom.   In order to understand the relationship between density and perceived control, let us begin with the simplest case—where a single individual must deal with a limited amount of available space. Freedom of choice (i.e., decision freedom) may be reduced simply because of spatial constraints introduced by features of the physical environment. For example, architectural features of a building may reduce the size of one's office to the point that it is difficult to carry out certain activities such as "pacing up and down." Thus reductions in physical space occasioned by properties of the physical environment may serve to interfere with one's ability to choose freely a range of behaviors. In addition, semifixed features of physical space such as a cluttered arrangement of furniture may also have the same effects. In both cases, it is hypothesized that a particular type of stress reaction will be instigated that is qualitatively and perhaps quantitatively different from reductions in freedom of choice that are attributed to interpersonal factors (i.e., the social environment). Further, it is suggested that the term *crampedness* be used when reductions in freedom of choice occur because of restrictions that are attributed to features of the *physical,* as opposed to the social, environment.

Feelings of reduced freedom of choice can also derive from perceptions of inequity regarding the amount of space that is presently available. Thus, whether one's frame of reference is one's own past experiences and/or one's present comparisons, any sized space will likely appear smaller and be aversive if one engages in social comparison and finds that people with similar or lower inputs (experience, skill, etc.) are given larger spaces to occupy or if in other, similar instances one has been used to more space. (Although this type of derivation has never been unambiguously tested, negative reactions in areas such as housing may be partly interpreted in these terms.) Moreover, relative deprivation effects are likely to be operative even without extended experience with how a given setting "works" for the occupants if the source of spatial inequity is highly salient (e.g., a high-level executive in a business organization is likely to be unhappy with a moderately large office if a junior executive has a larger office, despite the fact that the smaller office accommodates all physical space requirements).

Outcome Control.   Spatial restrictions may also contribute directly to diminished outcome control by blocking means—goal sequences. It may be assumed, for example, that people develop expectations concerning the range of behaviors that are necessary to attain important outcomes in a given setting that are based upon their past experience and/or their present social comparisons. If these persons then occupy a spatially restricted setting long enough to realize that the behaviors they have available are not adequate to yield control over valued outcomes, the loss in outcome control will produce crampedness stress. For example, as an academician begins to get oriented to a new office, he or she may realize that the storage space is inadequate to house the large numbers of books and journals one habitually consults when working on a manuscript. This limitation means that the person will have to sacrifice valuable writing time going back and forth to the university library. All of these spatially mediated problems may, in turn, be seen by the individual as limiting potential productivity. In this instance, crampedness stress is likely.

When considering the impact of physically mediated spatial restrictions, these problems of volitional interference also follow a temporal sequence, with different types of problems being salient for different temporal cross sections. For example, it is possible that the sheer number of activities performable in a given setting will be the most salient determinant of one's *initial* appraisal of a setting, whereas after *extended experience,* the sheer number of activities possible may become less important than the person's judgment as to whether the performable activities allow him or her a reasonable likelihood of achieving important goals. Specifically, appraising the relative desirability of distinctive outcomes as well as the ability to determine whether clear contingencies exist between one's actions and outcomes (Seligman, 1975) appears to require more extended information-processing time than the simple identification of action possibilities. Thus, over time, we would predict an increase in the importance of outcome control relative to decision freedom as an antecedent of crampedness stress. In support of this assertion, Sundstrom's (1975) data suggest that intrusions that impinge on problem-solving ability (outcome control) continue to generate stress over time, whereas those limiting decision freedom appear to become less important.

Social Stimulation and Crowding Stress

General Arousal Features of Social Stimuli.   Before beginning a discussion of the complications of adding social stimuli to a restricted space, it should be noted first that all face-to-face social encounters have certain properties that create increments in arousal. For example, the human face is such a complex source of stimulation (Izard, 1971; Tompkins, 1963) that even without the further complexities of attributional inference, it is likely to increase attentional arousal. Second, the passive presence of even a single other person creates problems of audience effects to the extent that people feel they are being evaluated (Henchy & Glass, 1968). Active interaction with other people involving the coordination of complex interpersonal plans or strategies is likely to function as a still greater source of stimulation and arousal (cf. Goffman, 1959).

Let us now deal with the complications that occur when two people are together in a restricted space:

1. *Intentionality.* It is predicted that social stimuli will be scanned for evidence of intentionality. A person's information-processing burdens are thus increased as a function of group size. This problem of having too much information becomes even more acute when the interaction is prolonged over time. In addition to creating quantitative problems of too much information, encountering people in a restricted spatial setting creates substantive problems concerning the *content* of the interpersonal data. The sharing of confined space with a few other people will focus people on issues regarding the attainment of goal-relevant outcomes. It is here that we see the clearest difference between a spatially and a socially mediated restriction in space. The presence of other people in a cramped space raises a whole set of problems involving perceived power relationships (e.g., does the other person intend to expand his or her territory at my expense, etc.). The presence of other people therefore decreases the ease with which freedom of choice can be exercised and may limit one's range of possible decisions. There is also a limitation in outcome control possible if the presence of another person implies that outcomes will be reduced or delayed.

The combination of hedonic relevance and the implied personalism of the dominance threat (see Jones & Davis, 1965) strongly suggest the possibility that social, as opposed to physical, limitations of space will lead to the arousal of a reactance motive (Brehm, 1966), with initial attempts to restore freedom of choice through direct confrontations with the perceived source of reactance arousal. For example, the person may attempt to expand his or her territory as the threat of territorial invasion becomes intense (see Edney, Walker, & Jordan, 1976, for evidence supporting a reactance interpretation of these phenomena). Thus it may be argued that a social restriction on a given freedom is more likely than a physical restriction to be seen as having possible implications for a wide range of related freedoms. Moreover, when the loss of outcome control is socially attributed, it is also more likely to be seen as a personal threat than when a physical attribution is made (Stokols, 1976).

2. *Audience effects.* It is hypothesized that the presence of an audience interferes with decision freedom when it restricts the *range* of one's public self-presentations (e.g., if one has to keep up appearances in dress, manners, etc.) in the context of trying to make a good impression (Goffman, 1959). Performing for others and the related problem of evaluation anxiety should become even more stressful when the plans or scripts a person sees as available (Abelson, 1976) are largely those that have *not* been associated with successful outcomes in the past. It should also be noted that the "audience type" effects can occur even when there are not intrusions (either implied or actual) of territory or violations of personal space boundaries.

3. *Boundary control.* The third possible consequence of spatial restriction when two or more persons share that space is territorial invasion. Although the negative effects of encroaching on someone's territory are much more likely if the exposure extends over time (Altman & Haythorn, 1967; Sundstrom & Altman, 1974), another type of negative invasion is possible with small numbers of people in restricted spaces even when the encounter is transitory. Specifically, we refer to invasions of personal space (e.g., physical touching by strangers). It appears that these intrusions have their maximal aversive effect initially and that over time such intrusions lose their negative properties unless they interfere with freedom of choice or outcome control. Data consistent with this interpretation were reported by Sundstrom (1975), who found that stress from physical intrusions (touching of knees) not relevant to problem solving adapted out over time, whereas problem-solving interference did not.

Finally, the entry of another person raises issues of *psychological* boundary control (Altman, 1975). As we see it, such boundary control is largely a matter of offset control or the problem of how to terminate or short-circuit an interpersonal encounter. It is a problem in the *magnitude* rather than the multitude of social stimulation. It is proposed that we label this configuration of problems of offset control and magnitude of stimulation, the problem of *privacy stress.* As indicated by the present conceptual analysis, privacy stress is most clearly seen in extended social interactions.

In sum, it is proposed that a demonstration that the presence of other people produces increments in arousal *in and of itself* is insufficient to support a stress interpretation of crowding; it is only when such socially mediated arousal limits personal control that stress reactions are likely to appear (the privacy stress effects found by Worchel and Teddlie, 1976, offer direct supporting evidence for this proposiiton). It is also quite possible that if physiological arousal itself occurs, it may occur at different points in time depending on whether personal control is constrained by the social or physical environment. That is, given the greater intrinsic arousal properties of social, as opposed to purely physical, stimuli, it is hypothesized that socially induced arousal is likely to precede and perhaps motivate labeling, whereas arousal may not occur until *after* the cognition of loss of control has been attributed to physical design features that constrain decision freedom or outcome control.

Dyads Versus Groups

It should be noted that all of the social density effects discussed thus far are possible in a group as small as a dyad. As we move, however, from a dyad to a small group, the possibility of negative consequences increases (e.g., Baron, Mandel, Adams, & Griffen, 1976). Specifically, with a group in a small space there are control problems of stimulus intensity and offset control (privacy stress) along with the beginning of group size problems related to the unpredictability and uncontrollability of social encounters. Here we begin to combine problems of offset control with problems of onset control and social overload effects, a constellation that we call *numerosity stress*. In larger groups, the potential for social overload exists because there can be too many social features to process and because social contact may become unpredictable (Milgram, 1970). The attributional salience of numerosity for the loss of control is apparently so strong that if differences in unit space are not extremely salient, group size effects may appear unaffected by variations in room size (Worchel & Teddlie, 1976).

When an individual must deal with a number of other people, a major functional problem involves his or her ability to predict the occurrence or relevant social cues (Baum & Valins, 1977). Unpredictability prevents the development of adequate problem-solving plans and thus potentially interferes with outcome control. Unpredictability also creates an *initial* strain of attentional channel capacity, which creates a strong increment in arousal and forces a selectivity in attention that favors tasks or stimuli high in salience and/or functional value. Such effects may be viewed as providing a further mechanism for Zajonc's (1965) social facilitation effect.

When numerosity is present, the inability to establish contingencies between one's behavior and one's outcomes may also become more salient. Consider studying, for example. When an individual has a private room or shares it with only one other person, a fairly reliable contingency may be established between numbers of hours of study and academic success. Living with more people, however, may disturb this relationship. Because of the increased difficulty in knowing when another person may enter, the person may have to study under a more vigilant state (i.e., expend more energy). Moreover, if other people are present, distracting noise, etc., may be greater. Further, the person may have to study at less efficient times because of the difficulty of adjusting his or her schedule to that of other people. Any or all of these interfering social factors may make it difficult for a person to establish a reliable contingency between studying and grades. This type of situation illustrates the potential disruptive impact of numerosity variables on the establishment of *intra*personal contingencies (e.g., between studying and grades). If social overload leads to a narrowing of attention, as Cohen (see Chapter 1, this volume) has proposed, the distinctiveness of various outcomes may also be blurred, thus limiting one's outcome control as well. Similarly, the number and range of outcomes possible may fail to be attended to as a result of stimulus overload.

Of perhaps even greater interest is the impact of the numerosity–overstimulation problem on the direct control over interpersonal outcomes. For example, moving from a smaller to a larger group greatly complicates one's ability to establish smooth interpersonal relationships (e.g., a high level of trust and sharing), given all the additional problems created by coalition formation (Komorita, 1974). Outcome control can also be greatly reduced if the effects of excessive social stimulation lead to uncertainty about the timing, meaning, or reliability of relevant social stimuli. For example, Valins and Baum (1973) suggest that high-density corridor-type dorm arrangements (as opposed to dorm suites) accentuate problems of not knowing when you will run into people you want to avoid. It is also more difficult to know if one's positive social overtures are being reciprocated when dealing with several other people. For example, it is more difficult simply on a time-sampling basis to get to know the meaning of feedback cues from many as opposed to a few other people.

In one dormitory study that assessed unexpected tripling, Baron et al. (1976) found that students in triples felt significantly less control over the use of study space, the time they could go to sleep, and their ability to invite people to the room. Thus, with an increase in group size, problems in crowding arose that were directly tied to differences in control. Moreover, the following differential patterns of correlation occurred for doubles as opposed to triples: For doubles, a measure of perceived control over the performance of a range of activities (e.g., use of study space, furniture arrangement, sleep, etc.) and a measure of satisfaction with privacy were not significantly correlated with a measure of perceived crowding. On the other hand, for triples, both perceived control and satisfaction with privacy were significantly correlated with less crowding stress. Additional data differentiating the control problems of doubles and triples were obtained from a factor analysis. Specifically, only for triples did dimensions such as perceived control, privacy, and perceived crowding load on the same factor. Each of these supposed key crowding stress dimensions loaded on separate factors for doubles.

These data support the desirability of attempting to disentangle problems of boundary control (problems of magnitude of stimulation and offset control) from problems of too many and/or unpredictable stimuli (the problem of onset control). We suggest that triples experienced greater stress than doubles because they had to deal with problems of both onset and offset control.

Onset and Offset Control

The preceding analysis suggests that the two types of uncertainty dilemmas with regard to outcome control — onset and offset — may have a different temporal course in their effect on level of crowding stress. Having onset control can actually make the initial impact of potential stressor less arousing (Staub, Tursky, & Schwartz, 1971). If onset control is lacking, stress arousal in the early stages of experience with environmental restriction is likely, even if one can eventually terminate the stress-producing aspects of the setting. Once exposed to the stimulus, however, the individual with termination control may begin to find the situation less aversive, partly because it is escapable and partly because he or she is no longer in a position of high uncertainty.

Two studies within the area of crowding appear directly relevant to the present distinction. Langer and Saegert (1977) found that subjects given information about the effect of potential overload in crowded situations were less adversely affected when they were actually exposed to high density. Because this set reduced uncertainty, it may be interpreted as functionally equivalent to providing a degree of onset control.

The problem of termination control was addressed by Sherrod (1974), who found that the introduction of a termination control option for some subjects did not reduce their level of initial crowding stress, relative to subjects who lacked this option. However, as in the Glass and Singer noise studies (1972), potential control over the termination of the aversive condition (high density) improved performance on posttreatment adaptation measures (e.g., these subjects showed greater tolerance for frustration). Termination control quite likely gave subjects a possible mode of *coping* with crowding stress, which was absent for subjects who did not have this option. Knowing that they could leave, subjects might have been less compelled to attend to the other people and the spatial constraints of the environment over time. Subjects without termination control may have been forced to be more vigilant, thus keeping the environmental stressors more salient.

Although the Sherrod study established density as a potential stressor that control may help to alleviate, it still did not address the question of whether a restriction in control produces crowding stress and its consequences in high-density conditions. To consider this question, Rodin, Metcalf, Prussing, and Solomon (1976) manipulated whether onset or offset control was available over group activities that occurred in high-density settings.

Male subjects participated in six-person groups and were asked to interact in a group discussion and physical touching task. They expected that several more sessions would follow. Density was varied by differences in room size (66 vs. 156 square feet), and control was varied by assigning to two people in each group roles that afforded them the opportunity to exert different kinds of control within the group. Functions that allowed him to exert onset control were given to a person labeled the *coordinator*. His role permitted him to initiate each activity and to determine the nature and quality of each member's participation. A second controlling role, which focused primarily on offset control, was assigned to the *terminator*. It was his function to stop each task and to halt the entire group interaction when and if he wished.

Rodin et al. (1976) found that, in general, the subjects with onset control felt significantly less crowded in the small room than did the group members who did not have control. In addition, subjects with onset control felt significantly less cramped, found the room less constraining, and experienced more predictability and control over others than any of the other subject groups. Subjects with offset control felt as cramped as subjects without control, yet they were able to tolerate this situation significantly more easily than subjects with no control. For example, they evaluated the small setting as more pleasant, freer, more exciting, and less distressing. These perceptions are consistent with an assumption that offset control may redirect attention so as to ameliorate potential social stimulation overloads (e.g., by reducing the amount of vigilant information processing that is required by high density).

The Rodin et al. study (1976) demonstrated that perceived lack of control was related to crowding stress in the small room. As predicted by the general model outlined previously, perceived crowding stress was significantly less for those individuals with onset control. Those with offset control experienced initial crowding stress but were able to tolerate that stress more easily than subjects with no control.

A more in-depth interpretation of these data is of interest in terms of helping to specify the possible psychological dimensions implicated in the present distinction between onset and offset control. Subjects without offset control experience more uncertainty as to when the experiment will end. Such uncertainty may further exacerbate the primary stressor experiences. For example, Farber (1944) found that the suffering of prisoners in a penitentiary was more influenced by uncertainty in future time perspective than by any aspect of past or present time perspective. In a study explicitly testing the effects of crowding, Worchel and Teddlie (1976) reported that high-density subjects who were not given a distractor significantly overestimated the time spent in the experimental situation and that they were also significantly more stressed. Because subjects with offset control can set the limits of exposure, they are likely over time to reappraise the crowding experience as less threatening (Averill, 1973; Lazarus, 1968).

From a phenomenological perspective, when offset control exists, subjects may become increasingly positive in outlook over time as they progressively shift from a pawn to an origin orientation (DeCharms, 1968). Conversely, subjects without termination control are likely to remain in or fall into a passive or pawn state as their lack of control becomes more manifest over time. In the context of Seligman's (1975) analysis of the development of helplessness effects, it is proposed that the phenomenological consequences of extended exposure to stress in the absence of offset control is, in effect, a crucial feature of learned helplessness.

Nowhere should these processes be more readily demonstrated than when people must live for a long time in highly dense home environments. In considering these effects, Rodin (1976) suggested that when privacy and numerosity stress are high and occur for an extended period of time, children may be strongly affected, because a major portion of their learning will occur under these conditions. In order to measure these residual stress effects that, it was hypothesized, arise from density-derived restrictions in prediction, choice, and control, Rodin (1976) tested children from homes that varied in density in two experiments involving choice and controllable and uncontrollable outcomes.

In the first study, children pressed a lever to obtain a candy as reinforcement and, in certain phases of the procedure, were able to press a second lever if they chose, which allowed them to pick their own candy rather than having the experimenter select candy for them. Controlling for socioeconomic status, Rodin found that children who lived in conditions of high residential density were significantly less likely than children from less dense homes to choose to control the administration of available outcomes themselves.

Why should it be the case that the more crowded children did not choose to control their own outcomes? First, they may have already learned that they have little control over most outcomes and thus did not even try to exercise control over them. Or, rather than having learned that they are unable to exercise control in general, they may have been exposed to a more specific type of learning as the result of residential density. It has been suggested that children who do not have adequate privacy at home will lack some of the cognitive skills necessary for self-initiated behavior (Altman, 1975; Laufer, Proshansky, & Wolfe, 1976). These children from high-density backgrounds who did not choose self-mediated rewards in preference to rewards administered by the experimenter may be demonstrating a failure to have acquired self-regulation skills (Bandura, 1971).

In addition to this type of possible developmental dynamic, there is a more direct application of the present derivation of learned helplessness from a model of attentional capacity that can be applied to the consequences of high-density living over an extended period of time.[5] Specifically, one could derive the failure of children from high room-density apartments to work for the self-administration of rewards when the alternative was to be rewarded by the experimenter by assuming that: (1) chronic high density lowers residual channel capacity by requiring excessive vigilance; (2) when outcomes are equal, persons with limited channel capacity will prefer the less effortful of alternative activities; and (3) self-selection of rewards may be avoided because it is a more effortful way of obtaining the same outcomes.

It is also possible that the effects Rodin obtained reflect a situation in which reduced channel capacity results in deficits in the accurate registration of the likelihood of environmental events (Brunswik, 1943), thus clearly limiting the exercise of both freedom and outcome control. More specifically, as a consequence of reduced channel capacity the person may: (1) fail to perceive the occurrence of an event and thus fail to attend to an opportunity to exercise decision freedom or outcome control; (2) perceived the opportunity but miscalculate the likeli-

---

[5]Relating the phenomenon of learned helplessness to the mechanism of reduced channel capacity suggests a possible way to reconcile Weiss' (1971) physiological and Seligman's (1975) cognitive approaches to learned helplessness effects. Specifically, it might be assumed that the shrinkage in channel capacity occasioned by extended overload conditions might be *physiologically* indexed by depletion of norepinephrine (related to deficits in the initiation of active behavior) and *psychologically* by perceived helplessness.

hood of being able to successfully accomplish a given action and thus underestimate the likelihood of exercising a high level of outcome control; and (3) perceived the correct likelihood function but be unable to expend the necessary energy to make the appropriate response.

Because the results of the first experiment were consistent with several interpretations, a second study was conducted to examine more directly the effects of high density on responses to controllable and uncontrollable outcomes. In this study, a randomly selected sample of junior high school students was tested. No social interaction was permitted throughout the task. Subjects were first asked to solve a series of either solvable or unsolvable problems, and then all were given a second series that was solvable. As Hiroto and Seligman (1975) have pointed out, unsolvability in a cognitive task is formally analogous to inescapability of shock, because in both, the probability of reinforcement (correct or incorrect or shock or no shock) is independent of responding. It was predicted that control-relevant experiences due to high residential density would influence expectancies formed in an experimental situation, which made uncontrollability between response and outcome salient. Specifically, Rodin expected that for all subjects, experience with uncontrollable outcomes would interfere with the acquisition of a subsequent response that could control relevant outcomes but that crowded children would be more strongly affected by uncontrollability.

Subjects participated in a series of experiments for 3 hours in either crowded or uncrowded same-sex four-person groups. At the conclusion of the experiment, each child was interviewed entensively, using both oral and written questionnaires, to establish demographic information relevant to family structure and residential density.

The results indicated that subjects had fewer answers correct on a solvable puzzle if they were living in high residential density or if they had just been asked to solve an unsolvable puzzle. Other factors such as race and parents' education level also explained significant portions of the variance in performance, but short-term crowding in the laboratory did not. The interaction of high home density and pretreatment with an unsolvable puzzle also strongly contributed to the variance in performance on the solvable puzzle.

Rodin's studies were not focused on differences between various kinds of control-relevant restrictions that may result from high-density living, and, indeed, it may be argued that high-density living has a range of correlates relevant to crowding stress. First, it generally restricts physical space, thus increasing crampedness stress. Second, by increasing the number of social encounters that may be difficult to terminate (and possibly difficult to predict), it creates privacy stress. Third, prolonged numerosity fosters stimulus overload, which may reduce onset and termination control and lead to postadaptational consequences resembling the helplessness-like effects described previously (Baum & Valins, 1977).

OVERVIEW OF THE COPING PROCESS

Let us assume that the antecedent conditions for the arousal of crowding stress have been met. We can now examine coping at two levels. First, we take a relatively molecular look at coping as an *online* process. For the purposes of this analysis, we focus primarily on issues of attributional mediation versus more automatic response patterns. A second level of analysis involves our examination of, within different types of crowding stress, the range of adaptations occasioned by people's attempts to readjust to density-induced shifts in environmental potential. In this second type of analysis, there is a greater emphasis on coping as an *achievement* than coping as a *process.*

Coping as an Online Process

Our description of the *online* properties of coping with crowding stress focuses on two issues. One basic problem concerns how active a role attributional decision making is likely to play in the coping process. A second question concerns the specific foci of the attributional process at various stages of coping.

With regard to the general role of attributions in the coping process, we can envisage three general patterns:

1. Coping processes may be directly mediated by the nature of attributional decisions.

2. Coping processes are directly instigated by the stress state; attributions become salient during the coping process as the individual observes the nature of his or her coping response [in this type of situation attributions may determine when stop rules are activated as opposed to determining the direction of coping as may occur in (1)].

3. The coping process proceeds relatively automatically without attributional mediation. For example, attributional mediation to instigate, terminate, or change the direction of plans or scripts may not occur for a threat to control that has been encountered many times before. In such situations, coping is still purposeful; it simply does not require conscious decisional guidance (Harré & Secord, 1973).

Attributions as Direct Mediators.   Direct attributional mediation is most likely to occur when persons are explicitly aware that changes in their potential for personal control have occurred. Two conditions are likely to facilitate awareness: (1) the presence of intrusive social stimuli; and (2) the unexpectedness of the event. First, with regard to the presence of other people, it has already been noted that people, as opposed to purely physical stimuli, are likely to be scanned for intent and be seen as potentially threatening to one's freedom of choice and/or outcome control. Second, the unexpectedness of the events producing changes in control potential is likely to directly increase awareness.

Here, both source and setting have to be considered. For example, we are more likely to expect to have our privacy invaded when riding the subway, a setting we occupy on a transient basis, as opposed to when we are working in our studies at home, a setting where continuity of occupancy exists (see Stokols', 1976, distinction between primary and secondary settings).[6] With regard to sources, it is more expected, for example, that a child will invade one's privacy (e.g., violate one's territorial perrogatives without permission) than an adult. Thus people will be much more conscious of a possible loss of control if an adult begins to rearrange their books or files.

Given a situation in which the person is explicitly aware that a loss of control has occurred, attributions can determine the nature of coping at two levels. First, attributions can function as an immediate source of cognitive control in Averill's (1973) sense of stress reduction accomplished by the person redefining the meaning of the aversive situation. Thus crowding stress is likely to be directly eliminated or sharply reduced if an individual is able to attribute a threat to unstable as opposed to stable entities in the environment. If an attribution is made to an unstable as opposed to a stable entity, response capability is likely to be only temporarily reduced and crowding stress short in duration. For example, the cause of a restriction in office space can be attributed to a cluttered arrangement of furniture, as opposed to room size, or to the addition of a person as a permanent office mate. This type of cognitive work can be viewed as a special case of Lazarus' (1968) secondary appraisal process.

If cognitive reappraisal has either not occurred or failed to reduce crowding stress sufficiently (e.g., loss of control is attributed to stable environmental entities), a different type of attributional decision becomes important as a guide to subsequent coping processes. Here, the crucial property of the attributional process is no longer the stability of the entities causing the loss of control; the critical feature now is whether crowding stress is primarily attributed to the social or physical environment.

One important implication of a social versus a physical attribution concerns whether the primary focus of coping will be on altering the adverse environmental condition or on attempting to improve one's own response capabilities. It is assumed that social environments will be perceived to be more malleable or pliant than physical environments. For example, self-presentations involving ingratiation tactics (Jones, 1964) are available to alter the "rewardingness" of social but not physical stimuli. Thus, when threats to control are seen as social as opposed to physical in origin, the perceived probability of successful modification of the environment is assumed to be higher. In general, then, social attributions are likely to result in more attempts to alter environmental properties,

---

[6]According to Stokols (1976), a primary environment is one in which person spends a large amount of time, relates to others on a personal basis, and performs personally important activities. A secondary setting is one in which a person spends relatively little time and relates to others on an impersonal, superficial level.

whereas physical attributions will result in modifications in response level ranging from lowered levels of activity to diminished expectancies. One consequence of this distinction is that reactions to the social environment may often involve more active and effortful responding.

Another basic difference between coping guided by attributions to the physical as opposed to the social environment is the likelihood that reactance will be aroused when one attributes loss of freedom to other people. For example, interpersonal power-assertion strategies are only likely to occur when one makes social attributions regarding the source of infringements on decision freedom or outcome control. By contrast, when reductions in control are attributed to interior or external architectural features, reactance processes will be irrelevant to both the arousal and reduction of crowding stress. It should also be noted that within social attribution, personal attributions involving reactance-type threats to power are more likely to occur when there are prolonged face-to-face contacts characteristic of privacy stress.

These assumptions also have implications for the relationship between reactance and learned helplessness (Wortman & Brehm, 1975). We suggest that when helplessness derives from an inability to achieve control over the social environment, it is more likely to be preceded by a reactance phase. This reactance phase, or active attempt to restore decisional and outcome control, is likely to occur because people are seen as potentially controllable. Moreover, reactance is likely to be aroused because the person is concerned that a loss of choice and/or control in a particular area will have implications for his or her ability to maintain control in other areas. The foregoing line of reasoning allows us to begin to specify conditions under which reactance arousal is and is not likely to precede learned helplessness effects.[7]

Nonattributionally Mediated Coping Processes.   First, it may be noted that even when attributional processes do determine the basic nature of the coping process, *initial* coping reactions may occur directly without attributional mediation. Thus density stress may have an immediate and direct effect on attentional processes. Indeed, because density stress in a number of its manifestations is likely to involve the person confronting highly complex focal stimuli, it is likely to entail stronger attentional demands than other potential environmental stressors such as noise. At least since Easterbrook's classic paper (1959), attention and stress have been linked . Cue utilization becomes restricted with increases in stress; for example, attention is focused on central stimuli that are high in visual salience, value, or function. Peripheral stimuli are missed or processed at levels that make them relatively inaccessible (see Chapter 1, by Cohen, this volume; Turvey,

---

[7]Wortman and Brehm (1975) propose that whether or not reactance will precede learned helplessness effects will be importantly affected by the strength of a person's expectancy for control in a given task situation.

1974). It is possible for a person to cope with crowding stress largely by narrowing his or her focus of attention. For example, a person attempting to study with other people in his or her dorm room may be able to block out their conversations by focusing attention solely on the work. No assumptions concerning attributional processes are necessary to explain this type of coping strategy. Moreover, attentional shifts may occur at a tacit level of informational processing (Shiffrin & Schneider, 1977).

When the person is not readily able to focus attention narrowly, attentional burdens may become too great. This is particularly likely to be true when the incidental stimuli have high perceptual salience (e.g., when social stimuli are present) and when the focal task is either highly complex (Paulus, Annis, Seta, Schkade, & Mathews, 1976) or requires complex coordination of efforts (Marshall & Heslin, 1975). In this type of situation, the attributional processes may be instigated only *after* attention shifting has proved unsuccessful (e.g., Worchel & Teddlie, 1976). Where this type of attentional strain is prolonged, delayed deficits may appear in the form of residual reductions in information-processing capabilities (Chapter 1, by Cohen, this volume). Under such conditions, attention deficits have likely produced interferences with outcome control (Rodin, 1976) (e.g., misperceptions of response—outcome contingencies, lowered incentive value for control, etc.).

A second type of nonattributionally mediated response to crowding stress involves the nonconscious or automatic instigation of scripts of plans of action (Abelson, 1976; Langer, 1978; Nisbett & Wilson, 1977). Although no one has explicitly treated coping with crowding stress in these terms, there are conditions under which this appears to be a highly likely event. First, there are likely to be certain situations in which the nature of the impact of high density is such that there is insufficient time for attributional mediation to emerge. For example, persons undergoing threats to personal space may begin to decrease eye contact and/or tilt of their bodies without the interventions of attributional processes.

Particularly in situations in which people have to deal habitually with crowding stress, it is possible that regular phases of awareness and unawareness occur in the course of the development of stable coping responses. For example, people who have to go to work using a mode of transportation that is typically highly crowded may develop "deindividuation scripts," which involve essentially treating other people as inanimate objects (see Milgram, 1970, and pp. 173–174, this volume, for an elaboration of this mode of coping). Historically, the original instigation of such a plan or script may have involved attributional processes. After a while, however, such processes are no longer necessary and indeed might interfere with the "plan's successful operation." Thus a chronic density problem may evoke general adjustive strategies that become routinized and automatic. In this type of situation, attributional processes are only likely to be reinstated when the "scripted response" no longer works (e.g., the person next to you in the subway attempts to be friendly).

Coping as an Adjustive Achievement

When people who are confronted with stable sources of stress have high comparison levels regarding the possibilities for decision freedom and/or outcome control in alternative settings (see Thibaut & Kelly, 1959), the most likely mode of coping is a shift to an alternative setting (e.g., a new job, etc.). When favorable *Comparison Levels* for *Alternatives* in regard to personal control do not exist, several general categories of corrective responding appear possible *within* the setting:

1. Withdrawal from social contact to avoid excessive stimulation is a possible coping mode for privacy and numerosity stress; this type of strategy is not applicable for crampedness stress.
2. Internal cognitive adjustments may occur that which involve a lowering of one's standards or expectancies for an acceptable level of decision freedom and/or outcome control.
3. The person may attempt to directly alter the properties or the physical or social environment to the point that a manageable level of environmental potential exists (i.e., changes in the availability of means, ends, barriers, or supports).
4. When persons expect to remain in a given setting for a substantial time period, they may seek to acquire new resources, skills, or interests that will better equip them to deal with an unalterable environmental situation (e.g., a prison inmate may learn to enjoy reading, a dorm resident may join a group, etc.). We now illustrate these types of coping strategies within specific situations of crowding stress.

Coping Under Crampedness Stress

Given that a state of crampedness stress and a low likelihood of shifting settings (e.g., a place to study outside of one's room) is either too costly (e.g., too much time is lost going back and forth to the library) or unavailable (e.g., alternative settings are too noisy), two major categories of coping are possible: (1) alterations of personal—internal properties to readjust; and (2) alterations of the physical setting. Attempts to modify the physical setting are generally assumed to precede internal changes, because changes in the physical setting are likely to be less costly and require less alterations in long-standing coping strategies (e.g., changes in one's style of work). Thus, given a situation in which the amount of space (e.g., size of the room) or arrangement of space (e.g., shape of room) adversely affects decision freedom and/or outcome control, the person will attempt to modify the physical environment so as to increase the amount of usable space. Thus he or she may attempt to restructure the environment to create more functional space. For example, furniture may be placed along the periphery of the room, piled vertically, etc. (Baum & Greenberg, 1975; Baum & Koman, 1976). If these attempts fail, the person has two major options. He or she may: (1) give up and adjust to a lowered level of functioning in terms of lowered expectancies for freedom of choice and/or outcome control; or (2) engage in aggressive acts against the physical environment.

In general, in this type of constrained situation, people are likely to adjust to lowered levels of decision freedom and/or outcome control. Although lowered control expectancies appear to be the most probable resolution, there are circumstances under which crampedness stress may result in aggression. Agression is more likely when people feel they were forced to enter a spatially restricted environment (deprivation of onset control) and feel they cannot leave the environment (lack of offset control). In this type of situation, there can be two levels of attribution: one for the immediate cause of one's distress (that is, the restricted physical environment), and the other, a broader nonphysical attribution involving a specific or generalized other (e.g., a specific absentee landlord or the political system). Here we have the possibility of reactance arousal occurring at a more molar, indirect level. As with other personally instigated losses of control, the possibility exists for both active coping (e.g., attempts to agress against the property of the absentee landlord) and helplessness exists (e.g., people's attempts at aggressive coping fail, and they simply give up). Aspects of this process may be seen in the vandalism that occurred in housing projects such as Pruit-Igoe in St. Louis. The precise conditions under which such aggression stops and turns into learned helplessness remain to be specified, although we suggest later that factors such as unclarity of results of one's coping, effortfulness, and success of the coping will be critical.

Coping Under Privacy Stress

It is expected that to reduce privacy stress two specific coping strategies will evolve: (1) increased territorial behavior; and (2) some type of filtering to reduce stimulus overload. Territorial boundaries may serve both as an instrument of dominance and as a buffer to decrease the likelihood that privacy will be violated (Altman, 1975; Edney, 1975; Proshansky, et al., 1976). In this regard, Mandel and Baron (1976) found that strategic placement of one's desk (e.g., near the door as opposed to the window side of the room) resulted in greater perceived control over the social environment. Such territorial buffers decrease the likelihood of unpredictable intrusions, thereby fostering onset control (see Schiffenbauer, 1976). A territory may also provide offset control by providing an "island of privacy," where an individual may withdraw in order to terminate an intrusive encounter. Thus territories can have two functions: to control both imminence of contact and duration of contact.

When defensible territories are not available, the high informational demands of intensive social interactions are likely to result in selective attention. In privacy

172 BARON AND RODIN

stress, the attentional filtering is intended primarily to modulate the intensity of the stimulation rather than the number of stimuli. Another filtering mechanism that would reduce the intensity of the stimulation is nonreciprocation of self-disclosure. For example, Aiello (1976) found that self-disclosure decreases over time for those individuals who remain in crowded living conditions for long periods of time.

Although filtering mechanisms of the type described earlier are likely to be readily available in secondary settings, they may be difficult to utilize under certain conditions in primary settings. For example, when interpersonal intrusions are unpredictable and territorial buffers do not exist, people are likely to abandon hope of maintaining any control over interpersonal contacts. Such situations are vividly depicted by Oscar Lewis (1961) in his account of the almost total lack of privacy in an impoverished Mexican family. These are precisely the types of conditions likely to have characterized the high-density living conditions that Rodin (1976) found resulted in the passivity of learned helplessness – that is, a world in which even the most basic privacy of withdrawal is difficult within the home. Privacy stress in secondary settings (e.g., overly close physical contacts such as touching by strangers in the laboratory, the subway, etc.) appear to be less serious because: (1) they are likely to be transitory; and (2) various perceptual filtering strategies are available (in particular, see the topic of deindividuation discussed later).

Coping Under Numerosity Stress

Three types of coping appear particularly relevant to understanding how people deal with stress occasioned by large group size. These are withdrawal, group formation, and deindividuation. Withdrawal and group formation are likely to appear in settings that have a certain level of stability in that one encounters the same *basic set of people over time* (e.g., the people one meets on a large dormitory floor with "double-loaded" corridor room arrangements). Because of this general continuity of interpersonal encounter, such a situation is closer to a primary than a secondary setting in Stokols' (1976) terms. Deindividuation, on the other hand, is most likely to emerge and be maintained as an adjustive strategy in secondary settings. These general propositions may be supported as follows.

Withdrawal Versus Group Integration. Baum and Valins and their associates (Baum, Harpin, & Valins, 1975; Baum & Valins, 1977) have observed that dorm residents faced with unpredictable encounters involving potentially large numbers of other students typically utilize one of the two types of coping strategies: withdrawal or group integration. Specifically, becoming a member of a cohesive group may serve to both increase the predictability of social stimuli (improve environmental potential) and increase response capability (e.g., one is allowed to use a group territory). In support of these assumptions, Baum et al. (1975) found that students in corridor-type dorms who were integrated into groups rated significantly lower on a number of indices of crowding stress than those who were not. For example, they were less competitive and less likely to distance themselves from others in their choice of seating arrangement.

Further, Baum and Koman (1976) found that developing a group structure was most effective in ameliorating subjective and behavioral manifestations of crowding stress in anticipation of interacting with a very large group. If this line of reasoning is correct, as environmental threat goes up there should also be increased attempts to assert leadership as a response capability-enhancing coping mechansim. Consistent with this assertion, Worchel and Teddlie (1976) found that a group leader emerged most often under conditions in which both numerosity and personal-space violations were present (as opposed to conditions in which numerosity existed without threat to personal space).

On the other hand, when coping with numerosity primarily involved withdrawing to one's room, there did not appear to be as much reduction of crowding stress. For example, Baum and Valins (1977) found that freshmen corridor residents, a group that tended to deal with unpredictability by withdrawal to their rooms attempted to avoid social contact when placed in laboratory situations with strangers. In some cases, this type of avoidance strategy occurred even when it reduced the likelihood of corridor residents attaining highly valuable prizes in bargaining games.

The superiority of group integration to withdrawal follows directly from the present model, because group coping processes are likely to affect both environmental potential and response capability, whereas withdrawal does not.

Deindividuation. There are two aspects of deindividuation relevant to crowding stress: One is related to environmental features; the other is related to response capability. One feature of deindividuation involves the attempt to deindividuate others. Specifically, one way to deal with social stimulus overload generated by lack of onset controllability is to begin to treat other people as if they were physical objects, a strategy that reduces the complexity of the social environment. Thus, if other people are reduced to physical objects, their stress-arousing properties may reduce to little more than the issues raised by crampedness stress — that is, interference-type effects of reduction in space.[8]

In support of this line of reasoning, Worchel and Teddlie (1976) found that recall of others' names (a measure that Zimbardo, 1969, cities as indicative of deindividuation processes) was lowest under conditions in which numerosity and physical contact were high and no distractor stimulus was available. It was in

---

[8]It is interesting in this connection that Worchel (1976) has proposed that deindividuation be increased in prisons as a means of alleviating perceptions of crowding.

this treatment that social stimulation was likely to have been the highest because filtering due to any kind of avoidance or withdrawal strategy was made almost impossible. Thus it might be predicted that deindividuation of others occurs when withdrawal becomes unavailable as a coping strategy.

Another aspect of deindividuation involves deindividuation of oneself in the sense that one attempts to achieve a state of anonymity. This aspect of numerosity coping is most possible in a large, public space where others exist as an aggregate rather than common group members (Jorgenson & Dukes, 1976). Here one is able to increase one's freedom of choice in the sense of being able to carry out behaviors that are normally inhibited when one is in an identifiable state (e.g., avoiding normative pressures to follow social etiquette) (Jorgenson & Dukes, 1976). In addition, self-oriented deindividuation, if successful, may provide another way of achieving privacy (Proshansky et al., 1976).

It should also be reemphasized that features of the setting are likely to be critical parameters of coping choice. For example, attempts at achieving group structure will probably be more successful the longer the expected exposure, whereas attempts at deindividuation will be increasingly unlikely. In general, deindividuation should occur more often in secondary than primary settings (Milgram, 1970).

Finally, at a more molar level, long-term density may be coped with in ways that have differential impacts on decision freedom and outcome control. Specifically, Booth's (1975) analysis of lower-class families suggests that they sometimes cope with large family size by ceasing to monitor the behavior of their children, a coping strategy that maximizes freedom of choice without providing the necessary skills to achieve outcome control. Similar patterns of reaction appear likely to occur with increases in classroom size (e.g., cessation of active monitoring by the teacher).

Appraising the Efficacy of Environmental Coping

Here we are concerned with the implications of the type of coping mechanisms we have previously described. Let us begin by looking at some concrete examples and then move to the issue of how different types of coping outcomes may influence: (1) postcoping behaviors; and (2) level and valence of postcoping arousal.

One very basic characteristic of any appraisal of the coping process is whether the coping mechanism has succeeded or failed. Success is seen as the extent to which coping has reduced the "demandingness" of the environment and/or increased, perceived response capability. For example, has rearranging the furniture yielded enough space to carry out actions that will allow one to attain important positive outcomes or avoid negative ones? When success has been achieved, we expect postcoping arousal, if it occurs, to be labeled positively.

Whereas perceived success or failure is likely to affect the *valence* of postcoping arousal, we propose that clarity of feedback and the effortfulness of the coping will affect whether or not this second order of postcoping arousal occurs. For example, as numerosity increases, the clarity of feedback as to the success of one's group-oriented actions may be reduced. When clarity is low, arousal is likely to be high (Averill, 1973). Moreover, increases in arousal are likely to occur as a function of the physical and psychological effort involved in coping (Houston, 1972). A critical determinant of effort is persistence. How long does one try? We may also think of effort in terms of the type of coping mechanism used. Here, the greater the difficulty of either discovering or using a particular coping device, the greater the effort expended. In general, it is expected that increases in social density will be more related to increased psychological effort, whereas decreased unit space may affect both physical effort as well as psychic effort.

In sum, it is assumed that level of second-order or response-mediated arousal is a joint function of effortfulness and clarity, whereas valence of the arousal is a function of success/failure of the coping. For example, second-order arousal is expected to increase as effortfulness goes up and clarity goes down, a situation likely to be true under high numerosity. Other situations likely to involve highly effortful coping include territorial expansion and invasion of another's personal space (Efran & Cheyne, 1974). Finally, clarity and effort may or may not be independent, because ambiguity of feedback may increase coping effort by forcing the person to try alternative coping processes.

Residual Stress Effects

It is assumed that postadaptation costs will be greatest when coping processes implicate prolonged arousal. When highly effortful coping has been successful, the individual should feel an increased sense of mastery. Nonetheless, the previous expenditure of effort may work to oppose new-found effectance. Because, in any situation, either the effort expenditure or the perceived mastery may be the greater, it is difficult to develop more than general hypotheses about this subsequent behavior. By contrast, when effortful coping has failed, the effects of effort expenditure and failure of coping summate and thus should produce straightforward effects. In this instance, we expect the individual to fail to cope well with even simple new challenges from the environment. That is, in a subsequent situation, the person may give up *without exerting any initial effort*. The purest form of this effect should occur when antecedent effortfulness has been accompanied by lack of clarity of feedback.

Temporal Factors and Coping With Crowding Stress

Most density studies have neglected to allow for the sequential—temporal character of density effects (see Sundstrom, 1975, for an exception). A close examination of the density literature suggests that this neglect has had serious negative consequences. It is to these problems that we now turn.

Variations in the Point of Impact of Density Effects

Despite the fact that many naturalistic density situations are characterized by extended anticipatory phases during which people may attempt to avoid, delay, or modify anticipated density effects (Baum & Valins, 1977), most laboratory studies of density provide little or no opportunity for onset control of any kind. Specifically, most laboratory studies force an immediate, inescapable confrontation. Interestingly, this is in sharp contrast to laboratory studies of other stressors such as electric shock; here, variations in onset control are quite common (see Averill, 1973, for a summary of the aversive control literature). Ironically, forcing an immediate confrontation with density situations may actually lower their threat value. For example, Lazarus (1968) purposes and cites supportive research to the effect that anticipating a threatening encounter is often more aversive than the actual encounter itself.

It also appears possible that whereas initial density stress effects are largely stimulus-mediated, distal or resultant stress effects are primarily determined by the availability and efficacy of offset control coping. Direct support for this proposal may be found in the research of Sherrod (1974), who found that whereas variations in the possibility of offset control affected postdensity encounter decrements in persistence of performance, no differential impact of offset control was found on distal self-report items that retrospectively assessed experienced discomfort. On the other hand, the failure of Paulus et al. (1976) to find a relationship between density-induced performance decrements and distal self-report mood measures may simply reflect the fact that maximal mood effects occurred early in the adjustive sequence. Similarly, it is possible that in Freedman et al.'s (1971) research, anticipatory discomfort was instigated but failed to be detected by performance and postperformance assessments. Thus it would appear critical to obtain multiple assessments of stress reactions, because a distal measure may only be sensitive to residual stress effects after corrective coping has occurred.

Finally, it is possible that certain types of density parameters vary as to whether they function as transitory or persistent stressors. It is to this problem that we now turn.

Transitory Versus Persistent Density Effects

It appears likely that certain types of crowding stress are, in general, more likely to create both high initial (e.g., anticipatory) and resultant stress, although any such general proposition must be understood to involve a statement not only of the likely *antecedent* conditions for stress arousal but also of the likely coping strategies possible. For example, privacy stress in a residential setting for persons too young to leave home is likely to create high resultant stress in terms of chronically reduced capacities for exercising control (e.g., Rodin, 1976). On the hand, if the problem is primary one of crampedness stress, anticipated loss of control is likely to be much stronger than the actual loss, leading to little resultant stress. It is also possible that whether a given parameter of density will have transitory or persistent effects may be affected by the task situation. For example, if one is willing to assume that convergence of negative experiential and task performance effects is indicative of more persistent density effects, it appears that density situations that involve tasks requiring close, as opposed to little or no, interpersonal coordination may produce more persistent effects (e.g., Worchel & Teddlie, 1976).

In control terms, we may describe all of the foregoing situations as differing in the extent to which a given type of density problem implicates anticipated and/or actual loss of control. Furthermore, it appears that this control problem often takes the form of the absence of onset and/or offset control. In support of this general line of reasoning, it may be noted that in situations in which physical proximity is not likely to affect outcome control over time (e.g., where the task involves interpersonal coordinations), physical touching does not adapt out as a stressor (e.g., Worchel & Teddlie, 1976).

With these temporal boundary conditions in mind, we may now summarize the basic substantive features of our crowding-control model (pp. 152–155 may be viewed as a process summary).

Overview of Model and Supporting Evidence

Table 8.1 summarizes the model by providing illustrative environmental ante-cedent conditions for crowding—stress arousal, control-relevant mediators, and coping mechanisms for the three major types of crowding stress previously described. Of particular interest is the unified treatment accorded processes such as reactance, overload, and learned helplessness.

Given these basic features, the usefulness of the model in describing conditions under which high density creates stress effects may be assessed at two levels. In the following paragraphs, we first briefly review the empirical evidence for asserting that control is implicated in generation of crowding effects. Second, we compare the present model with other approaches to crowding in order to establish further its unique features. Finally, we examine the applicability of the model to large-scale crowding problems.

Control and Experienced Discomfort

Significant correlations between perceived control and indices of perceived crowding and discomfort have been found by Baron et al. (1976) and Schif-fenbauer (1976). Similarly, Mandel and Baron's (1976) finding that indices of crowding and discomfort are inversely related to people's ability to establish a gate-keeper role through the positioning of their furnishings near the entrance to the dorm room, although it is correlational, points to a possible behavioral

TABLE 8.1
Types of Crowding Stress

	Crampedness Stress	Privacy Stress	Numerosity Stress
Illustrative conditions of instigation of stress	1. Lack of adequate space due to limitation in fixed properties of the built environment (e.g., small room size). 2. Lack of adequate space due to poor organization of semifixed physical environment (e.g., cluttered arrangement of furniture).	1. Mere presence of other people lowers freedom of choice. 2. Invasions of personal space or territories in primary environments. 3. Overly intensive social-interaction—high-magnitude-of-stimulation from limited number of sources. 4. Beginning of group size problem if moved beyond dyad in restricted space.	1. Group size – large number of inputs to be processed. 2. Unpredictability of inputs. 3. (1) and (2) together create high environmental complexity affecting amount and rate of processing.
Illustrative intervening processes	1. Relative deprivation of decision freedom due to social comparison with one's own spatial history. 2. Nondirected frustration due to perceived blockage in outcome control, which is attributed to stable features of the physical environment.	1. Evaluative apprehension due to mere exposure effects. 2. Arousal of reactance motive due to attribution to social environment of intentional violation of buffers. 3. Overstimulation due to lack of termination control.	1. Lack of onset control interfering with stable contingencies for social contact. 2. Unpredictability increases effortfulness of information processing due to continued viligance.

3. Directed frustration—aggression analogous to reactance arousal if second-order social attribution made. 4. Apathy analogous to learned helplessness if aggression is effortful and fails to raise response capability.	4. Learned helplessness if: (a) violation of buffers is temporally prolonged; (b) coping in response to magnitude of stimulation effect is effortful and unsuccessful. 5. Lack of onset and beginning of loss of onset control due to unpredictability if dyad expanded without increased space.	3. In secondary environments, reactance is not likely to be instigated; when overstimulation occurs, freedom of choice may even increase as outcome control decreases.
Illustrative coping mechanisms	1. Restructure semifixed environment to create more functional space (increasing freedom of choice and/or outcome control). 2. Seek alternative setting to decrease environmental potential and/or response capability. 3. Lower expectancies for choice and/or outcome control to adjust to low environmental potential.	1. Selective inattention (decrease environmental demands). 2. Withdrawal (decrease environmental demands). 3. Setting up of territorial buffers in attempt to increase freedom of choice and outcome control (reactance reduction mechanisms).	1. Withdrawal from unpredictable setting (decrease environmental complexity). 2. Deindividuation of self and others (decrease environmental demands, increase freedom of choice decrease outcome control). 3. Group formation and integration (decrease unpredictability and increase outcome control; possible loss of freedom of choice).

179

mechanism for control (see also Edney, 1975). Furthermore, Rodin et al.'s (1976) demonstration — that lower levels of perceived crowding and discomfort occur for a person's assigned onset control — puts us in a position to argue that there is a causal link from control to reductions in density-aroused discomfort (see pp. 162–163, this volume).

Control and Interpersonal Reactions

The Baron et al. (1976) study also provides suggestive data regarding the impact of control on interpersonal functioning. Specifically, Baron et al. (1976) found that when persons who see themselves as personally responsible for the outcomes that accrue to them (internals) perceived that they lacked adequate space, they preferred greater interaction distance than persons who attributed control over outcomes to external causes (e.g., luck). Furthermore, Baron et al. found that persons in crowded dormitory conditions were lower in perceived control over room activities and preferred greater interaction distance for roomates than friends. Persons who were less crowded (e.g., persons sharing their room with one as opposed to two other persons) were (1) higher in perceived control, and (2) preferred *closer* interaction distances for roomates than friends.

Control and Task Performance

Illustrative evidence consistent with the present model also exists for task performance. For example, Sherrod (1974) demonstrated that giving people perceptions of potential control over the *termination* of an unavoidable high-density interpersonal encounter (e.g., a small room for a large group of people) ameliorated postdensity decrements in persistence in problem solving. Support for cumulative effects of density on problem-solving ability can also be adduced from Mandel and Baron's (1976) finding that students who established gate-keeping control over their dorm rooms both studied more in their rooms and obtained better grades than students who failed to establish territorial control. Furthermore, Langer and Saegert (1977) found that providing the equivalent of onset control to consumers who were to shop under highly crowded conditions improved their ability to utilize bargain price information in their shopping. Rodin's (1976) study also bears directly on the presumed link between control and performance deficits, because she established that children from high-density homes: (1) preferred lower levels of control; and (2) were more susceptible to learned helplessness effects on solvable anagrams.

   A discussion of the relevance of the control model for understanding relationships between crowding and health is postponed until the final section on the implications of the model for more molar crowding problems in natural settings. We are now, however, ready for a preliminary summary of our position.

Both direct and indirect evidence from our own and other research programs have been cited to demonstrate links among density, control, and stress. These data, which have been taken from both laboratory and field studies and from both long- and short-term exposures to density, appear to establish the case for control mediation as a sufficient condition for high density to produce crowding stress effects. Moreover, it appears that when density variations have no direct implications for control as in certain of the studies involving manipulations of room size (e.g., Freedman et al., 1971; Marshall & Heslin, 1975; Sundstrom, 1975), variations in density do not produce differential stress effects. Thus there is a preliminary indication that the density-control link may not only be a sufficient condition for stress instigation but a *necessary* condition. Considerably more research is needed, however, before one could safely assert that the density-control link is a necessary and sufficient condition for crowding stress effects to occur. Further support for the generality of control as *the* crucial mediator of stress effects can be gleaned from a comparison of control with other current explanations of crowding effects.

A COMPARISON OF THE PRESENT CONTROL-CROWDING MODEL WITH ALTERNATIVE FORMULATIONS

Control Versus Intensification Interpretations of Density Effects

We begin this comparison process by juxtaposing the present model with Freedman's (1975) intensification theory of crowding, a theory that asserts that density per se is not a stressor but merely a condition that intensifies pre-existing or typical reactions to the situation; that is, density by itself has neither good effects nor bad effects on people. According to Freedman, if the typical situational reaction is pleasantness, high density will make the situation more pleasant; if it is unpleasant, high density will make it more unpleasant. Freedman leaves open the question of whether density is arousing. He concedes that it may be but points out that increments in arousal are not necessarily stressful.

We agree with Freedman on two basic points: First, high density may have positive *or* aversive consequences. Second, we share his view that not all arousal is indicative of stress. We basically differ with Freedman in that we believe that there are specifiable circumstances under which density effects are not merely intensifiers of typical or pre-existing states; on the contrary, it is the fact of high density that creates conditions that have the capacity to transform typical or baseline conditions. Specifically, it has been proposed that because variations in social or spatial density may either enhance or interfere with decision freedom and/or outcome control, the potential exists for density to enhance or interfere with ongoing task performances and interpersonal relationships. We also argue shortly that in natural settings involving high-density living conditions, the potential exists for control-relevant aspects of density to increase the negative impact of other environmental stressors (Levi & Anderson, 1975). Moreover, a knowledge of the control-relevant properties of density allows one to differentiate the potentially separable effects of density on attentional-arousal and crowding-stress types of arousal.

Control and Other Models of Crowding

Overload.   Although Milgram's (1970) analysis served as the initial stimulus for the contemporary interest in overload as a model of urban stress, Saegert (1976) has provided the most comprehensive conceptual and empirical work with this concept (see also Desor, 1972; Cohen, Chapter 1, this volume). Saegert (1976) proposes that three distinct kinds of overload can occur: stimulus overload (e.g., meaningless noise); information overload (e.g., too many signs on a highway); and decisional overload (e.g., competing and unpredictable social and nonsocial task demands). Crowding, viewed as a special case of overload, is said to arise when the number of potential or actual social interactions that involve or impinge on a person is so great that it taxes his or her information-processing capacity. Reduced residual information-processing capacity is, in turn, assumed to result in deficits in cognitive performance, withdrawal, reduced prosocial behavior, etc. (Cohen, Chapter 1, this volume).

There are two problems associated with overload models, both of which are substantially remedied by the application of a personal control model. The first problem concerns how to predict a priori when overload effects will occur. This is a rather acute problem, because people appear able to tolerate a wide range and intensity of stimulation (Glass & Singer, 1972). That is, it appears that within wide sensory limits too much stimulation has no real meaning in an absolute sense. This specification problem can be dealt with from a control perspective. In essence, the clearest and most psychologically interesting examples of overload effects appear to occur when high levels of stimulation are unpredictable and/or uncontrollable (Cohen, Chapter 1, this volume). Such effects occur both with high levels of noise (Glass & Singer, 1972) and high levels of density (see below). Thus it appears that the same number of people will differentially affect immediate or delayed information-processing capacity depending on whether or not they are encountered in a context that allows for predictable and/or controllable interactions.

In adition to its usefulness as a model of the generative mechansims underlying overload effects, the control concept helps to better specify the dimensions of overload. For example, definitions of overload constantly fluctuate between stimulus-and-response—oriented formulations (e.g., excessive stimulation versus reduced attentional capacity or experienced overload). Such issues are clarified if social overload is viewed as a property of settings rather than as a commentary on the limitations of the perceiver. That is, overload effects are most likely to occur when there is a poorly structured (e.g., unpredictable) stimulus array and/or a situation that restricts the person's opportunities to become freely and fully acquainted with the people to be encountered (e.g., high-density encounters in dormitory corridors and in public territories in general).

Control Models. Now we turn to the somewhat more difficult task of differentiating the present model of personal control from other control-type models of crowding. In general, the issue here is not a matter of conflicting formulations but of the advantages of a more differentiated and integrative interpretation.

Altman's Privacy Model. According to Altman (1975), crowding arises from a breakdown in self—other boundary regulation. Crowding effects are predicted to arise whenever the individual's *desired level of privacy* is greater than the achieved level. This presumably occurs when privacy regulation mechanisms such as territories, nonverbal gestures, etc., fail to provide the desired level of social interaction. When this occurs, no matter how ample the space or few the stimuli in absolute terms, the *person* or *group* will experience crowding.

With regard to the present model, the first point to be made is that Altman is singling out a particular type of goal-privacy and making the control problems around it central to the creation of crowding effects. From Altman's perspective, control gains its importance from its instrumental value to privacy attainment. We, on the other hand, *see the attainment of personal control as a significant adjustive problem in its own right, which cuts across a number of goals including but not limited to privacy-oriented concerns.* Thus, from the present perspective, crowding can arise in situations that are *not* interpersonal in character (e.g., the problem of crampedness) and in interpersonal contexts where privacy attainment is not a crucial goal (e.g., in the course of group problem solving). Furthermore, because Altman's (1975) model makes control a secondary concern to the maintenance of optimal self—other distance, it does not treat control per se in a highly differentiated manner. This is unfortunate even within the context of Altman's interpersonal concerns, because it is quite likely that problems of making initial contact with others (onset control) are quite different from problems of terminating contact with them (offset control).

We wish to emphasize, however, that we have been stimulated by several aspects of Altman's formulation. He has emphasized the importance of (1) treating crowding as a process that involves coping over time, and (2) of viewing crowding as a multivariate phenomenon involving many levels of responding. Moreover, it is perfectly reasonable strategically to focus on a particular subset of density problems as long as one does not assume that all crowding effects must be of this character. Finally, it should be noted that whereas our approach to coping with crowding has been at the individual-cognitive or small-group level, Altman more than anyone else in the crowding area has been sensitive to the role of cultural factors in the coping process.

Behavioral Constraint Models.   The present approach may also be compared to a type of control interpretation of crowding effects that Stokols (1972) has labeled a *behavior constraint model.* According to this type of treatment, the earliest example of which was Proshansky et al.'s (1976), high density is stressful to the extent that it imposes restrictions on behavioral freedom. Thus, although Stokols (1972, 1976) emphasizes the importance of the demand for space and Proshansky the intrisiveness of people, both treat the loss of freedom of choice as the crucial proximal mediator of a personally experienced sense of crowding.

Our formulation differs from Proshansky et al. (1976) and Stokols at a number of levels. First, we differ from their interpretation of crowding as a subjective experience. As a number of investigators have noted, conscious reports typically contain the *results* or products of cognitive processes rather than capturing the nature of the processes themselves (Neisser, 1967; Nisbett & Wilson, 1977). We are attempting to understand the process as opposed to the product of the control-crowding interphase.

Proshansky et al. were the first to use control to integrate a range of phenomena related to crowding such as privacy and territory. However, they limited themselves to losses of behavioral freedom in situations where a stable pattern of occupancy exists and personal territories are claimed. Although these may indeed be the situations where loss of freedom of choice is most disturbing (see Stokols, 1976), loss of decision freedom may also produce crowding effects in settings where no territories exist (e.g., in public or secondary settings). Perhaps even more important, it appears necessary to differentiate between the impact of territorial invasions on freedom of choice and on outcome control (e.g., the threshold for crowding effects may be lower for outcome than decisional control). Although Proshansky et al. (1976) propose that interferences with both goal attainment and freedom of choice can produce crowding, only the treatment of choice is integral to their model of crowding; that is, goal blockage is treated on an ad hoc basis as opposed to the present integrated framework. Finally, the temporal–sequential coping aspects of crowding are ignored by Proshansky et al. For them, crowding has an "all or none" character.

Stokols' work has been important to the present formulation at two levels: (1) he has urged differentiating between density and crowding; and (2) he has also treated crowding in terms of a process-oriented, temporally-sensitive information-process framework.

Two major problems, however, characterize Stokols' treatment of crowding. First, he perhaps more than anyone else is responsible for crowding being viewed in primarily subjective terms. Second, although Stokols has tried to incorporate

control within his crowding model (e.g., Stokols, 1972), he blurs the point somewhat by falling back on the need for space as the crucial defining condition for
crowding to be experienced. For Stokols, control is important in order to provide
adequate space, a position that is formally similar to Altman's treatment of control as instrumental to the attainment of privacy. We, on the other hand, see
space as relevant only insofar as it impinges on control.

Control and Large-Scale Crowding Problems

One reader of an earlier draft of this control-crowding model raised the following
question: "How do you handle the fact that people in ghettos and in other long-
term crowding situations adapt to and cope with their circumstances?" First,
it appears that many of the pathological effects of high density occur more
readily with populations that have minimal control over environmental events
(Cohen, Glass, & Phillips, in press). Thus aversive consequences of high-density
living have been found for the young (Booth, 1975; Rodin, 1976), the lower
class (Mitchell, 1971), ship crews (Dean, Pugh, & Gunderson, 1975), and prisoners
(Paulus, Cox, McCain, & Chandler, 1975). It is in such populations that high
density and lack of control are inextricably bound in the sense that high density
both creates less control and enhances pre-existing limitations in control.

Perhaps an even more convincing argument concerning the relevance of the
present control-crowding model to real-world crowding dilemmas is evident
when adaptive costs are examined. It is possible for adaptations that are functional at one level of behavior to be dysfunctional at another level. Thus Baron
et al. (1976) found that in a crowded dorm room, good interpersonal adjustment
was related to lowered academic performance. Furthermore, Rodin's (1976)
findings — that children from high-density apartments assigned lower incentive
value to choice and were particularly vulnerable to learned helplessness effects —
may be seen as direct evidence for a delayed-cost view of density-control effects.

It also appears possible to explain within the present framework why certain
demographic studies such as Freedman, Heshka, and Levy (1975) failed to find
evidence of crowding—stress effects. First, these studies have typically looked at
evidence of links between census tract indices of high density and molar indices
of stress, such as disease and crime, for only a single census period. If one assumes
that the loss of control is the major mechanism mediating stress effects, analysis
of randomly selected single periods may be insufficient. Loss of control should
be maximal during periods of rapid population explosion, because such phases
of population growth pose the greatest readjustment strain (see Levi and Anderson, 1975, for supportive data regarding the relationship between stress and
rate of population increase). That is, demographic studies of density appear
obliged to utilize a time series mode of analysis to be methodologically adequate.

Finally, it may be argued that many "real-world" studies of crowding have
looked at the wrong indices of crowding stress. Thus much as we distinguished

between initial and resultant consequences of stress for the individual, at the societal level we may also have to differentiate between the initial consequences of rapid population increase and the more subtle erosions in the quality of life created by the cumulative costs of adjusting to density-induced reductions in control. Specifically, more dramatic indices of social disorganization such as crime statistics may be most strongly associated with population density during periods of rapid population build up. Once the rate of increase slows down and corrective coping processes come into play, the most persuasive evidence for the impact of high-density living is likely to be found in indices of "quiet desperation" such as chronically elevated levels of blood pressure (e.g., D'Atri, 1975), impaired reading achievement scores (e.g., Cohen, Glass, & Singer, 1973), and density-induced breakdowns in prosocial behavior (Milgram, 1970; Chapter 1, by Cohen, this volume). At this stage of the adaptation process, as Renee Dubois (1965, 1968) has so eloquently stated, the real issue is not one of adaptation or survival, but of cost.

ACKNOWLEDGMENTS

The writing of this manuscript was supported by Grant #273 to Reuben M. Baron from the University of Connecticut Research Foundation, and to Judith Rodin by the Yale University Morse Faculty Fellowship.

Requests for reprints should be addressed either to Reuben M. Baron, Department of Psychology, U-20, University of Connecticut, Storrs, Conn. 06268, or Judith Rodin, Department of Psychology, Yale University, New Haven, Conn. 06510.

REFERENCES

Abelson, R. P. Script processing in attitude formation and decision-making. In J. S. Carroll & J. W. Payne (Eds.), *Cognition and social behavior.* Hillsdale, N.J.: Lawrence Erlbaum Associates, 1976.

Aiello, J. R. Personal communication, November 10, 1976.

Aiello, J. R., Epstein, J. M., & Karlin, R. A. *Field experimental research on human crowding.* Paper presented at the Eastern Psychological Association, New York, April 1975.

Altman, I. *The environment and social behavior.* Monterey, Calif.: Brooks/Cole, 1975.

Altman, I., & Haythorn, W. W. The ecology of isolated groups. *Behavior Science,* 1967, *12,* 169–182.

Averill, J. R. Personal control over aversive stimuli and its relation to stress. *Psychological Bulletin,* 1973, *80,* 286–303.

Bandura, A. *Social learning theory.* New York: General Learning Press, 1971.

Baron, R. M., Mandel, D. R., Adams, C. A., & Griffen, L. M. Effects of social density in university residential environments. *Journal of Personality and Social Psychology,* 1976, *34,* 434–446.

Baum, A., & Greenberg, C. I. Waiting for a crowd: The behavioral and perceptual effects of anticipated crowding. *Journal of Personality,* 1975, *32,* 671–676.

Baum, A., Harpin, R. E., & Valins, S. The role of group phenomenon in the experience of crowding. *Environment and Behavior,* 1975, *7,* 183–197.

Baum, A., & Koman, S. Differential response to anticipated crowding: Psychological effects of social and spatial density. *Journal of Personality and Social Psychology,* 1976, *34,* 526–536.

Baum, A., & Valins, S. *Architecture and social behavior: Psychological studies of social density.* Hillsdale, N.J.: Lawrence Erlbaum Associates, 1977.

Booth, A. *Final report: Urban Crowding Project, 1975.* Ministry of State for Urban Affairs, Government of Canada, 1975.

Brehm, J. W. *A theory of psychological reactance.* New York: Academic Press, 1966.

Brunswik, E. Organismic achievement and environmental probability. *Psychological Review,* 1943, *50,* 255–272.

Chein, I. The environment as a determinant of behavior. *The Journal of Social Psychology,* 1954, *39,* 115–127.

Cohen, S., Glass, D. C., & Phillips, S. Environment and health. In H. H. Freedman, S. Levine, & L. G. Reeder (Eds.), *Handbook of medical scoiology.* Englewood Cliffs, N.J.: Prentice-Hall, in press.

Cohen, S., Glass, D. C., & Singer, J. E. Apartment noise, auditory discrimination, and reading ability. *Journal of Experimental Social Psychology,* 1973, *9,* 407–422.

Crandall, V. *The current status of the locus of control construct.* Paper presented at the annual convention of the American Psychological Association, Chicago, August 1975.

D'Atri, D. A. Psychophysiological responses to crowding. *Environment and Behavior,* 1975, *7,* 237–252.

Dean, L. M., Pugh, W. M., & Gunderson, E. Spatial and perceptual components of crowding: Effects on health and satisfaction. *Environment and Behavior,* 1975, *7,* 225–236.

DeCharms, R. *Personal causation.* New York: Academic Press, 1968.

Desor, J. A. Toward a psychological theory of crowding. *Journal of Personality and Social Psychology,* 1972, *21,* 79–83.

Drabek, T. E., & Quarantelli, E. L. Scapegoats, villains, and disaster. *Transactions,* 1967, *4,* 12–17.

Dubois, R. *Man adapting.* New Haven, Conn.: Yale University Press, 1965.

Dubois, R. *So human an animal.* New York: Charles Scribner's Sons, 1968.

Easterbrook, J. A. The effect of emotion on cue utilization and the organization of behavior. *Psychological Review,* 1959, *66,* 183–201.

Edney, J. J. Territoriality and control: A field experiment. *Journal of Personality and Social Psychology,* 1975, *31,* 1108–1115.

Edney, J. J., Walker, C. A., & Jordan, N. L. Is there reactance in personal space? *Journal os Social Psychology,* 1976, *100,* 207–217.

Efran, M. G., & Cheyne, J. A. Affective concomitant of the invasion of shared space: Behavioral, physiological, and verbal indicators. *Journal of Personality and Social Psychology,* 1974, *29,* 219–266.

Erdelyi, M. H. A new look at the new look: Perceptual defense and vigilance. *Psychological Review,* 1974, *81,* 1–25.

Farber, M. L. Suffering and time perspective of the prisoner. *University of Iowa Studies in Child Welfare,* 1944, *20,* 155–227.

Festinger, L. *Conflict, decision, and dissonance.* Stanford, Calif.: Stanford University Press, 1964.

Freedman, J. L. *Crowding and behavior.* San Francisco: Freeman, 1975.

Freedman, J. L., Heshka, S., & Levy, A. Population density and pathology: Is there a relationship? *Journal of Experimental Social Psychology,* 1975, *11,* 539–552.

Freedman, J. L., Klevansky, S., & Ehrlich, P. I. The effect of crowding on human task performance. *Journal of Applied Social Psychology,* 1971, *1,* 7–26.

Geer, J. H. & Maisel, E. Evaluating the effects of the prediction–control confound. *Journal of Personality and Social Psychology*, 1972, *23*, 314–319.

Glass, D. C., & Singer, J. E. *Urban stress*. New York: Academic Press, 1972.

Goffman, E. *The presentation of self in everyday life*. London: Penguin Press, 1959.

Hamilton, V. Socialization anxiety and information processing: A capacity model of anxiety-induced performance deficits. In I. G. Sarason & C. D. Spielberger (Eds.), *Stress and anxiety* (Vol. 2). New York: Wiley, 1975.

Harré, H., & Secord, P. F. *The explanation of social behavior*. Totowa, N.J.: Littlefield, Adams & Co., 1973.

Harvey, J. H. & Johnston, S. Determinants of the perception of choice. *Journal of Experimental Social Psychology*, 1973, *9*, 164–179.

Henchy, T., & Glass, D. C. Evaluative apprehension and the social facilitation of dominant and subordinate responses. *Journal of Personality and Social Psychology*, 1968, *4*, 446–454.

Hiroto, D. S., & Seligman, M. E. P. Generality of learned helplessness in man. *Journal of Personality and Social Psychology*, 1975, *31*, 311–327.

Houston, K. B. Control over stress, locus of control, and response to stress. *Journal of Personality and Social Psychology*, 1972, *21*, 249–255.

Izard, C. *The face of emotion*. New York: Appleton-Century-Crofts, 1971.

Jones, E. E. *Ingratiation: A social psychological analysis*. New York: Appleton-Century-Crofts, 1964.

Jones, E. E., & Davis, K. E. From acts to dispositions: The attribution process in person perception. In L. Berkowitz (Ed.), *Advances in experimental social psychology* (Vol. 2). New York: Academic Press, 1965.

Jorgenson, D. O., & Dukes, F. O. Deindividuation as a function of density and group membership. *Journal of Personality and Social Psychology*, 1976, *34*, 24–29.

Kelley, H. H. Causal schemata and the attribution process. In E. E. Jones D. E. Kanouse, H. H. Kelley, R. E. Nisbett, S. Valins, & B. Weiner (Eds.), *Attribution: Perceiving the causes of behavior*. Morristown, N.J.: General Learning Press, 1972.

Komorita, S. S. A weighted probability model of coalition formulation. *Psychological Review*, 1974, *81*, 242–256.

Langer, E. J. Rethinking the role of thought in social interaction. In J. Harvey, W. Ickes, & R. Kidd (Eds.), *New directions in attribution research* (Vol. 2). Hillsdale, N.J.: Lawrence Erlbaum Associates, 1978.

Langer, E. J., & Saegert, S. Crowding and cognitive control. *Journal of Personality and Social Psychology*, 1977, *35*, 175–182.

Langer, E., & Rodin, J. The effects of choice and enhanced personal responsibility for the aged: A field experiment in an institutional setting. *Journal of Personality and Social Psychology*, 1976, *34*, 191–198.

Laufer, R. S., Proshansky, H. M., & Wolfe, M. Some analytic dimensions of privacy. In H. M. Proshansky, W. H. Ittelson, & L. G. Rivlin (Eds.), *Environmental psychology: People and their physical settings* (2nd ed.). New York: Holt, Rinehart & Winston, 1976.

Lazarus, R. S. Emotions and adaptation: Conceptual and empirical relations. In W. S. Arnold (Ed.), *Nebraska Symposium on Motivation* (Vol. 16). Lincoln: University of Nebraska Press, 1968.

Lefcourt, H. M. The function of the illusions of control and freedom. *American Psychologist*, 1973, *28*, 417–425.

Levi, L., & Anderson, L. *Psychosocial stress: Population, environment and quality of life*. New York: Halsted Press, 1975.

Lewis, O. *The children of Sanchez*. New York: Random House, 1961.

Mandel, D. R., & Baron, R. M. *Environmental determinants of student study habits*. Paper presented at the annual convention of the American Psychological Association, Washington, D.C., September, 1976.

Marshall, J. E., & Heslin, R. Boys and girls together: Sexual composition and the effect of density and group size on cohesiveness. *Journal of Personality and Social Psychology,* 1975, *31,* 952–961.

McGrath, J. E. A conceptual formulation for research on stress. In J. E. McGrath (Ed.), *Social and psychological factors in stress.* New York: Holt, Rinehart & Winston, 1970.

Milgram, S. The experience of living in cities. *Science,* 1970, *167,* 1461–1648.

Mitchell, R. E. Some social implications of high-density housing. *American Sociological Review,* 1971, *36,* 8–29.

Neisser, V. *Cognitive Psychology.* New York: Appleton-Century-Crofts, 1967.

Newtson, D. Foundations of attribution: The perception of ongoing behavior. In J. Harvey, W. Ickes, & R. Kidd (Eds.), *New directions in attribution research* (Vol. 1). Hillsdale, N.J.: Lawrence Erlbaum Associates, 1976.

Nisbett, R. E., & Wilson, T. D. Telling more than we can know: Verbal reports on mental processes. *Psychological Review,* 1977, *84,* 231–259.

Paulus, P. B., Annis, A. B., Sęta, J. J., Schkade, J. K., & Mathews, R. W. Crowding does affect task performance. *Journal of Personality and Social Psychology,* 1976, *34,* 248–253.

Paulus, P., Cox, V., McCain, G., & Chandler, J. Some effects of crowding in a prison environment. *Journal of Applied Social Psychology,* 1975, *5,* 86–91.

Pervin, L. A. The need to predict and control under conditions of threat. *Journal of Personality,* 1963, *31,* 570–587.

Polyani, M. *Personal knowledge: Toward a postcritical philosophy.* Chicago: University of Chicago Press, 1958.

Proshansky, H. M., Ittelson, W. H., & Rivlin, L. G. Freedom of choice and behavior in a physical setting. In H. M. Proshansky, W. H. Ittelson, & L. G. Rivlin (Eds.), *Environmental psychology: People and their physical settings* (2nd ed.). New York: Holt, Rinehart & Winston, 1976.

Rapoport, A. Toward a redefinition of density. *Environment and Behavior,* 1975, *7,* 133–158.

Rodin, J. Crowding, perceived choice, and response to controllable and uncontrollable outcomes. *Journal of Experimental Social Psychology,* 1976, *12,* 564–578.

Rodin, J., & Langer, E. J. *Long-term effects of a control-relevant intervention among the institutionalized aged.* Unpublished manuscript, Yale University, 1976.

Rodin, J., Metcalf, J., Prussing, S., & Solomon, S. *Effects of onset and termination control on perceived crowding.* Paper presented at the Annual Convention of the American Psychological Association, Washington, D.C., September 1976.

Saegert, S. Crowding: Cognitive overload and behavioral constraint. In W. Prieser (Ed.), *Environmental design research* (Vol. II). Stroudsburg, Pa.: Dowden, Hutchinson, & Ross, 1973.

Saegert, S. Stress inducing and reducing qualities of environments. In H. Proshansky, W. H. Ittelson, & L. G. Rivlin (Eds.), *Environmental psychology: People and their physical settings* (2nd ed.). New York: Holt, Rinehart & Winston, 1976.

Sarason, I. G. Anxiety and self-preoccupation. In I. G. Sarason & C. D. Spielberger (Eds.), *Stress and anxiety* (Vol. 2). New York: Wiley, 1975.

Schiffenbauer, A. *The amelioration of crowding through design decisions.* Paper presented at EDRA 7, Vancouver, British Columbia, May 1976.

Seligman, M. E. P. *Helplessness: On depression, development, and death.* San Francisco: Freeman, 1975.

Seligman, M. E. P., Maier, S. F., & Solomon, R. L. Failure to escape traumatic shock. *Journal of Experimental Psychology,* 1967, *74,* 1–9.

Selye, H. The evolution of the stress concept. *American Scientist,* 1973, *61,* 692–699.

Shaw, J. D., & Skolnick, P. Attributions of responsibility for a happy accident. *Journal of Personality and Social Psychology,* 1971, *18,* 380–383.

Sherrod, D. R. Crowding, perceived control, and behavioral aftereffects. *Journal of Applied Social Psychology*, 1974, *4*, 171–186.

Shiffrin, R. M., & Schneider, W. Controlled and automatic human information processing: II. Perceptual learning, automatic attending, and a general theory. *Psychological Review*, 1977, *84*, 127–190.

Staub, E., Tursky, B., & Schwartz, G. Self-control and predictability: Their effect on reactions to aversive stimulation. *Journal of Personality and Social Psychology*, 1971, *18*, 157–162.

Steiner, I. Attributed freedom. In L. Berkowitz (Ed.), *Advances in experimental social psychology*, (Vol. 5). New York: Academic Press, 1970.

Stokols, D. A social–psychological model of human crowding phenomena. *Journal of the American Institute of Planners*, 1972, *38*, 72–83.

Stokols, D. The experience of crowding in primary and secondary environments. *Environment and Behavior*, 1976, *8*, 49–86.

Sundstrom, E. An experimental study of crowding: Effects of room size, intrusion, and goal-blocking on nonverbal behaviors, self-disclosure, and self-reported stress. *Journal of Personality and Social Psychology*, 1975, *32*, 645–654.

Sundstrom, E. Crowding as a sequential process: Review of research on the effects of population density on humans. In A. Baum & Y. Epstein (Eds.), *Human response to crowding*. Hillsdale, N.J.: Lawrence Erlbaum Associates, 1978.

Sundstrom, E., & Altman, I. Field study of dominance and territorial behavior. *Journal of Personality and Social Psychology*, 1974, *30*, 115–125.

Taylor, S. E. On inferring one's attitudes from one's behavior: Some deliminating conditions. *Journal of Personality and Social Psychology*, 1975, *31*(1), 126–131.

Thibault, J. W., & Kelley, H. H. *The social psychology of groups*. New York: Wiley, 1959.

Tompkins, S. S. *Affect, imagery, consciousness* (Vols. I and II, *Positive and negative affects*). New York: Springer, 1963.

Turvey, M. T. Constructive theory, perceptual systems, and tacit knowledge. In W. Weimer & D. Pelermo (Eds.), *Cognition and the symbolic processes*. Hillsdale, N.J.: Lawrence Erlbaum Associates, 1974.

Turvey, M. T. Preliminaries to a theory of action with reference to vision. In R. Shaw & J. Bransford (Eds.), *Perceiving, acting and knowing: Toward an ecological psychology*. Hillsdale, N.J.: Lawrence Erlbaum Associates, 1977.

Valins, S., & Baum, A. Residential group size, social interaction, and crowding. *Environment and Behavior*, 1973, *5*, 421–440.

Weick, K. E. The "ess" in stress: Some conceptual and methodological problems. In J. E. McGrath (Ed.), *Social and psychological factors in stress*. New York: Holt, Rinehart & Winston, 1970.

Weiss, J. M. Effects of coping behavior in different warning signal conditions on stress pathology in rats. *Journal of Comparative and Physiological Psychology*, 1971, *77*, 22–31.

Weiss, J. M. Effects of coping response on stress. *Journal of Comparative and Physiological Psychology*, 1968, *65*, 251–260.

Worchel, S. Discussant's comment delivered as part of a symposium on human crowding at the meeting of the Eastern Psychological Association, New York, April 1976.

Worchel, S., & Teddlie, C. The experience of crowding: A two-factor theory. *Journal of Personality and Social Psychology*, 1976, *34*, 30–40.

Wortman, C. B., & Brehm, J. W. Responses to uncontrollable outcomes: An integration of reactance theory and the learned helplessness model. In L. Berkowitz & E. Walster (Eds.), *Advances in experimental social psychology* (Vol. 8). New York: Academic Press, 1975.

Zajonc, R. B. Social facilitation. *Science*, 1965, *149*, 269–274.

Zimbardo, P. G. The human choice: Individuation, reason, and order vs. deindividuation, impulse, and chaos. In W. J. Arnold & D. Levine (Eds.), *Nebraska Symposium on Motivation* (Vol. 17). Lincoln: University of Nebraska Press, 1969.

INDEXES

Author Index

Italicized numbers denote pages that contain complete reference information.

Subject Index

24 JA

34,756

in Environmental

vol. 1.